Eureka!

Eureka!

Earthquakes, Chicanos, Celebrities, Smog, Fads, Outdoor Living, Charles Manson's Legacy, Berkeley Rebels, San Francisco Scenes, Southern California Style, Ronald Reagan, and Other Discoveries in the Golden State of California

STEVEN V. ROBERTS

QUADRANGLE/The New York Times Book Co.

Most of these articles originally appeared in *The New York Times*, sometimes in a different form. "Cop of the Year" appeared in *Esquire*, "High on Revolution" in *The New Leader*, and "Your Friendly John Birch Bookstore" in *Commonweal*. Permission to reprint them here is gratefully acknowledged.

Interior Design by Mary M. Ahern

LIBRARY OF CONGRESS CATALOGING IN PUBLICATION DATA

Roberts, Steven V   1943–
  Eureka!

  "Most of these articles originally appeared in the New York Times."
  1. California—Addresses, essays, lectures.
I. Title.
F861.R74   917.94'03'5   74–77948
ISBN 0–8129–0465–6

For Cokie

Contents

Acknowledgments

Any book is a cooperative effort, but one that is based on newspaper and magazine pieces involves more cooperation than most. Innumerable people at *The New York Times* have helped me along the way: Scotty Reston, who first hired me as his research assistant ten years ago; A. M. Rosenthal, who agreed to take me on as a reporter at age 22; Harrison Salisbury, who sent me to California; Dave Jones, Doug Kneeland, Irv Horowitz, Evan Jenkins, Tom Wark, and a dozen other sensitive and creative editors; Wally Turner, Glad Hill, and other colleagues on the national staff; Ellen Johnson, Judy Kinnard, and Leslie Ward, my assistants in the Los Angeles bureau; and D. Gorton, my photographer and companion. Many California friends provided affection and advice over the years; a few of them include Milly Harmon, Tom and Meredith Brokaw, Roy Aarons, John and Susan Wilhelm, Lucy and David Eisenberg, Geoff Cowan, Aileen Adams, Carol Powers, Monroe and Aimee Price, Joe Russin, and my brother, Glenn Roberts. Jon Segal and Roger Jellinek at Quadrangle helped make a book out of five years of yellowed clippings.

Several other people deserve special mention. Gene Roberts, the national editor of *The New York Times* for four years, taught me where to find the real America. Gerry Walker, my editor on *The Times Magazine*, where many of these longer pieces appeared, gave me the confidence to write about it. From the day I wrote a composition about Yellowstone Park in the fourth grade, my father, Will Roberts, has encouraged and supported my writing; long before that, my mother, Dorothy Roberts, was imparting a sense of discipline and responsibility. I am grateful beyond words to them both. My twin brother, Professor Marc J. Roberts, has always been one of my best teachers. My sister, Laura Beth Roberts, has been an ardent member of the family debating society that has long provided me with tough and constructive criticism. My in-laws, the late Representative Hale Boggs, and his successor, Representative Lindy Boggs, enlarged my family and my understanding of the country they loved so much. My children, Lee and Rebecca, made me laugh and not take myself too seriously. Above all, I must thank my wife, Cokie Boggs Roberts. I have read such sentiments in many books, but I can only say that I have never meant anything more. She co-authored one of these pieces and helped edit many of them. She maintained two full-time careers—as a mother and a television producer—and still found the time and energy to give me more love, understanding, humor, and insight than I thought possible. Ours is a marriage of equals, and this is her book as much as it is mine.

S.V.R.

Introduction

One day in late October of 1968 I took my wife and our first child home from the hospital, and then went to work in the city room of *The New York Times*. As I walked in, Arthur Gelb, the metropolitan editor, darted over and said, "I have some exciting news—we want to send you somewhere." I had been getting a taste of national politics during the presidential election and I answered quickly, "Where? Washington?" Gelb seemed taken aback. "No," he replied, "Los Angeles." On my way home that night, dubious and disappointed, I bought two books: Dr. Spock, and Tom Wolfe's *The Pump House Gang*. The first was confusing enough, but Wolfe was writing about all those Southern California kids who kept staring at the ocean and saying "mysterioso." It did not help a bit.

At that point I was still not sure where Los Angeles was. I had been west of the Mississippi for exactly one day in my entire life—about a month before, when I had been following Senator Edmund Muskie's campaign for vice-president, and had gotten a glimpse of three hotels in San Francisco and a field house in Provo, Utah. Before that, my closest contact with California had been a tall, blond surfer-type who lived a floor above me during my freshman year in college. And all I knew about him was that he wore madras bermuda shorts and sneakers with no socks.

I had been born in New Jersey, had studied in Massachusetts, and had worked in Washington and New York. At age 25 I was already suffering from an advanced case of Eastern Myopia, a crippling affliction that puts its victims under the delusion that the center of the world is somewhere around 50th Street and Madison Avenue in Manhattan and that almost any idea of any importance originated on the banks of either the Charles or Hudson River.

When I eventually accepted the Los Angeles assignment, I decided the "exile" would not have to last more than two years; then we could get back to Washington. We wound up staying for five, enjoying every day of it and hating to leave, even when we knew it was time to do something else. During that period, California might have been the best place in the world to be a reporter, and to grow as a person. There were many "big" stories, of course: the trials of Daniel Ellsberg and Charles Manson, earthquakes and brushfires, the election of a black mayor in Los Angeles, and the return of the prisoners of war. I still remember the night at a dinner party when a friend told me that UCLA had just hired a black girl named Angela Davis and that she was a Communist. But even more interesting were the little stories, the ones about suburbs and shopping centers, about the housewives and hippies and whores who were living their lives, day by day, on the shores of the Pacific.

This book contains a sampling of the hundreds of articles I wrote during those five years in California. Every one was originally written for a newspaper or a magazine, sometimes against a tight deadline, so this volume might lack the precision or detachment of a book written at a more leisurely pace, and in one piece. But hopefully these chapters have the immediacy and vitality that sometimes can be lost when a writer sits and ponders too much, and maybe decides he knows more than he does. This book is not a hard-edge drawing but a montage, bursts of overlapping colors and shapes, an impressionistic portrait of places and people I came to know well, and love deeply.

Reading over the portrait, several features seem particularly noteworthy. It's a cliché to say that things happen first in California, but it's often a valid one. Most Californians are from somewhere else; I remember the Thanksgiving when only one of the eight adults at our table was a native, and her parents had left Germany a few years before her birth. By definition, Californians are a restless and rootless breed, open to change and experimentation. They came to California in the first place to start a new life, not to repeat the patterns of the past.

This helps create a certain freedom in California, a wider sense of the possible. Established ideas and institutions are not nearly as powerful as they are in the East, and this flexibility shows up in many ways. In New York, for instance, the newspapers are being strangled by deeply entrenched unions; the *Los Angeles Times* does not even have a union, but it does have the most efficient automated equipment around. Politics in states like Pennsylvania and New Jersey are still heavily influenced by party organizations that command sizable loyalty and demand sizable payoffs. In California the parties are so weak that the state could elect a conservative Republican governor and a liberal Democratic senator at the same time. Fortunes are seldom based on the old industrial empires of heavy industry;

many of the richest and most influential barons on the West Coast made their own money in such postwar booms as computers, real estate, savings and loans, and insurance. The former head of the Los Angeles Urban Coalition owns a business that sells chemical toilets for pleasure boats.

There is more space in California, physical as well as psychic. There is room to breathe—at least when the smog is not too bad. Few buildings are more than two or three stories, and an "old" house is one built before 1962. Things are so spread out that you have to spend hours in the car, but you never have some grimy skyscraper looming over you, and you can always see the sky. I remember the first time I went to the University of California at Berkeley and saw Sproul Plaza, the center of the campus. My image of college had been Harvard Yard, a graceful but gloomy place, where I had lived in a building that had been housing students for 200 years or so. Sproul Plaza was light and airy, all molded concrete, not a red brick—or a hallowed tradition—in sight. No wonder the era of college rebellion started there in 1964, a time when students were still obeying "keep off the grass" signs back in Cambridge.

Take something as simple as dress. A colleague of mine came to California on assignment and soon after his arrival he went out to dinner at a good restaurant. "I wore a blue suit," he recalls. "When I go out in New York I always wear a blue suit. But when I looked around the restaurant I was the only man wearing one." Within weeks he was wearing jeans and open-necked shirts to work. That can become a uniform too, of course, but in California there is no "style"; you basically dress the way you want to.

You also live the way you want to, and California can have an enormous impact on personal relationships. Since most people are so far from their old friends and families, churches and neighborhoods, there is no one looking over your shoulder. There is no one to enforce traditional codes of conduct, no Aunt Bessie to go clucking all over town if you get divorced, no parish priest to conjure up visions of hell if you move in with your lover. Many find this exhilarating, a chance to explore new worlds of feeling and behavior. Others find it profoundly unsettling. They mourn the loss of such concepts as sin and sacrifice, and they worry that taken to an extreme "doing your own thing" can become mere selfishness.

But practically everyone feels a little lost. Freedom can be a tremendous burden, after all, and much of what happens in California is a search for new rules, new structures. Health foods, psychotherapy, surfing, drugs, mysticism, politics, demonstrations, even sailing and tennis—they all help provide a new identity, a raison d'être for people separated from their past. I was talking to a friend who had been through a messy divorce and had then plunged into various forms of analysis. She was trying something called "rolfing," a very physical form of therapy, and she was very excited. "I hear it works!" she said. Her words were really an updated version of California's official motto, taken from the gold rush days: "Eureka! I've found it!" What did you find? What works? Gold? Happiness? The journey continues.

In one sense, then, this book is about how people have been using their freedom in California, about the changes and experiments that flourished out on the western edge of the continent and ultimately made—or will make—their way eastward. But in another sense California is not a forerunner but a microcosm, a piece of the country as a whole. It is not one state at all, actually, but at least five—the northern and southern coasts, the deserts, the mountains, and the fertile central valley. Anything that is grown or made or thought elsewhere is grown or made or thought by some of the 20 million people who live in what is now our largest and most important state. Time and again during my tenure there, *The New York Times* found that when it wanted to know what the country was doing about a particular subject, the best place to find out was California. Whether the issue was riots or religion, inflation or elections, work or leisure, marriage or divorce—if it happened anywhere during the late sixties and early seventies, it happened in California. Thus this book is not just about one state, but about an entire nation. In searching for California, I was searching for America.

—*Steven V. Roberts*
March, 1974

SOUTHERN CALIFORNIA: LIFE ON THE LAST FRONTIER

The mobile, free-wheeling life-style described in "Ode to a Freeway" was seriously threatened by the gasoline shortage of early 1974. Suddenly 30 miles was too far to drive for dinner; instead of heading for the mountains on Sunday you had your picnic in the backyard; we sold our Karmann Ghia for almost as much as we had paid for it three years before but took a big loss on a new Ford station wagon. The crisis provoked new efforts to form car pools and subscription bus services, and more talk about a rapid transit system in Los Angeles. But a lot of it was just talk. As long as any gas is available, and the freeways are still there, Southern Californians would no sooner give up their cars than they would give up sex.

Two years after the earthquake piece appeared, there was a major tremor in Southern California that caused considerable damage and several dozen deaths, many of which resulted when a nursing home collapsed, and again, there was more talk—this time about improved construction standards—but little action. Yet the quake somehow symbolized the impermanence and instability of life in the Southland, and some residents were so unnerved that they suffered mental breakdowns and left the state.

Civilization does seem a bit fragile as it clings precariously to the Western coast. If it isn't earthquakes, then it is a flood or a fire or a landslide. The blaze described here came within a mile of our house and the piece was written while my family was still evacuated.

The popular mythology of a state seething with right-wing kooks has never been very accurate, but the John Birch Society endures, secure in its faith that a moral earthquake is on its way, and that Sodom is an exit on the Hollywood Freeway. Probably the best symbol of California is Disneyland, a whole world created out of nothing, rootless, disembodied, yet full of promise. When you wish upon a star, goes the theme song, it makes no difference who you are.

Ode to a Freeway

Los Angeles

Several years ago, the magazine *Cry California* ran an article about a family that lived most of its life on the Los Angeles freeways. Mike and Merilee Farrier, said the story, could not afford both a home and a camper, so they opted for the vehicle. At night, they parked in a deserted lot near downtown. At 7 A.M., Merilee arose, changed the baby, plugged in the coffee, and headed for the Hollywood Freeway. Halfway to Burbank she woke up Mike, and when they arrived at the factory where he worked, they shared breakfast in the parking lot. Then Merilee dropped the baby off at her mother's and went to a half-day job. Later, she reversed her trip—128 miles in all.

"One day is about the same as another: about 10 gallons of gas," Mike Farrier said. "We've begun to feel that the freeways, particularly the Hollywood Freeway, belong to us. It's not the same feeling that you get about a house on a lot, but it's definitely a sense of ownership. We don't have any neighbors, of course, but actually we had a few neighbors before that we were happy to leave behind."

When the story appeared, the journal's editor, William Bronson, was swamped by newsmen wanting to interview the Farriers. It was all a hoax, he said—"I thought it was obvious." But the reporters were not satisfied. "My bet," wrote Art Seidenbaum in the *Los Angeles Times*, "is that there really is such a family, eating and bathing and meshing gears and staying one ramp in front of the bill collectors."

Seidenbaum was right, of course; the Farriers do exist, figuratively if not literally. Freeways shape and mold the life of Los Angeles, and every other once-virginal city that has now been penetrated by the interstate highway system. In the car-centered culture of suburbia, our vehicle can be a restaurant or a living room, a pew or a movie theater, even a boudoir. In the confines of our own little steel cell, we eat breakfast, flirt with fellow drivers, catch up on the news, think great thoughts, fantasize a bit. There is

a favorite story among highway patrolmen about the cop who found a
blouse tossed out on the freeway. A mile or so farther he found a bra, then a
skirt, then panties, and so on. Despite the officer's valiant efforts, however,
the litterbug was never apprehended. We also pollute the air—so badly that
the Environmental Protection Agency has threatened to ration gasoline in
Southern California during the height of the smog season.

Freeways are the new Main Streets of America, the heart of our
commerce, an experience we all share. Around Boston, the Route 128
beltway has spawned a tremendous complex of electronics and computer
companies. In Washington, Houston, and dozens of other cities, developers
have followed the freeways and constructed huge shopping malls on the
outskirts of town, modern-day bazaars where you can buy a bag of
gumdrops at a candy store or an airplane at Neiman-Marcus, self-contained
worlds where you can eat chow mein or lasagna or enchiladas, cash a check,
lose weight, go ice skating, play pool, meditate, consult a machine that
analyzes your handwriting. Few of them have mortuaries, but that is only a
matter of time.

In my hometown of Bayonne, New Jersey, the thing to do on a Friday
night was cruise up and down Broadway, or maybe hang out at Irv's candy
store or Dido's pizza palace, home of the wateriest Cokes on the East Coast.
In San Jose, California, where I recently spent some time on assignment, the
kids drive out Route 101 to the Eastridge shopping center. There they cruise
the mammoth parking lot, or wander up and down the shiny corridors,
gathering occasionally in the sunken "conversation pits" that surround the
modernistic sculpture and spouting fountains. I don't know if the Cokes are
any better in Eastridge than at Dido's, but the object of the game is clearly
the same.

Freeways are now familiar phenomena across America, but in Los
Angeles they have reached their highest stage of development, victors in a
Darwinian struggle over various forms of trains, trolleys, and traffic lights.
Here, they are such a pervasive influence that they stand as the symbol of
the city, sources of mythology, objects of esthetic appreciation and
ecological anger, man-made monuments of such an elemental force that
they might have heaved up out of the earth eons ago. The freeway is our
Mother!

Indeed, there are those who see these spans of molded concrete as
works of art, functional forms of lean beauty and sweeping grace—"a new
form of urban sculpture," in the words of architect Lawrence Halprin. Jack

Smith, a local columnist, thinks they will endure as some sort of "West Coast Parthenon." Reyner Banham, a British architectural critic, has written that "the wide-swinging curved ramps of the intersections of the Santa Monica and the San Diego Freeways . . . immediately persuaded me that the Los Angeles freeway system is indeed one of the greater works of man." Ed Ruscha, an artist known for his photographic study called "Every Building on the Sunset Strip," now wants to do a similar pictorial panorama of the Hollywood Freeway. But he is mainly interested in the road itself, not the cars on it, and there is no time of day when the Hollywood Freeway is even close to being empty. Ruscha also would like to photograph a freeway wreck from the air, and has even thought of causing one himself—all for the sake of art, of course.

"Freeway" has become an emotional word in recent years, like "hippie" or "mugger." To their critics, these roads cause an almost endless catalog of social ills: smog, congestion, urban sprawl, erosion of local tax bases, decimation of pleasant neighborhoods, destruction of natural beauty, a dependence on the automobile that is considered insidious, even immoral. As Art Hoppe, writing from the self-satisfied, if overbuilt, heights of San Francisco, has said, the typical citizen of Los Angeles is "a well-preserved, middle-aged, middle-class, two-door Chevrolet."

But there is another side, a viewpoint that does not square with most liberal rhetoric. The fact is that freeways work, and damn well. Most of the time they are fast and efficient. And even at their most congested, they provide a wider variety of options than just about any other transportation system. The word "free" should refer not to their cost but their character. And this freedom forms the foundation of the Southern California life-style. As Richard Austin Smith put it in a *Fortune* magazine article eight years ago, "Whatever glass and steel monuments may be built downtown, the essence of Los Angeles, its true identifying characteristic, is mobility. Freedom of movement has long given life a special flavor there, liberated the individual to enjoy the sun and space that his environment so abundantly offered, put the manifold advantages of a great metropolitan area within his grasp."

The definition of a freeway is rather simple: at least two lanes in each direction, no lights, tolls or stop signs, limited access at specific points, and no grade crossings. The state master plan of 1959 called for 1,550 miles of pavement in the Los Angeles area alone—a road about every 5 miles—and while only about 600 miles have been built, the statistics are already overwhelming. Every day, 220,000 cars use the Santa Monica Freeway, 38 million vehicle-miles are driven throughout Los Angeles County, etc., etc.

In order to gain a better sense of the freeway phenomenon, I hitched a ride one afternoon with Kelly Lange, who at the time zipped around in a single-engine Cessna doing traffic reports for radio station KABC. Since so many people spend so much time in their cars, radio is a very important medium in Los Angeles, and at least a half-dozen stations provide airborne reports on the latest traffic conditions. In fact, it got so crowded up there that the pioneer of this journalistic genre, Captain Max Schumacher, crashed into a police helicopter several years ago and was killed. Now, to avoid mishaps, the reporters have agreed to fly only on the right side of the freeway.

Out at Van Nuys Airport, in the San Fernando Valley, I met our pilot, Rod Ibers. As we waited to take off, the west end of the valley, swept clean by winds, looked crisp and lovely all the way to the surrounding mountains. But to the east, the brownish smog billowed up, as if a huge herd of strange animals were racing across a dusty plain toward us. I asked Ibers what he thought of, watching the traffic every day, and he replied, "I'm glad I'm up in the air."

As the engine revved up, Kelly arrived, a friendly, almost cherubic-looking girl with streaked hair, who got her first job six years ago in typical Hollywood fashion—she walked in off the street one day and defeated hundreds of other girls in a contest to become KABC's "Ladybird." We took off toward the south and the first thing I noticed was the parking lots, found op art, straight and slanted lines of white and yellow on black, with a variety of curves and wedges at the end of a row.

Directly ahead was the great slash of the San Diego Freeway, crossing the Santa Monica Mountains through Sepulveda Pass, linking the valley's million residents with what passes for a central city. To the west trickled the Ventura Freeway, headed for outlying areas just now being developed. I recalled a conversation with Edgardo Contini, a noted transportation planner, who said that the growth of Los Angeles was dictated by the freeways—even though highway engineers seldom took land-use questions into account. "When we build a shopping center, the first thing we look at is what freeway is there or will be there," said Mr. Contini, whose architectural firm, Gruen Associates, has designed many. "We don't look at any master plan or what SCAG [Southern California Association of

Governments] has to say. Freeways decide what happens."

As we neared the smog-shrouded hills, I could make out regular bursts of oddly shaped blue color, the ubiquitous Los Angeles swimming pool, symbol of the region's devotion to privacy. After her first report, Kelly pointed out some oddities. In one tunnel on the Pasadena Freeway, she said, "the traffic is always heavy going in, and always light going out. It kind of blows your mind." Nearby was The Stack, the famous four-level interchange that is said to be the busiest in the world. But to the connoisseur of congestion, the worst bottleneck is the East Los Angeles "connector complex," variously known as the Spaghetti Bowl, the Rat's Nest and other, less printable epithets. It looked to me like tracks from my son's model railroad, after his sister had scattered them aimlessly around the room. Here, four different freeways converge into an area so tangled and tricky that sometimes it takes a seasoned aerial observer ten minutes to figure out the exact location of a stalled vehicle, even if it's plainly visible. Possibly the most fiendish Christmas present of the year was received by one of my co-workers: a jigsaw puzzle of the L.A. freeways, featuring the Spaghetti Bowl.

By now, traffic was slowed to a crawl on most roads. "If I had to drive the freeways every day, I just wouldn't stand for it," mused Kelly, gazing down. "I'd figure out another way, or I'd go at a different time." Then the radio crackled with a highway patrol advisory: A girl was stalled on the center divider of the Golden State Freeway, and would someone please call her mother to come get her. The cops have become particularly protective of young women since a tragic incident several years ago. After her car broke down, a girl accepted a ride from a stranger and was never heard from again. The call also reminded Kelly of a more amusing occasion: A striking redhead in hotpants got out to look at her smoldering auto and four would-be good samaritans, if that's what they were, crashed into each other trying to come to her aid.

The blood-red sun snuffed itself out in the Pacific, and gradually the nightly Los Angeles light show made its appearance. As we turned back toward Van Nuys, along the Hollywood, even a jaded veteran like Rod Ibers could not contain his appreciation. "On clear nights," he enthused, "those roads look like long strings of red and white jewels." I noticed something else, a plague of brightly lit golden arches twinkling across the basin, the McDonaldization of America. At the off and on ramps, the rows of lights flowed together and parted, a gentle ballet that might serve as a metaphor for this strange, amorphous town, where so little is settled and stable, including the hillsides.

From up there, you can forget that each of those lights represents a car, and a driver. But negotiating those ribbons of molded concrete can be a very individual and intense experience. The myth, of course, is that they are only slightly less dangerous than a kamikaze run over a SAM-missile base. In fact, they are quite safe, about five times safer than conventional roads. Compared to the narrow, angular confines of a monstrosity like the West Side Highway, the broad swath of a California freeway feels open and easy. For the neophyte, though, things can get pretty scary. A friend of mine arriving after a trip from the East got four tickets here before she arrived at her destination, including one for changing lanes too timidly and another for going only 55 miles an hour in the fast lane. A colleague, Gladwin Hill, remembers seeing a befuddled visitor drive into a wedge-shaped no-man's land between the roadway and an off-ramp, and just sit there, paralyzed. It took a kindly cop to guide him back into the stream of traffic.

In general, California drivers are able and courteous. Maybe it's because most have been "trained in the bush leagues" before coming to the big time, as one friend commented, or because some process of natural selection has weeded out the incompetents. But to someone used to the search-and-destroy tactics of New York cab drivers, California motorists approach saintliness.

Another favorite myth is that freeway driving is an arid, soul-destroying punishment that robs you of two or three hours a day. A typical comment comes from Neil Morgan, a San Diego columnist, who calls the experience "chillingly impersonal, suicidally frenetic, and so vacuous as to make its inhabitants appear as the robots of a city that has become a puppet of technology."

There are many things I'd rather do than drive on the freeway (even take out the garbage), and it can be a very impersonal exercise, but that is not necessarily bad. As my wife puts it, only half in jest, "I think it makes the city friendlier. Keeping people apart keeps them from killing each other. Anyone who talks about how sterile the freeways are hasn't been felt up on the subway recently." Indeed, Ms. Roberts finds that her driving can be a pleasant, private time, a rare experience for the mother of two small children. Jack Smith of the *Los Angeles Times* adds, "It's perhaps the only time we're really alone, unavailable to neighbors, wives, the telephone. It's the only time we're really disengaged. If you're in the office or at home, you're harassed by feelings that you ought to be doing something. All of us have moments when we're putting off something that should be done—reading a good book, or writing a column, or pruning the trees. Now that women are liberated, we feel we ought to be doing the dishes. But if you get in your car, and you know you have forty-five minutes to get there, no one can touch you."

Like many people I talked to, Smith uses his freeway time for contemplation. "I sort of get things in order, and remind myself of what I have to do next week," he said. "Sometimes on long trips I come close to engaging in philosophical thought—like, what do I really think about the bombing of Vietnam? Usually I just have instant reactions to issues, and I wonder, 'Is it possible to give some thought to this while I'm driving along here?' After a while, you sort of conk out, and start thinking about how long it's been since you've been to a pornographic movie or something. Pure thought doesn't hold up very long, but at least you can make the attempt."

Joan Didion, whose novel *Play It As It Lays* helped foster a rather sinister view of the freeways, remembers having one of her "great experiences" in the middle of a traffic jam on the Harbor Freeway. "I had an interview at 9 [A.M.], and I was all tensed up," she recalled one afternoon, as the Pacific curled against the beach behind her. "I was afraid I'd miss the interview, and I was feeling sorry for myself for being up so early. Then it hit me—what difference did it make whether I sat on the freeway or went to the interview? The whole thing about Los Angeles fell into place. Every minute is a *tabula rasa*. There it is—by itself—no back or forward references. Just Right Now."

John Gregory Dunne, her husband and collaborator, loves feeeways. "When I'm having trouble working, I get in my car and drive," he said. "My whole mind opens up. I'm so aware of things; it's a strange kind of highway narcosis. Once, I went out for a loaf of bread and wound up in San Francisco. So I got the loaf, turned around and came back."

That episode might have suggested a well-known passage in Didion's novel, in which the heroine, Maria Wyeth, is described this way:

In the first hot month of the fall after the summer she left Carter (the summer Carter left her, the summer Carter stopped living in the house in Beverly Hills), Maria drove the freeway. She dressed every morning with a greater sense of purpose than she had had in some time, a cotton skirt, a jersey, sandals she could kick off when she wanted the touch of the accelerator, and she dressed very fast, running a brush through her hair once or twice and tying it back with a ribbon, for it was essential (to pause was to throw herself into unspeakable peril) that she be on the freeway by 10 o'clock. Not somewhere on Hollywood Boulevard, not on her way to the freeway, but actually on the freeway. If she was not, she lost the day's rhythm, its precariously imposed momentum. Once she was on the freeway and had maneuvered her way to a fast lane, she turned on the radio at high volume and she drove. She drove the San Diego to the Harbor, the Harbor up to the Hollywood, the Hollywood to the Golden State, the Santa Monica, the Santa Ana, the Pasadena, the Ventura. She drove it as a riverman runs a river, every day more attuned to its currents, its deceptions, and just as a riverman feels the pull of the rapids in the lull between sleeping and waking, so Maria lay at night in the still of Beverly Hills and saw the great signs soar overhead at 70 miles an hour, "Normandie ¼," "Vermont ¾," "Harbor Fwy 1." Again and again she returned to an intricate stretch of the interchange where successful passage from the Hollywood to the Harbor required a diagonal move across four lanes of traffic. On the afternoon she finally did it without braking or once losing the beat on the radio, she was exhilarated, and that night slept dreamlessly.°

Some read that passage as anticipating the day when a sign on the San Diego Freeway will announce "Oblivion ½." Joan has always liked the radio station that follows its call letters with the eerie phrase "Freeways Are Forever. . . ." But, essentially, Maria drove the freeways because they were there. "She didn't have anything to do; she was kind of in limbo," Joan explained. "When you're in that state, marking time and trying to stay together, you've got to have something to do to organize your day. The freeways give you a spurious sense of organization. You do have to be organized and in control. You're using skills that you have, and you do well or badly. You have a sense of accomplishing something."

Freeway driving can be exhilarating, too. When columnist Jack Smith takes the transition road from Santa Monica westbound to San Diego southbound, he feels as if he's soaring, about to take off. Architect Lawrence Halprin writes, "The great excitement is in the travel—a kind of free-wheel-

° From *Play It As It Lays* by Joan Didion, published in 1970 by Farrar, Straus & Giroux, Inc.

ing, fast-moving mobility in which the sense of motion and speed is important. The quality is something like swimming with fins; the water buoys you up and the slightest effort propels you forward."

Some freeways are almost like movable galleries, wonderful places to sense the pace and texture of the city. One of the best ways to see L.A. is to drive the Santa Monica from downtown to the ocean; when the air is clear, the city unfolds in an ever-changing panorama of buildings and mountains, a linear way to see a linear city. My wife's favorite spot is Sepulveda Pass on the San Diego, heading north. Open, mountainous terrain walls you in on both sides, giving a glimpse into California's unspoiled past. Then you reach the crest and suddenly, spread at your feet—or rather, tires—is the San Fernando Valley, the quintessential American suburbia, land of Chevron and *der Wienerschnitzel,* all the way to the looming mountains beyond.

When the driving becomes automatic, people regularly eat breakfast, comb their hair, put on make-up, shave with portable razors in their cars. Paul (Panther) Pierce, who reports freeway conditions for radio station KMPC, tells about a group that plays cards every morning in the back of a van on the San Bernardino. Every policeman I talked to has, at one time or another, followed the crazy meanderings of a driver he thought was drunk. When he finally stopped the car, up popped the head of a woman who had been administering her own form of roadway service. (I'm told it also happens with the sex roles reversed, but not as often.) An acquaintance who grew up here said such antics were common practice among local teen-agers. "It's all part of the lust and violence thing," he said casually, as if I were supposed to know what that meant.

Anything that can be spilled on a freeway has been. Kelly Lange recalls seeing a briefcase and a bag of golf clubs, the kinds of things that don't usually fall out of a car by themselves. "It seemed as if somebody had just said, 'To hell with it,' and tossed them out," she said, laughing. One day, half a dozen steers tumbled out of a truck on the Ventura, and presented an unusual problem for patrolmen who had done most of their horseback riding on the merry-go-round in Griffith Park. One amateur cowboy was so eager to help he stopped his horse trailer right in the middle of traffic, saddled up his palomino, and took off down the center divider, whooping it up and waving a lasso. Hours later, when the critters had finally been corralled, the budding Hopalong Cassidy was given a ticket.

Freeway drivers have wonderful fantasy lives, and sometimes they act them out. Larry Deitz, editor of a new magazine called *LA Is*, told me the story of a girl who was driving along the Hollywood Freeway and saw a man in a Ferrari passing and waving to her. After a while, he motioned for her to pull over, and when she did, he invited her out for a drink. They went to a bar near the ocean, had a few, and wound up in bed. Larry, who got the story from the girl, asked her why she had pulled over in the first place? "I was lonely," she told him, "and besides, he had a nice car."

Listening to the radio is another favorite diversion. The top-rated program these days is called "The Feminine Forum" and features a middle-aged pseudoswinger named Bill Ballance, who asks women to call in and talk about a particular subject, usually something to do with their sex lives. (The show was recently criticized by the Federal Communications Commission and was toned down by the station, KGBS.) One day he did a show on freeways, and when it was over, he exclaimed, "Those girls are always on the prowl! They're out there looking for romance!" Ballance's station has even institutionalized the game by assigning a girl named "Little Fanny Freeway" to ride around—her car is called "Big Red Cruiser 41-D," in honor of her measurements—flirting with commuters and handing out prizes.

One of Ballance's callers, named Peggy, said she was creeping up Sepulveda Pass in heavy traffic one day when the man in front kept slipping back and almost hitting her. Finally he did, and motioned for her to pull off. He was very apologetic, and asked for her name and phone number so he could "take care of everything." When he asked her for a cigarette, she got nervous and jumped back into her car. Another day, "a real nice-looking man in a Cadillac" started flirting, and on impulse she passed him her phone number across a crowded lane. When Ballance expressed amazement at her adventures, she sighed. "I spend my whole life on the San Diego Freeway," she said.

Automotive amours do not always work out. One girl had a delightful time flirting down the freeway with a man who followed her home. As they walked toward each other, they stopped in astonishment, and then laughed. She was 5-foot-11, he was barely 5-foot-6. Another caller, named Nava, reported that she was followed off the freeway once, and when she stopped for a light, the man struck up a conversation. Several months later, she married him, but she's not very happy. "Next time I stop at a red light, I won't look around," she insisted.

Like the girl picked up by the Ferrari-driving stud, most of the callers remembered in great detail the cars their suitors were driving. When we talked after the show, Ballance went over some old broadcasts, and was surprised to realize how many stories involved vehicles. Favorite fantasies? "So many of them dreamed about having Porsches or Mark IVs," Ballance remembered. "They dream about cars, man! I said to one, 'Can I name you Miss Pistonhead of 1972?' They even mention colors. One said she wanted a long Mercedes limousine. I asked what color, and she said, 'Magenta.'"

Car advertisements obviously play on the dreams of their customers— "Buy a Hupmobile, and that gorgeous creature off in the distance will fall right into your bucket seat"—and the pitch apparently has a point. When Ballance asked women how they could tell if a man would be a good lover, many of them mentioned cars. "If you see a man driving a VW, you know he's not much of a stud," said one. "But if you see a guy cruising around in a big Buick, you know he's got to be a virile swinger." (I must confess that I feel much spiffier driving my burnt-orange Karmann Ghia than the dilapidated Ford Falcon I used to own. So does my wife. She keeps stealing my car when I'm not looking and leaving me with the Popsicle-smeared station wagon.)

No doubt, freeways have their drawbacks. One study showed recently that freeway fumes aggravate existing heart conditions in many patients. When my wife has to commute to Burbank at rush hour, it can be a nerve-frazzling experience. We have one friend who drove 150 miles a day just taking her three children and herself to school, and then picking the kids up.

The car culture does erode a sense of community. In New York I walked several blocks from the subway at 72nd and Broadway to our apartment, and while I had to dodge an occasional addict anxious for a fix, I loved the liveliness and richness of Broadway. I miss buying a paper at a corner stand, going to the movies or a Chinese restaurant across the street, picking up flowers from a sidewalk vendor. My wife did not have to cross a street to do most of her shopping, and when our first child was born, the local merchants knew her so well they bought presents for the baby.

Here, you get into the car in your own driveway, and you have no contact with anyone. The only neighbors we know have teen-agers who baby-sit, or subteens who shoot BB's through the picture windows. The nearest store is 3 miles away, and the nearest place anyone will deliver *The Sunday New York Times* is 5 miles in the other direction. About the only person I greet regularly when I go to work is the parking-lot attendant, and to him, I'm just another orange Karmann Ghia or sticky blue Volvo. When we were talking about freeways, Edgardo Contini, the planner, mentioned a recent trip to Rome. "It reminded me of something I had forgotten," he said, "the pleasure of urban noise. I heard a carpenter sawing, a mother calling her children in the street, someone singing. Those are all experiences of which we are deprived."

The way we live here tends to have an antisocial effect. People do not care about Los Angeles and its problems. They do not even think of themselves as living in Los Angeles; they live in Highland Park or Van Nuys or Pacific Palisades, and the rest of the place can go to hell. Four years ago, Thomas Bradley, a black city councilman, ran for mayor of Los Angeles on the platform of bringing the city together. He lost then for a variety of reasons, but one of them was that people did not want to be brought together; they wanted to be left alone. Sam Yorty has been the perfect mayor for most Angelenos. He seldom does anything—except snip ribbons at freeway openings—and half the time he is not even here.

But when you give up the flower vendor on Broadway and the mother calling her children in Rome, you gain a lot of other things. The freeway allows you to create your own life. Your community is formed not by geography or ethnicity but by common interests, and it is not unusual to drive 45 minutes for a casual dinner with friends. Because of the freeways, I can live in Malibu, in the hills overlooking the Pacific, and work downtown. No Chinese restaurants, but plenty of horses. That's 25 miles from the office, but only 30 minutes by freeway, at off-hours. My wife is 30 miles from work, and it takes 45 minutes, but that is the same time it took her to go crosstown on a bus in Manhattan.

The freeways can be miserable at rush hour, but everybody is not going to the same downtown core. While planners are struggling to spread out the flow and commerce of other big cities, Los Angeles has already achieved that diffusion. Life is not a series of competitions; even the best restaurants and theaters are seldom as crowded as they are in New York. You never have to wave at a disheartening series of cabs with "off duty" signs in the rain, and you can always get a parking spot. You might miss some of the vitality of other cities, but you also avoid the tension.

Not everybody can afford a car, or is physically able to drive one; some freeways are used far beyond capacity already, and if the opposition to new roads continues—as it should in many places—there must be some form of mass transit. But that is no panacea for smog, or congestion. If given any kind of a choice, most people will drive their own cars. Everybody wants the other guy to take the bus.

"We find it hard to live with the freeways, but it would be far worse without them. In one light, they are monuments to our rapacity, bullish self-righteousness, and materialism. Norman Mailer used a big-game hunt as a metaphor in his novel *Why Are We in Vietnam?*; one could also use the story of a freeway cutting through a residential neighborhood, a neighborhood that has to be destroyed in order to be saved. Yet these infuriating hunks of concrete also express some of our better traits: the quest for independence, for self-reliance. Horace Greeley told young men to go west. Now that they're here, they can go in any direction they want. On the freeway.

1973

Disneyland Is the Heart of America

Anaheim

The Hunters looked like classic Disneyland visitors: handsome parents in their 30s, with two boys, ages 3 and 7. The younger child clasped a plastic copy of a familiar little mouse, which he called "Donald Duck." Mom held a balloon. Dad held a wallet. The unusual thing about the Hunters is that they are from Australia. "This is the only reason we came to L.A.; we checked into a hotel and came straight here," said Steve Hunter, who still seemed a bit disoriented. "This place is really well advertised overseas, through Disney's films and TV, and everybody said you can't go to North America and not see Disneyland."

The Hunters were among close to 100,000 people who poured through the gate of the "magic kingdom" during the Labor Day holiday. This weekend, if you went looking for the heart of America, you might have found it reposing in a 7-year-old boy at Disneyland, eating a hot dog, with mustard on his face and Mickey Mouse ears on his head.

Sixteen years after its opening, Disneyland has achieved a singular success. That tinkling sound you hear is not childish laughter, but money. Earlier this year, the 100-millionth guest passed over the castle drawbridge into Fantasyland, with the strains of "When You Wish Upon a Star" lilting in her ears.

Why? For one thing, Disneyland pioneered a whole new concept in family entertainment, the "theme park," with enough rides and restaurants and rest rooms to keep everyone happy. Second, say park officials, Disneyland is a triumph of merchandising. Every Disney venture—from T-shirts to TV—"plays off" the others, generating new interest and audiences. Third, the place is immaculate. Every cigarette butt and candy wrapper is considered an offense to the memory of Walter Elias Disney himself.

But the real secret of Disneyland is that people feel transported into another world, out of their own, ordinary lives. It is not an image on screen or a picture in a book. You can touch it and smell it and breathe it. Disneyland is fake, and everyone knows it is fake, but it is real fake. Out here in Orange County 27 miles from the center of Los Angeles, you can ride on Tom Sawyer's raft or climb in the Swiss Family Robinson's tree house.

When Disneyland opened in 1955, it had twenty-two attractions and an investment of $16 million. Today it has fifty-three features representing $128.5 million, and as one official said, "Technological progress is as important to family recreation as to the space industry." The important innovation has been Audio-Animatronics, a patented process that makes possible an extraordinary range of three-dimensional animation. A figure of Abraham Lincoln in one exhibit is capable of 275,000 different movements. One lady recently insisted on getting the "actor's" autograph.

Another concession to modernity is the introduction of rock music shows, although it is definitely "clean-cut rock," more like the Carpenters than, say, Grand Funk.

Despite its efforts to change with the times, Disneyland is not immune to trouble and criticism. In the last year or two, park officials have started enforcing an "appearance code." Long hair on boys is not an absolute bar to admission, but the freakier-looking types are screened pretty closely.

The park is still shaky from an incident last summer, when a crowd of self-styled "yippies" staged an "invasion." Robert Jackson, director of publicity, soberly describes the day as "Disneyland's most difficult, but finest hour."

"We get 10 million people through here a year, and they're really actors on a stage," explained Mr. Jackson. "Anything that grossly interferes with the enjoyment of a large majority of the people should not be allowed."

Some critics contend that the Disneyland dress code is an extension of the management's basic outlook, that it caters to a white, middle-class—and distorted—view of the world. Many attractions, they complain, depict American Indians and African natives as "wild savages," thus perpetuating racial stereotypes imbedded in the mass culture. As one young woman put it, "We went on the jungle boat ride, and saw all those natives in masks shaking spears, and I looked around to see if there were any blacks on our boat. I felt very embarrassed for them."

Nevertheless, these 72 acres of fantasy—and 107 acres of parking lots—have become an international institution. In the next century when a park is built to recreate contemporary America, one of the exhibits will probably be Disneyland.

One reason is its incredibly wide appeal. There are 4.7 adult visitors here for every child, and one of the biggest groups is young adults in their 20s. Take Bill McGillivray, who posed happily with his arm around the life-sized figure of Pinocchio while his wife, Linda, snapped a picture. "We come from Boston," he explained, "and you hear so much about the place, you have to see it when you're here. There's always a little bit of kid left in all of us."

"Even someone like me, who's a real cynic, can get something out of it," added Mr. McGillivray. "There are a lot of places you hear a lot about, like the Grand Canyon. When you get there you're often disappointed, but not here."

The essence of Disneyland is still children; even people without their own like to look at others'. As the Reverend Ken Mulder, a blond minister with two young charges, said, "The whole trip from Oregon was worth watching the expressions on their faces—they were thoroughly enraptured and enthralled."

Chris King, who is 7, was down for a weekend from Oakland. He liked the "scary" rides. "It's fun when you know it's not real," said Chris, between bites of a french fry, "but when it's real it's not fun." After the "scary rides," the most popular attraction seems to be the food. Tommy and Billy West, 4-year-old twins, were waiting in line for the jet rocket ride. What did they like best at Disneyland? "I like the hamburgers," said one. "I like the hot dogs," answered his brother.

As Mr. Jackson, the publicity director, said, everyone at Disneyland is on stage, entertaining everyone else. They laugh and shriek and wear funny hats. Sometimes they cry, or fall asleep, or spend too much money. Mostly they just enjoy themselves.

"It's happy out here," said Cheryl West, the mother of the twins. "Everyone is smiling, everyone is happy. Everyone is excited because they're at Disneyland."

1971

Your Friendly
John Birch Bookstore

Costa Mesa

Dorothy Seeley is the mother of four teen-agers and the wife of a roofing contractor, almost middle-class, almost middle-aged, and very upset. The other day she was browsing in the American Opinion Bookstore, which is run by the local chapter of the John Birch Society. After several minutes she selected a pamphlet attacking President Nixon for being too liberal and a bumper sticker which read, "Help! Get U.S. Out of U.N." I asked her why she was there and she replied, "I'm looking for an answer to what I feel is wrong with things as they are, the present lawlessness of the country, an answer to why I believe it's happening. I want an answer to why our country appears to fight communism but in actuality we aren't."

Mrs. Seeley is a rather typical customer of the American Opinion Bookstore here in Costa Mesa, a town of about 75,000 in the middle of Orange County, California, an area whose reputation rests more on conservatism than citrus. Like Mrs. Seeley, many of the patrons seem to be looking for "answers," simple explanations for the confusing changes that are battering their world out of shape: drugs and crime, long hair and dirty words, presidents in China, businessmen in Russia, guitars in church, and sex education in the schools.

There are about 450 American Opinion outlets, making it the largest bookstore chain in the country. Each one is organized by a local Birch Society chapter, which donates time and money to get it started. The group in nearby Garden Grove, appropriately enough, held a fireworks sale on July 4 to raise funds. This store got its carpeting at cost from a society member, and the manager, a retired funeral home director, built the shelving himself. All the clerks are volunteers, usually housewives with time on their hands. Most of the stock comes from an approved society list, and local managers, who also serve without pay, are discouraged from making independent judgments.

The stores serve as libraries for society members and as public outposts in the community. "It's a meeting place, an open place," explained Bob Gogley, a telephone repairman who heads the Garden Grove chapter. "It's a way of saying, 'Here's Garden Grove, here's the John Birch Society.' If people can see it, they won't be so afraid of it."

But the main reason for the bookstores is the conviction that the "Establishment" press and publishing houses do not tell the truth. The right holds this belief as fiercely as the left; if the two political extremes can agree on one thing it's their hatred of *The New York Times*, CBS, and *Newsweek*. Hal Tibbetts, a retired business school teacher, was in the store with his wife to buy ten copies of *None Dare Call It Treason*, one of the best-selling conservative books of all time, "the carefully documented story of America's retreat from victory." Mr. Tibbetts, who was going to give the books to friends, pointed to the shelves and said, "This tells what the government is trying to do—destroy the United States—and you can't get that information anywhere else. They suppress it in other magazines and bookstores and newspapers. It's pretty well known you can't get it out of the *Los Angeles Times* or the *Washington Post* or *The New York Times*—they're the worst papers in the country."

The Costa Mesa store is located in a long, one-story building divided into a dozen small examples of free enterprise: a record store called the Licorice Pizza, a German delicatessen, a failing income tax service, and a thriving barber shop. Inside, the decor runs to American eagles and prints of Mount Rushmore. One volunteer had cross-stitched two large portraits of Civil War soldiers, one Union and one Confederate. A bulletin board near the door displayed a newspaper cartoon with the adage, "Any government big enough to give you anything you want is powerful enough to take away everything you have." Below that were arrayed the right-wing entrants in the Great Bumper Sticker War, including "Remember the Pueblo," "POWs Never Have a Nice Day," and a picture of the flag with the admonition, "Honor—Defend."

Next to the cash register was a selection of patriotic jewelry: gilded birch leaves (pins from $2.50 to $5.50, earrings $7), a variety of flags, and an eagle with a red glass eye, marked down from $2.50 to $1. Also on the counter was a petition to the president, which urged him "to have our government stop, promptly and completely, giving aid in any form, directly or indirectly, to our Communist enemies." A dozen signatures were affixed to the bottom. One whole bookcase held Bibles, at least ten different editions. A stack of free palm cards explained that the peace symbol was really a broken cross and represented "anti-Christ, anti-religion, and anti-everything that is decent."

One wall held dozens of political pamphlets, mainly reprints from *American Opinion*, the Birch Society magazine, and *The Review of the News*, its weekly paper. Most of them looked the same—large block letters blaring forth the titles like tabloid newspaper headlines; no illustrations, as if the slightest ornamentation would smack too much of frivolity. Most of them also carry the same message—things are not what they seem; all those new ideas are just further examples of the Communist conspiracy at work. The titles provide a rundown of current concerns: "FIFTH COLUMN, Subversion In the U.S. Military"; "HATE THERAPY, Sensitivity Training for 'Planned Change' "; "RICHARD NIXON, Professor Galbraith Calls Him a Socialist"; "THAT MUSIC, There's More To It Than Meets The Eye"; "PHONEY EXPRESS, Revolutionaries Playing Post Office."

Record albums are another staple. You can find "God Bless America" by the Mormon Tabernacle Choir, General Douglas MacArthur's farewell speech to the cadets at West Point, and "Folk Songs for Taxpayers," by Wini Beatty and the Folkniks. The liner notes for "Folk Songs" complain that the " 'Think Pink' characters" have usurped the folk song, and that "in less than a generation, happy, hand-clapping folk forms have degenerated into the angry sounds of unrest and defiance." What is needed, the notes contend, is a return to bluetail flies, amorous bullfrogs, and "even happy musical forecasts of the hereafter." The record albums can be rented for meetings and parties, as can a large library of film strips.

The book selections contain a few surprises—George Orwell's *Animal Farm* and *1984*, and the novels of Taylor Caldwell, one of the right wing's more devoted and vociferous supporters. Louisa May Alcott and Mark Twain are also available, presumably under the category of "wholesome" reading. A scattering of classics include *The Communist Manifesto*—know your enemy—and John Stuart Mill's *On Liberty*. Mill's *Autobiography*, however, in which he describes his conversion to socialism, is not offered.

Most of the books are didactic tacts published by conservative houses: Henry Regnery, Devin-Adair, Arlington House, and the Birch Society's own imprint, Western Islands. Many of them fall into broad categories, both in substance and style. Some I noticed include personal revelation (*F.D.R., My Exploited Father-In-Law*), foreign disaster (*Africa's Red Harvest*), attacks on liberal issues (*The Bondage of the Free, A Critical Examination of the*

Misnamed "Civil Rights" Cause), attacks on liberal heroes (*Little Cesar*, about Cesar Chavez), urgent alarms by high-ranking generals (*Design for Survival*, by General Thomas S. Porter), and Robert Welch's own Birch Society manuals. Right-wingers never seem to let an issue die, and browsing through the titles is a little like reading musty old newspapers, sprinkled with names only half-remembered: Peress, Hiss, Chambers, Otepka, Harry Dexter White.

The best seller in the store right now is called *The Naked Capitalist*, by one W. Cleon Skousen, who also wrote *The Naked Communist*. Mr. Skousen, who appears fully clothed in the jacket photograph, spent sixteen years with the FBI and now teaches at Brigham Young University. His book is actually a review of a much longer work, *Tragedy and Hope*, by Carroll Quigley, and one reason for its popularity, according to a clerk, is that "it's not too long; people don't like to read too much." Another reason is that Mr. Skousen does not settle for another exposé of the Communist conspiracy. His thesis is summed up in a quote from Bella V. Dodd, the Communist-turned-conservative: "I think the Communist conspiracy is merely a branch of a much bigger conspiracy!"

The other big seller is *Teddy Bare*, by Zad Rust, which goes to show that readers of *Photoplay* and *Esquire* are not the only ones mesmerized by the Kennedys. Mr. Rust alleges that some "organized Force" conspired with "official authorities" to cover up the real story behind the death of Mary Jo Kopechne at Chappaquiddick.

The bookstore is also a floating debating society and counseling service, and as I scanned the shelves I overheard some conversations that provided a sort of counterpoint to the titles: "Here's a leaflet against UNICEF; that's important now that Halloween is coming. . . . My boy has become a Jehovah's Witness, and I have mixed emotions about it. I was told they had known Communists on their writing staff. . . . My son ran away and they brought him into juvenile court. I said I wouldn't have anything to do with him, but he went to work with his brother in Hawaii and it worked out fine. . . . They finally decided where they're going to build the freeway, and it's going right next to my house. . . . I've got a black man living on my property and I don't think anyone else in Garden Grove can say that. . . . I grew up believing that America was the good guys, that they didn't take anything off anybody. . . . If a guy commits a crime, they study his sociological background, they excuse him for everything he did. . . . It all comes down to this, do you want to be taken care of, or do you want to take care of yourself. . . ."

These are the voices of people who want answers. At the American Opinion Bookstore, some of them find what they're looking for. As Kay Goode, a clerk in a blue print dress and white tennis shoes, put it, "I believe in the Birch Society, and we're trying to educate the people. We want to get this literature out to them. I think it's the truth.

1972

Fire!

Malibu

The Presbyterian Church had given Amelia Harrison a pair of blue jeans and a work shirt, but they could not give her back her house. That was gone, a big mound of smoldering, ashen rubble. "I thought I might find some piece of metal that meant something to me," she said helplessly. "But I couldn't find anything. I'm in the same boat as everyone else. A lot of people lost their whole lives."

Hundreds of families are in that boat with Mrs. Harrison, burned out of their homes by the worst series of brush fires ever to hit Southern California. Most of the blazes were under control today, but since last Friday they have ravaged more than 600 square miles, killed ten persons, and done inestimable damage. President Nixon has proclaimed Southern California a major disaster area, making fire victims eligible for low-cost federal loans.

Mrs. Harrison's was one of about a dozen homes destroyed here on Malibu Road, a street whose ocean beaches and salt breezes provide a refuge from the harassment of life in Los Angeles, 15 miles down the Pacific Coast. One house belonged to Tuesday Weld, the actress. Another, according to Mrs. Harrison, was where Elizabeth Taylor lived "when she was sixteen and making all those horse pictures." But today, Malibu Road was a street not of dreams but of memories, memories of terror and of loss.

"I wasn't the least bit hysterical," recalled Mrs. Harrison, a former actress who retained her regal bearing despite the red kerchief tied around her head. "I was outside watering down the house and I figured someone would come along to help. But the last twenty minutes all happened so fast. I had a suitcase packed. But suddenly I couldn't breathe, and I decided I couldn't go back inside the house. It was just instinct. I couldn't go back in. I lost the portraits of my two daughters, old theatrical photos, mementoes from a trip I took to Russia, things from my childhood, from Stanford, all sorts of things," she said. "My dog, Irving—he died last March—is buried right there in the front yard. He was very well known around here. People called him 'The Mayor of Malibu.' Everyone knew Irving."

Somehow, Mrs. Harrison has retained her sense of humor. "We should start naming our fires, like hurricanes, so we could get a little status," she laughed. "Now we just call them by the years."

A few doors down, or what used to be doors, a young doctor was carrying a carton of charred metal to his red sports car. "It's just junk," he said, "but I thought that some day I might make a sculpture out of it for my new garden—if I build one." The doctor considered himself lucky. On one side, a young couple who had been married for three weeks have lost everything. On the other side lived a man who had recently moved to Malibu Road. His previous home had been destroyed in a mudslide.

Many people here fell prey to the delusion that if you ignore something it will go away. One young couple, for instance, had no insurance. "It was like expecting a fire to have insurance," the wife explained.

Even when they heard that the fire was approaching, some residents failed to take precautions, hoping somehow to stave off the holocaust. "I guess," said Mrs. Tess Weiner, whose house still stood, "that I didn't really give credence to the fact that it might happen." When it did happen, it came with such speed and force that little survived.

Mrs. Suzanne Odekerken poked through the ruins of the house she had grown up in and found a few pieces of old Limoges china a great-aunt had stored there. But there was no hope for a painting of her great-great-great-grandmother or her great-grandfather's Confederate uniform. Others lost a life's work. The doctor could not save 6,000 medical slides he had collected from all over the world. And many shuddered at the thought of replacing all the papers and numbers and forms that seem to spin a web around modern life.

Some had strange thoughts. Mrs. Sandra Janson, whose house did not burn because it had asbestos siding, remembers fleeing the flames at the last moment. "We got to the end of the road, and I started to think, 'Why didn't I take my sewing machine?' I guess I figured that if we were destitute I could always make our clothes."

On Malibu Road, life continues. A little girl sells orange juice for 5 cents a glass and throws into the deal a look at a "fossil"—a seashell encrusted with mud. Mrs. Janson, who is several months pregnant, reads the instruction booklet for a new washing machine that was delivered today. But some people here have a new idea of what is important to them.

"It's funny," said Mrs. Weiner, "I looked at everything and there's a lot here I enjoy, paintings and antiques I collected for thirty years. But in the long run, I don't think they're irreplaceable." "A friend of mine up the road was asked what she wanted," said Mrs. Odekerken, "and she said, 'There's a lot of things I want, but I found out there's very little I need.' "

At least for the moment, the heat of the fire seems to have fused the people of Malibu Road together. Neighbors who never exchanged more than a curt nod before have become friends. People seem to relish the excuse to make contact with each other.

"Sometimes we need our values shaken up a bit," said Mrs. Bunny Sexton, as she brought some cold soda pop out to Mrs. Odekerken. "I hate to think you need a catastrophe like this to make you realize it. But you've just got to help your fellow man. That's all there is to it."

1971

Earthquakes
as an Art Form

"There will be a great rain, and oil upon the waters, before the great wave."

—Hopi Indian prophecy as translated
by the Arch Druid Morloch

Los Angeles

You're driving home along the Pacific Coast Highway. The moon is up and the waves are slapping gently against the beach—which is covered with sticky black oil from a leaking offshore well. The traffic slows to a crawl. A house high on a hill above the highway has slipped loose in recent rains and threatens to fall, so only two lanes are open. As you creep along, a disk jockey's voice comes from the radio. "How's the old San Andreas Fault holding up tonight?" he asks cheerily, and then proceeds to play a familiar calypso song: "Day after day, more people come to L.A. Shhh, don't you tell anybody the whole place's slipping away." The bouncy tune goes on: "Where can we go, when there's no San Francisco? Better get ready to tie up the boat in Idaho. Do you know the swim? You'd better learn quick, Jim. Those who don't know the swim, better sing the hymn." ° Your mind wanders. That old Indian prophecy can't be right. Can it? CAN IT?

California today bubbles with talk about earthquakes. Prophets of doom are as common as girls in bikinis (there are even a few prophets in bikinis). Some predict the whole state will break off and sink into the Pacific—probably this month. Why April exactly is a bit of a mystery. Some mystics just have a "feeling" about it; others point out that the sun and moon will line up in such a way as to exert considerable magnetic force on

° From "Day After Day" by Stuart Margolin, Jerry Riopelle and Tommy Reynolds. Copyright 1969, Irving Music, Inc. and St. Croix Music Co. (BMI). All rights reserved. Used by permission.

the earth. Anyway, it's a veritable festival of calamity. Even the straight people—those without visions or premonitions, tea leaves or astrology charts—are a little worried. Can all the kooks be wrong? Even a stopped clock is right twice a day.

There are nervous little jokes. "California is perfect to a fault," goes one, or "California will lose by default." "Howard Hughes is buying up all that property in Nevada so he'll have ocean frontage" is, for some reason, a particular favorite in barber shops. Newspaper columnist Herb Caen suggests that, "If you feel queasy at the thought of April, ask your doctor for earth control pills." A *Los Angeles Times* cartoonist recently pictured a robed seer carrying a sign with the legend, "Warning! California will fall into the ocean in April!" Two elderly ladies are gazing in horror at the poor fellow, and one says, "Heavens! I hope it doesn't happen before the Academy Awards presentations!"

The *San Francisco Chronicle*'s inquiring reporter asked seven people if they thought there would be an earthquake, and four admitted they were worried. One, a girl with the unlikely name of Friday Coyle, said, "Yes. I'm leaving California. I'm going to Oklahoma. I don't think the whole state will drop into the sea but I think San Francisco will." Practically everybody professes to know somebody who is getting out while there is still time—or at least is laying in some extra Band-Aids and canned food.

The airways are plagued with the talk. A recent song by Mama Cass, called "California Earthquake," blares forth the somber news: "Atlantis will rise. Sunset Boulevard will fall. And where the beach used to be won't be nothing at all. That's the way it appears. And they tell me the fault line runs right through here." ° "Sin City," by the Flying Burrito Brothers, warns enigmatically, "On the thirty-first floor, a gold-plated door. Won't keep out the Lord's burning rain." †

Earthquakes have replaced the sexual revolution as Topic A on women's talk shows. Books on earthquakes are grabbed off the shelves as if they were free. One of them, *The Last Days of the Late, Great State of California*, by San Francisco journalist Curt Gentry, has run through five printings since November. When a local newspaper ran a front-page story on earthquakes and told concerned citizens to consult the Civil Defense office for advice, more than 1,000 calls flooded the switchboard in a single day.

Of course, there are aspects to life out here that can stir qualms in the calmest of hearts. The rains and mudslides of the last few months have toppled dozens of homes from their cliffside perches and damaged hundreds more. Geologists trying to stem the oil leak in the Santa Barbara Channel reported ominously that the crude sludge was escaping not from the well itself, but from a fault in the ocean floor. Similar, if somewhat larger, faults are the main cause of earthquakes.

The fever has produced a windfall for Ben Harris, a bearded young man in paint-stained jeans, who runs the Timeless Occult shop on Sunset Boulevard. He has sold out his entire stock of ephemerists (charts that show the positions of the planets), and such items as magic candles are moving fast. Another big seller is books by and about Edgar Cayce, the "sleeping prophet," who foresaw California's demise in 1941. "Some people just wander in and want to know how far they should drive inland," Harris said. "I tell them not to worry. This one won't be so bad. Utter devastation won't come until 1972."

Astrologers are also cashing in on the rumors, but at least one prominent star-gazer in town, who wishes to remain anonymous, will not comment on earthquakes. "Every time I've predicted an earthquake, it hasn't happened," he said sadly. "Although one time I predicted a quake and we had the Watts riot instead."

One group that is intent on doing something about the earthquake is the Fellowship of the Ancient Mind, a Druidic order which claims to be telepathic and traces its lineage back 6,000 years. The fellowship caused a bit of a stir recently when several members appeared at Los Angeles City Hall and applied for a salvage permit that would allow them to rescue great works of art when the tremor strikes. The group's plan, according to its leader, Arch Druid Morloch, is to send the objects out of state by teleportation. "We've already moved a car from Los Angeles to Palm Springs in twenty minutes, but we need more practice," the Arch Druid said the other day, sucking thoughtfully on a pipe. "We tried to move an Etruscan vase and broke it."

Morloch is a pleasant young man of 27, who wears a clerical collar and a silver pendant that represents the jabberwock, "a sign of office." Unlike many doom-sayers, he plans to stay around for the cataclysm. "We're doing a study of the earthquake as an art form," he said. "You've heard of destructive art—you know, people chopping up pianos and things. Well, this will be the greatest example of destructive art in history."

California has always had more than its share of mystics. They seem to thrive on the climate, like oranges, and many of them have been prophesying the end of the Golden State for years. So why the sudden panic?

Some people trace it to a lady named Elizabeth Steen, who claims she felt bad vibrations when she placed her hand over the Fresno section of a map. A 28-year-old housewife from San Francisco, Mrs. Steen declared last summer that disaster would strike this April and promptly decamped with her family and several others for Spokane, Washington. A number of ministers have also abandoned California in the past year and herded their congregations to such safer, and apparently holier, places as Kennett, Missouri, and Murfreesboro, Tennessee. Followers of Mrs. Steen point out gloatingly that these ministers variously pinpointed the day of doom in either October or February. Hundreds of hippies have also fled, but they are just as anxious to escape the local cops, who are likely to bust you on a pot charge if you're smoking a Chesterfield and not wearing shoes.

Another great cause of consternation is the prophecy of Mr. Cayce, who told a visiting businessman in 1941 that "Los Angeles, San Francisco, most all of these will be among those that will be destroyed before New York even." Mr. Cayce would only say that the trouble would begin sometime between 1958 and 1998. However, Mr. Cayce's prediction is recalled by Mr. Gentry in his book, which only uses the idea of an earthquake as a literary device to excuse a history of the state as if it had already been destroyed. Mr. Gentry says that followers of Cayce put the hour of disaster at 3:13 on a Friday afternoon in 1969. Although he has promised not to reveal the date, the author hints it is December 12. Gentry is a serious journalist, whose angry book charges that California is being destroyed even without an earthquake by such individuals as water polluters, redwood choppers, and John Birch Society members.

Scientists at the California Institute of Technology in Pasadena, meanwhile, have released the following statement: "Wild predictions of disastrous earthquakes—issued by self-proclaimed oracles and other visionaries—are not supported by scientific evidence and are frightening many Californians needlessly." On the other hand, one thing remains indisputable: If scientists cannot predict when an earthquake will strike, they cannot predict when one won't strike, either. Moreover, there is considerable evidence that California is due for a major tremor almost any time now.

About 90 percent of the country's earthquakes occur in California. There are thousands here every year, although only about 500 can be felt by the average person, and only one in every 10,000 is capable of causing damage. The worst quakes happen along cracks, or faults, in the earth's crust. Normally, each side of the fault moves slowly, either vertically or horizontally, in relation to the other. But if the two sides somehow get "locked," and cannot move, pressure builds up. When the two sides finally break apart, a quake occurs.

The state's largest and most famous fault, the San Andreas, which runs for 600 miles from Mendocino to the Gulf of California, last caused a major earthquake in 1906; most of San Francisco was destroyed by the tremor and the ensuing fire. The San Andreas also shook Southern California severely in 1857. That's a long time for the pressure to mount. On top of the natural causes, scientists believe that atomic blasts in the Nevada desert and attempts to dispose of contaminated water in deep wells have both helped cause small quakes.

In a frank moment last year, Dr. C. F. Richter of Cal Tech, one of the world's leading seismologists, said that in California "every community is within striking distance of one or more of the important faults." Because of the long period since the last big tremors, he added, "we must expect repetitions of the great earthquakes of 1906 and 1857." In his well-regarded book, *Earthquake Country*, Robert Iacopi wrote, "California's next great earthquake may take place while you are reading this book, or it may not come during our lifetime. But one thing is sure: It is definitely on the way." And a few days ago in Washington Dr. William T. Pecora, director of the U.S. Geological Survey, told the Senate Interior Appropriations Subcommittee that California was in a "steady state of restlessness" and predicted "another massive earthquake, certainly within the next thirty years and probably within the next decade."

Thus you do not have to be crazy to worry about earthquakes. In fact, many experts are concerned that people are not worried enough. Construction codes were adopted after the Long Beach quake in 1933 to guarantee that buildings could withstand earthquakes. But the codes are administered sloppily and do not retroactively affect buildings built before 1933. Housing developments have been put up right over the San Andreas and other faults, and in San Francisco an allegedly "quakeproof" skyscraper stands midway between the San Andreas and a branch fault, the Hayward, which runs through Berkeley across the Bay. Dr. Richter warns that most injuries come not from a quake itself but from falling debris.

However, precautions for disaster seem to be minimal. The Los Angeles Civil Defense office will send you, on request, a booklet about what to do in various emergencies. Only two of the book's ninety-two pages deal with tremors, and the advice can be summed up in two perceptive words: "Keep calm." In San Francisco, city officials and businessmen wince when you refer to the earthquake of 1906; they prefer to call it the "fire." The reason for all this reticence is obvious: Talk about earthquakes is bad for business, especially the tourist business. (Of course, they could always try the slogan, "Come see California while it's still here," but that, too, has its drawbacks.)

Real estate companies have, according to reports, threatened to sue radio stations that play earthquake songs. A spokesman for San Francisco Mayor Joseph Alioto seemed to take a question about earthquake preparations as a personal insult. "We are continually aware of the possibility of an earthquake," he said huffily, "but the city goes about the job of living and prospering and building and moving ahead. We simply can't live under the cloud of fear that something might come tumbling down on us." Presumably, the spokesman will be attending a chamber of commerce convention in Miami Beach when the quake comes.

One theme runs through virtually all the commentary on California earthquakes: This is a sinful place that deserves all the calamity it gets. California is, simply, too nice a place to live for some children of the Protestant ethic. A few sunny days in February and they start lashing themselves with guilt. But the fascinating thing is that everybody thinks California must pay for a different crime.

The *Express Times*, an underground paper in San Francisco, gives the possibility of a quake a leftist political slant. "Like if it hits the San Andreas Fault," asserted a recent article, "certain portions of San Francisco will probably fall into the ocean. . . . But they're not going to do anything about it because that would require social planning. And that would be socialism. And this is the U.S.A. We only plan wars." The *Express Times* goes on to hint darkly that all the earthquake talk might be the devious work of the "Power Centers," which somehow have a large stake in continued "hysteria" among the populace.

Ben Harris at the Timeless Occult shop gives a rather traditional religious version: "From the spiritual aspect—you know, I practice a little mediumship myself—there have to be sacrifices in this world. The Sodom and Gomorrah of the United States must be Los Angeles and New York. They're the two places where moral degradation, the loss of the unity principle, the loss of communication between people, that sort of thing, are at their highest." Harris noted, however, that a quake might be forestalled because "Buddhists all over are chanting to stop it."

Harris thinks that people are actually looking forward to a quake. "This society is fear-oriented," he said; "they seem to get a religious sensation out of catastrophes." Columnist Caen tends to agree: "The quake of 1906 was really our finest hour. It was considered the Golden Age of San Francisco, something like the Battle of Britain. People camped out in Golden Gate Park and apparently lived by the slogan, 'Eat, drink and be merry, for tomorrow we may have to move to Oakland.' Everyone had a high old time—except, of course, the people who were killed. Everybody looks back on it all with nostalgia; it was the high point of their lives."

What is certain is that someday, somewhere, a major earthquake will hit California. What remains uncertain is the result. Some anxious types are encouraged by the observation of Greg Chursenoff of Van Nuys, who recently wrote to a newspaper, "It is true that a disastrous earthquake will split California in half at the San Andreas Fault. However, there is no reason for alarm because it is the eastern section of the United States that will sink into the ocean."

1969

TRANSITION IN SAN FRANCISCO

The era of revolution seems far away now. If the watchword in 1969 was "from dissent to resistance," today it could be "from resistance to indifference," and there are a number of reasons for that. After "High on Revolution" was written, things got even more violent for a time; there were riots over People's Park in Berkeley, and a Bank of America branch was burned down in Isla Vista. But as their frustrations grew, the rebels turned inward, to more traditionally political, and even personal, concerns. Tom Hayden waved a rifle in 1969, but handed out election leaflets in 1971, and by 1973 he was bouncing a baby on his knee. Above all, the Vietnam war finally ended. Young people no longer faced the draft; neighbors were no longer coming home in boxes. The sharp edge of anger and fear that had prodded so many thousands into the streets was rubbed smooth by an apparent peace. Charges against the Oakland Seven were eventually dropped, and the Presidio mutineers, as far as I know, are now free. The Black Panthers are little more than a name and Huey Newton lives in a penthouse, but those turbulent years left many scars. The University of California, for example, is still suffering from budget cuts pushed through by Governor Reagan. More important, a whole generation learned to be skeptical of any authority—professors or politicians or priests—and that is a useful lesson.

Every generation thinks its own ideas are unique, but they seldom are. Skepticism was one of San Francisco's major exports long before People's Park, and the remnants of the beat movement still survive in North Beach. So do topless dancers and Italian clerics, and one of these days, one of the girls is going to bill herself as The Dancing Nun and read Jack Kerouac in nothing but a wimple.

High on Revolution

A group of pacifists recently marched up from Carmel and staged an all-night vigil in front of City Hall, demanding clemency for twenty-seven soldiers charged with mutiny in the stockade of the Presidio, the army base overlooking the Golden Gate Bridge. Their candles flickered and danced in the cool evening air, and snatches of the old movement songs floated up from small knots of people clustered around strumming guitars. The scene was joyous and peaceful—and very out of place. It seemed more like an old newsreel clip than a contemporary political event, a film that evoked considerable nostalgia for a time pleasantly remembered but definitely over.

San Francisco is well beyond the days of "We Shall Overcome," and even those of flower children and love-ins in Golden Gate Park. The city is on a "bummer"—a bad trip. It appears locked in an increasingly vicious cycle of violence and counterviolence, and the end all remains very unclear. What is certain, however, is that between the young radicals and the Establishment the lines are hardening, the rhetoric and the action escalating. The peace-makers are now the villains, vilified by extremists on both sides eager for conflict. "Compromise" has become an obscenity.

The repressive actions of the "power structure," civil and military, have accelerated rapidly. Across the Bay in Oakland, seven young men are being tried for conspiracy to trespass and obstruct policemen, felony charges that could result in three-year jail sentences. The charges stem from their activities during Stop the Draft Week, a major series of antiwar demonstrations in the Bay area in October 1967.

In the past, demonstrators have usually been charged with misdemeanors, which seldom carry sentences longer than ninety days. The suit was clearly brought against the Oakland Seven to intimidate future political protests, since the state conspiracy laws are very vague and could probably apply to almost anyone who helps organize a demonstration. Indeed, the prosecution is basing its case on the fact that the defendants performed such insurrectionary acts as renting buses and opening bank accounts. Recently Alameda County officials also brought conspiracy charges against three

more radicals for participating in protests last fall in support of Eldridge
Cleaver's lectures at the University of California in Berkeley. And they have
persistently hunted down Cleaver and his fellow Black Panthers.

At the Presidio, the mutinous soldiers were tried for the crime of
staging a peaceful sit-down demonstration and asking the base commandant
to listen to a list of grievances they had prepared. Among their demands was
the investigation of the killing of a fellow prisoner, more psychiatric help for
inmates, and improvement of medieval conditions one lawyer has called
"worse than our soldiers experienced in Japanese prison camps."

Like the Alameda County officials, the army brass seems eager to set an
example of harsh reprisal and deter further dissent. Before the first of the
twenty-seven was sentenced, the prosecutor urged the court-martial not to
stress the seriousness of the actual offense. "It is the attack on the system
that counts," he said—and less than an hour later a sentence of fourteen
years at hard labor was returned.

Meanwhile, Governor Ronald Reagan is taking every available opportunity to denounce radicals at San Francisco State College and Berkeley, and
his rating in the public opinion polls is soaring. Laws to restrict the student
demonstrators stand a good chance of passage in the legislature, which also
holds the enormous power of the purse over the state college system.
Reagan has proclaimed an emergency at Berkeley and moved national
guardsmen to the campus.

Chancellor Roger Heyns at Berkeley and Acting President S. I.
Hayakawa at San Francisco State have not hesitated to use force against
students, and each clash gets a little more violent—on both sides. Police are
now regularly called to put down fracases at local high schools (there was a
particularly bad one over a basketball game between white and black
schools) and even junior highs.

The young radicals, of course, are hardly innocent. Stop the Draft
Week, for instance, represented a definite intensification of student tactics.
Instead of merely protesting the injustice of the draft, the demonstrators
actually tried to block the entrance to the Oakland induction center. Thus
they started moving "from dissent to resistance," and they have traveled
very swiftly along that road in the last seventeen months.

This year, acts of violence and vandalism, mainly on college campuses,
have risen sharply. A 19-year-old State student lies blinded and crippled in a
local hospital because a bomb he was planting in the creative arts building
exploded prematurely. The next day, shots were fired into several other

campus buildings. These incidents follow a long series of bombings at induction centers and similar establishments. Some students in the Bay area carry more rocks and stink bombs to class than books.

When Tom Hayden of the Students for a Democratic Society (SDS) spoke recently at a birthday party for Huey Newton, the Black Panther leader now in jail for shooting an Oakland policeman, he made an impassioned appeal for revolutionary struggle. To emphasize his point, he left the stage and returned brandishing a rifle. There is a lot of talk about guns among the radicals, and some have bought them and are taking lessons. One member of the Oakland Seven explained: "People are losing their fear of violence. They know it's insane to go out with a gun and snipe at the cops, but right now guns represent an extension of the concept of self-defense, which started with Stop the Draft Week. In Mexico City, students were machine-gunned in the streets, and they started shooting back. Obviously the situation is very different here, but when it's necessary to launch an attack, that will happen. That's history."

The roots of this mood in San Francisco are jumbled and obscure. But a few tentative explanations are possible. Among white students, the move toward active resistance was motivated mainly by the feeling that they could not influence Vietnam policy through peaceful protest. This has come out clearly during the Oakland Seven trial. A stream of witnesses has testified that they participated in the demonstrations because they felt "there was nothing else to do."

In the case of the black students, many who are now pouring onto college campuses were recruited from the ghettos and are used to a much more aggressive and physically violent style of expressing themselves than the average white, or middle-class black, collegian. As one student said, "Berkeley thought it was getting 300 Roy Wilkinses, but it wound up with 300 Eldridge Cleavers." The blacks, and their allies in the Third World movement, are bent on demonstrating their power, sometimes merely for the sake of showing that they have it. "They have been dominated by whites for so long," one college administrator said, "that they just want to show they have some control over their own lives."

In addition, young people of all races have become entranced, even intoxicated, with the rhetoric of revolution. They imbibe it like older generations slurped beer. Instead of empty cans on their mantelpieces, they tack up posters of Ché Guevara—whom they conveniently forget was a rather unsuccessful guerrilla. It is largely talk, but occasionally it provokes an eruption. Sometimes one gets the impression that the movement is like a kid who started on fairly mild drugs, then looked for something more powerful when they lost their kick.

For many young people, radical protest is an end in itself. They find a new purpose and feeling of community merely by participating; the larger and more distant goals of social change often recede into the background. The emotional content of the movement is terribly important, therefore, and "revolution" is a first-rate high. As for ego gratification, getting beaten up by a cop is an uncomfortable, yet incontrovertible, way of proving not only that you exist but that you matter. Why else would the cop have bothered to hit you?

On the Establishment side, the growing repression obviously springs from the same climate in the country that spawned the "law and order" campaign appeals of Richard Nixon and George Wallace. "People just want to clamp down," one Democratic politician commented. Why? Apparently because the young people are defying not just the politics but the essential values and life-styles of an older generation. Moreover, they are challenging something very dear to a generation nurtured on the patriotic formula of World War II—faith in the country. When Alameda County officials talk about the Oakland Seven in private they start sputtering words like "sedition" and "treason," not "trespass."

The opposition to the militant and intractable young radicals, though, is not confined to Reaganites and other troglodytes. Many liberals who have been deeply sympathetic to student demands for university reform and an end to the war are now cringing at the violent tactics used at Berkeley and State. They are seriously worried that the integrity of the institutions and their essential commitment to rationality are being threatened. And continuing turmoil, they fear, will only produce a ferocious counterattack that could destroy the universities.

San Francisco is still beautiful and vibrant, a rare place which pulses with the juices of urban life at its best, and yet avoids many irritants endemic to the big city. But churning in its streets today is an ugly mood, a mood of bitterness and violence that chills the first warmth of spring.

1969

Worlds Apart in North Beach

North Beach has many worlds, many faces; its people are neighbors, yet strangers. They walk the same steep, crooked streets, but like parallel lines, they never meet. They speak the same language, but they do not understand each other's songs: the wail of a rock singer, the lyrics of a lonely poet, the chants of a fruit peddler, the slogans of an angry radical.

This old neighborhood, tucked between Nob and Telegraph Hills in downtown San Francisco, was the haven of the "beat generation" of young writers in the 1950s. Five years ago came the topless dance clubs. Then it was the hippie-types, refugees from Haight-Ashbury, pushing pot and revolution.

But before them all came the Italians. As poor immigrants they lived in the small pastel houses that creep up the side streets, almost as if they were trying to escape the threadbare gaudiness of the Broadway "strip" and its faintly sinful, neon-splashed night life.

Now most of the young families, with their college degrees and union pay scales, have moved to the new subdivisions where the plumbing is better and their children can play on grass, not broken concrete. But something remains.

A few old women still plant vegetables in their tiny backyards and a few little girls still skip home yelling to each other, "Anyone who made her communion at St. Peter and Paul raise her hand." The freshening evening breeze still wafts the aroma of simmering pasta through the gathering darkness.

Those who stay have familiar complaints: "You can't walk on the streets anymore—they'll kill you." "A lot of beautiful girls are going with the niggers." But they also have the old ways—ways that do not transplant well to suburbia.

The Molinari delicatessen, a symphony of smells, a temple of tastes, has stood on the same spot for more than fifty years. Here one can find fifteen different kinds of sausages and cold cuts, macaroni sculpted with the frills and curlicues usually found on Roman palaces, 4-year-old Parmesan cheese served by a friendly clerk on the end of long, flat knife.

They don't make salami in the back anymore, but they still turn out homemade ravioli on a weird machine that looks something like a pants presser with blades. Eddie Cereghino, a butcher in Rossi's Market next door, came in for some cold cuts. He rubbed his hands on his bloody apron and said, "I was born here on Green Street in 1904, before the fire. The neighborhood's deteriorating; a new class of people has moved in. The old people have passed on and the young ones don't care to stay; they don't like the old houses."

Mr. Cereghino surveyed his purchases and asked for some more of the spicy, motley-colored meat. "I've got a priest coming tomorrow," he laughed. "I'll be in good company for a change. Maybe I'll go to heaven."

Less than one block from Molinari's is the Condor Club, a garish, purple-fronted establishment on the corner of Broadway and Columbus. Here, in 1964, a waitress named Carol Doda first danced on a piano in a topless swimsuit. Broadway soon nurtured more than a dozen topless clubs—which later started baring bottoms as well when the topless novelty wore off. But today the clubs are faced with a threat even more serious than boredom.

Governor Ronald Reagan signed a bill this fall allowing local committees to outlaw topless clubs, and a zealous county supervisor, running for reelection, has vowed to push for such legislation.

Dave Rosenberg, a portly press agent who first dreamed up the topless gimmick, is a little surprised that the clubs have lasted this long. "Usually a fad like this lasts one, maybe two years," he said, as visitors crowded his tiny office above Tipsy's, one of the smaller clubs. "I think this lasted because of the name itself. Some entertainers just electrify a crowd, like Sinatra. Well, this name, topless, electrified the crowd. It's magnetic, it's phenomenal."

Broadway has been called "Disneyland for Adults"; it offers modern jazz, grand opera, and pornographic movies as well as undraped females. But the street characters are as intriguing as any formal entertainment: old Chinese men playing pinball machines, pregnant hippies begging for spare change, fresh-faced coeds staring at their dates over espresso cups and having "serious talks."

The biggest group is the conventioneers, knots of three or four men in white shirts and business suits, nudging each other as they pass the barkers ("all nude, right inside") straining to see, trying to laugh. Usually they go in.

"Let's face it," said Jerry Morris, who owns five clubs, "they can't see this in Iowa."

Another thing they cannot see in Iowa is *Oh Calcutta*, the nude review that opened here recently. Marvin Boyd, who owns the El Cid, watched the gyrations of one of his dancers, billed as Nude Orphan Fanny, and said, "I've been in this business six years and I was embarrassed by *Oh Calcutta*. I live with this stuff, but to me that was plain dirt. Burlesque has been around for years and you're used to seeing girls without clothes. But to see men and women together without clothes—that shocked me."

A visitor was strolling along Broadway with Dave Rosenberg and asked him if he remembered Jack Kerouac. "Who?" replied the press agent. Not many people in North Beach remember Jack Kerouac, the man whose novels of youthful wanderlust made him an oracle of the "beat generation." By the time Mr. Kerouac died last month many of the bars and coffee houses made famous by the beats had long since closed. One gathering place that remains is the City Lights Bookstore on Columbus Avenue; one can see it from Dave Rosenberg's window, but it could be light-years away.

The bare brick walls and simple wooden bookcases remain. One can still find crudely printed books of obscure poems (*Separate Voices. An Anthology of New Jersey Shore Poets*) and sit at little round tables in the basement to read them. Shigeyoshi Murao, his black beard thick and straight, is still the manager. But many other things have changed. "The hippies are not as intellectual as we were," recalled Mr. Murao, known to everyone as Shig. "The whole scene is anti-intellectual. They don't read as much poetry. We sell them *Zap* comics and the underground papers and books on astrology—it has to be happening at the moment for them to be interested."

"You go to a college today and it looks like Haight-Ashbury," he went on, sitting in his basement office with an old magazine photo of Marilyn Monroe pinned to the wall. "We used to call that look 'college crummy.' We sneered at the weekend bohemians, but now that whole style has been taken over by the bourgeois middle class. The underground is no longer underground."

Mr. Murao was asked about Jack Kerouac. He hesitated and then said, "Jack always kept to himself. You were with him but then you weren't with him. I don't remember a serious conversation we had in fifteen years—he was always kidding around. But then you can know a lot of people for fifteen years and not really know them, and yet call them friends. Sometimes you call them parents."

He smiled, showing several missing front teeth. Did he think Jack Kerouac's work would last? "*On the Road* is a very important novel—the way it was written and the attitude of the people in it. It was the first genuinely picaresque bohemian novel about a generation people didn't think existed. It was written in the days of so-called affluence. People didn't think there was anything to dissent against, remember?"

1969

THE BERKELEY SCENE

Since 1970, ecology has changed from an elitist fad to a mass phenomenon. After the California legislature refused to limit growth along the Pacific Coast, a citizens' group gathered enough signatures to place an initiative on the ballot. Despite the well-financed opposition of big business it passed overwhelmingly, and today California has a Coastline Commission that must approve all construction along the shore. The last I heard, the Humphreys, chief characters in "The Better Earth," had moved to Modesto, a farming community in the central valley, where Cliff ran unsuccessfully for Congress. Many of the institutions mentioned in "Halfway Between Dropping In and Dropping Out" undoubtedly have folded, but others have sprung up in their place. The issues and the rhetoric might change, but Berkeley remains "one big social laboratory." The search for alternatives goes on.

The Better Earth

The house at 3029 Benvenue is out of an earlier, quieter time. High-pitched roof; brown shingles; large, airy rooms; bright flowers in the yard. It is the kind of house that sends real estate developers scurrying for their adding machines, their heads whirling with estimates on how many cinder-block apartments they could cram onto the lot. Near the door, drawn in black script on white cardboard, is this sign: "If you came by car to Benvenue, in the future we would appreciate it very much if you would come by some alternate locomotion—walking, bicycle or public transportation. If coming by car is unavoidable, please remember, as a courtesy to neighbors who would like us to minimize noise and fumes, to park on College (near Woolsey is generally easy) and to walk around to the house. Enjoy the walk!"

This is the headquarters of Ecology Action, one of dozens of groups now fighting the battle for a better environment in the San Francisco Bay area. What makes Ecology Action different is its style—brash, activist, radical. If the Sierra Club is the NAACP of environmental groups, Ecology Action is a cross between SNCC—when it was still nonviolent—and the Yippies. Its activists generally share neither the bitterness nor the violence of some New Leftists; they'd sooner say, "Enjoy the walk," than scream, "Up against the wall." Ecology Action was started by Cliff Humphrey, a student of archeology, and some friends two years ago, long before even the sophisticated denizens of Berkeley (which has been called "one big social laboratory") knew what "ecology" meant—the study of man's relationship to his environment. "When Cliff first started talking ecology," says his wife, Mary, in a voice still reminiscent of her Boston Irish heritage, "they thought he was an idiot."

But today, Ecology Actionists find themselves riding a tidal wave of interest in the environment, a wave that threatens to drown them even as it hurtles them toward prominence. Each day's mail—it is carted from the post office by bike—contains a flood of requests for information, literature, or speakers. Humphrey likes to talk about Ecology Action as "a movement rather than an organization," and local groups—there are more than 100, and new ones form weekly—are virtually autonomous. But they invariably look to the founding fathers for guidance, and the pressures are enormous.

The house on Benvenue provides office space as well as living quarters for the Humphreys and about ten full-time volunteers. Many of them are conscientious objectors who—with the approval of their draft boards after the state decided that the project served the national interest—are performing their two years of alternate service.

The center of activity in the house is the basement. After getting past the sign at the door, the visitor is confronted with a large poster of a noble, if somewhat apprehensive, Indian. The first Americans have become the culture heroes of the ecology movement. As Mary explained, "The Indians lived in harmony with this country and they had a reverence for the things they depended on." There were petitions to sign—against smog and a new bridge over the Bay, for the "valid claims" of the Indians on Alcatraz—and a canister for contributions to the "Planet Earth Defense Fund." A hand-printed sign warned, "We are already five years into the biosphere self-destruct era."

Cliff and I went upstairs to talk. He is 32 but looks older, with a rough complexion and longish, sandy hair. He was dressed in a beige knit shirt, adorned with dirt spots and a little hole, and brown slacks; on his belt he wore a leather holster that carried a notebook. After junior-college training in engineering and three years in the army he worked, he hesitates to admit, checking freeway construction as an inspector for the State Division of Highways. He went back to the University of California here to study archeology, and in his first course wrote a paper on the Cheyenne Indians. "That was the switch, right there," he explained in his rapid, excitable way. "A lot of things fell into place. I realized the importance of ecology—and the relation of the Plains Indians to their environment." The era of confrontation politics was starting in the Bay area, and Humphrey, although never a leader, was "in the streets" for many of the antiwar, antiuniversity demonstrations. A combination of these political activities and his academic interests led to the formation of Ecology Action.

The basic point, Humphrey said, "is that the biosphere, the life-support system for the earth, is finite and fragile. Once you understand that, the ethics of the movement follow. Through the fifties and sixties, the basic premise of our society was that growth was good—bigger and better everything! But now that premise is changing; it's being replaced by an idea more simple and more universal: The ability of the planet to support life can't be diminished. You can have complete freedom as long as you don't destroy the common life-support system.

"Everywhere I speak I say we have a vested interest in our own destruction," Humphrey went on. "When the stock market goes up it is a signal device warning us of the imminent destruction of some part of the environment. Capitalism is predicated on money and growth, and when you're only interested to maximize profits, you maximize pollution. We need a system that takes maximum care of the earth."

Despite such statements, Humphrey is hardly a doctrinaire Marxist or a knee-jerk America-hater. He is simply an ecologist, and ecologists tend to ignore political barriers; their enemy is man himself.

"You can't really blame the stock market," Humphrey continued. "Our culture evolved in almost total ignorance of ecological absolutes. The New Left rhetoric is so simplistic. There was no conspiracy to get us into this mess. People in the Establishment never had a choice. Henry Ford never realized when he started the assembly line that in 1970 people in Los Angeles would be dying from emphysema caused by his cars. But injecting our new understanding into an old value system will cause a lot of tragedy. Take a guy who owns a hardware store. He's probably honest as the day is long—he'd run after you with your change. But his idea is to maximize his profit. How do you tell him that if the best interests of the people were considered, he should probably sell as little as possible?"

This is one of the great debates in the ecology movement: Growth versus the Good Life, Quantity versus Quality. Most Americans, it seems, still believe that technology can eradicate the problems it has caused. As Dr. Lee S. DuBridge, President Nixon's science adviser, told a conference in Los Angeles recently, "I strongly reject the idea that we have to destroy our technological civilization, deflate and decrease the standard of living, to improve the quality of life. There may be a few who would like to return to the days of the caveman, but most of us believe that men live healthier, more pleasant lives than they did ten thousand years ago, or even a hundred years ago."

Cliff Humphrey thinks DuBridge is not only wrong, but irrelevant. What he and many ecologists believe is that society must undergo a "cultural transformation," a move away from the ideals of growth, consumption, and progress. "At this moment, Western society is having a cumulative impact on the planet," he explained. "If we continue this way we'll run the life-support system down to zero. Survival can't be voted into existence; it has to be lived."

For the Humphreys, ecological soundness begins at home. The residents of Benvenue live on a budget of about $1,500 a month, including $500 for mortgage payments. The $4,000 down-payment on the house, like almost all their income, came from donations, which are seldom enough. "We spend zero for salaries," Humphrey said. "If we have to fix a bike, or someone needs a new pair of pants, we do it, but no salaries."

The household is now down to two gasoline-powered cars, one truck—which runs on propane gas—and eight bikes. They have to allow more time for travel than they would with a more conventional fleet, but there are advantages. "The pace has gotten so fast around here there is a great lack of privacy," Cliff said. "Now most of the time the family is together is when we're traveling around on some public transportation system." Mary has four children, but she quickly points out that three are by a previous marriage and don't live with them. "Cliff's not guilty, he has only one natural-born son," she says, as if one were about to question his ecological credentials.

The house buys food in bulk when it can—rice, sugar, and flour are available—both to save money and to avoid the containers that hold prepackaged foods. Plastics, in particular, are shunned because they're virtually indestructible. Residents of the house take along their own shopping bags or knapsacks to carry their purchases; when they have to accept paper bags they usually return them to the store. Several Ecology Actionists startled a grocer the other day when they bought some potato chips for a picnic, emptied the contents into their own bags and returned the wrappers on the spot. Though the returnable glass bottle is about as rare these days as a beach without oil, the house finally found a dairy that will deliver milk in reusable containers (waxed paper cartons are almost as hardy as plastic). All cans are crushed and saved in two boxes—one for tin-plated steel, one for aluminum—and eventually sold for recycling. Paper is also divided into categories—newsprint, magazines and "mixed"—then resold. All glass that cannot be returned is broken for easy storage, then sold.

The organic garbage is buried in the backyard with lawn cuttings to form a compost heap that will eventually decay and enrich the soil. The yard is not big enough for a garden, however, and the group is looking for some land outside town on which to grow their own vegetables—without pesticides, of course. The group members also bake their own bread, which is cheaper and healthier than the store-bought kind, but they are not maniacal about health foods (witness the potato chips).

The use of drugs is a personal decision. Cliff says he has tried marijuana and decided "it does nothing for me," but others feel that such drugs as mescaline, widely known as a "good high," improved their sensitivity to nature and the "unity of all living things."

Considerable energy is spent conserving other kinds of resources. Most of the Ecology Actionists' clothes are candidates for the rag bag—Mary wears a uniform of a red shirt, denim skirt, and hiking boots, all spotted with white paint—and everything is repaired until it is totally unusable. The toilet tank is filled with bricks; less water is allowed in, and thus wasted, with each flush. Residents are also urged not to bathe every day, and some cynics feel this precept helps account for ecology's popularity among the young.

Old pieces of machinery are saved. One resident recently made a new bike from used parts, but the amateur mechanics of Benvenue tried to fix a car with a second-hand clutch plate recently and realized only after four hours' work that they had the wrong size. Driving is considered a rather sinful act, and when someone does take a car out he usually runs a long list of errands to avoid wasteful trips. When the temperature drops, residents put on sweaters instead of turning up the heat.

The office is another bastion of economy. The mail boxes are old tin cans. Envelopes are opened carefully, then reused—with the legend, "Save trees, reuse envelopes." "It won't save a hell of a lot of trees," Cliff concedes, "but it is a conspicuous act of conscience." Much of the organization's literature is printed on paper donated by other groups; when I was there, a stack of old computer paper about 3 feet high was standing in the hall, awaiting reuse. Sometimes second-hand paper already has a message on one side, and that can cause problems. A batch of ecological tracts showed up at a local high school recently with a Black Panther harangue on the back, and a teacher was almost fired.

A growing number of people around Berkeley practice some of these tricks, but few are as devoted as the Ecology Actionists. Benvenue has become a sort of moral touchstone for the movement. "Everytime I go visit the Humphreys," said one girl in obvious discomfort, "they make me feel like a pig."

Despite the economy measures, money is always scarce, and the group is beginning to look for foundation support. "We're exploring what jobs we can do," Humphrey added. "We might go paint a house together, or learn to convert vehicles to propane, but we won't do it unless we have to. We'd rather stay small and a little on the hungry side."

In addition to the Humphreys, the residents include one other married couple. The rest are young men, most of whom would like to see the sexual imbalance corrected. "It's a little too much like the Boy Scouts," one complained.

Each volunteer is developing a specialty—recycling materials, fund-raising, speech-making—but the group seems to take its character from Humphrey. In line with his theory that survival has to be lived, Ecology Action has staged a series of demonstrations—a sort of guerrilla theater—to dramatize the crisis.

One of the Humphreys' early extravaganzas was the public destruction last June of their 1958 Rambler station wagon—which, they quickly note, had a new transmission. "I saw myself talking about ecology and urging people to drive less, and here I had this car," Cliff recalled with obvious relish. "It was so great! We had a minister from some church in Berkeley read something from Isaiah about not worshiping the works of our hands. Then I ceremoniously raised the hood, removed the air filter, and smashed the carburetor with a sledge hammer." Mary added, rather sheepishly, "We thought other people would give up their cars, too, but no one did."

The car-smashing was followed in September by Smog-Free-Locomotion Day, a demonstration of fumeless alternatives to the automobile. Hundreds of people paraded through Berkeley on bikes, pogo sticks, stilts, roller skates, shopping carts, skate boards, baby carriages, golf carts, and feet. A coffin on wheels, containing an internal combustion engine, led the line of march.

One of the big issues here has been the gradual filling-in of San Francisco Bay. A bill was introduced in the state legislature to stop the practice, and ecologists of all stripes joined the fray. One Sunday, Ecology Actionists loaded twenty canvas money bags with mud—"unfilling the Bay"—and delivered them to companies with Bay-front real estate who want to continue the filling. The story won front-page headlines.

"Those executives had to face not just a bag of mud, but a bag of mud a million people knew about," Humphrey exulted. "If we're going to get the culture changed, each of us can't just have private knowledge of the problem. Everyone has to know that everyone else knows—that they're being watched—it has to be a public thing." The bill passed.

Humphrey also worries that people are not adequately prepared for the next earthquake, and he is trying to warn them. Ecology Actionists invaded a breakfast given by Mayor Joseph Alioto commemorating the last San Francisco earthquake and handed out little black crosses. The group also staged a march along the Hayward Fault, an earthquake line running through Berkeley, and marked the route with purple crepe paper. It ran, Humphrey recalled, through a hotel, a number of residence halls, the California School for the Blind and Deaf, the university football stadium, and the Berkeley City Hall.

In October, the group proclaimed Damn DDT Day in San Francisco. An Ecology Action volunteer, Kathy Radke, dressed as the Grim Reaper, carried a scythe in one hand and her 3-month-old son in the other as she walked through the financial district at lunchtime. She was accompanied by Malvina Reynolds, a folk singer, and several people who handed out leaflets detailing the evils of the pesticides. "People pretended not to notice," Kathy remembered recently, "but I caught them looking out of the corners of their eyes."

Ecology Action's antics have spawned imitators. At San Jose State College, for instance, students recently contributed $2,500 to buy a new yellow Maverick, which they buried at the climax of a week-long "Survival Faire." Some students complained that the burial was "ecologically unsound" because the car was not "biodegradable"—it would not return to its natural components. Black and Chicano (Mexican-American) students argued that the money could be better spent helping blacks and Chicanos. In the end, a vote was taken and the car was buried after the students, at the Chicanos' insistence, put a box of grapes in the back seat as a show of support for striking farm workers.

Future demonstrations could get more disruptive. One idea is a "traffic seminar," in which a large number of people would drive to San Francisco early one morning and occupy all the parking places. The ensuing traffic jam, it is felt, would dramatize the need for more rapid-transit facilities.

Now that ecology has become so popular—the Sierra Club gets at least six job applications a day, and the editor of a music magazine was heard to say recently, "Someday ecology might be as important as rock 'n' roll"—one crucial job is to provide information on what people can do in their own lives. Ecology in Action has developed the concept of a "life house," essentially an information center for a neighborhood. The operators of the "life house" would urge their neighbors to demand returnable containers at the supermarket and tell them how to save refuse and sell it for recycling, to find soaps that do not contain phosphates, to garden without pesticides, form car pools, obtain free trees and plant them, get birth control information, and generally reduce their consumption. Several are functioning in Berkeley and nearby communities. As part of their information program, a contingent of Ecology Actionists are staging a six-week march this spring through California's San Joaquin Valley, stopping in each city to hold a fair or a meeting for local residents.

Life on the ecology front these days is not always peaceful. The field is getting crowded, and some groups are on "power trips," as the local jargon puts it. Humphrey concedes that organizations "tend to horde money and good organizers," but each faction is gradually working out its own role. For example, the Sierra Club, which fought so many conservation battles alone for so long, is now concentrating on legal actions and has more than fifty suits in the courts, including half a dozen against cabinet officers. "If the Sierra Club didn't exist we would have to be much more structured," Humphrey admits, "and we would have to get into some of the things they're doing. This way we have freedom to do what we want to do."

There are at least three major criticisms of Ecology Action's approach. One is that too many people are too enamored of the "throw-away society" to make many changes in their lives. Humphrey tacitly acknowledged this when he talked about high school students. "They're so much less rigid; they're open to new ideas," he said. "They don't have any vested interests yet. They're not employed and they're not into buying cars."

The second criticism is that a "cultural transformation" and small personal acts might make people feel good, but won't have any significant impact on the chemical companies, the auto manufacturers, the timber companies, and other huge polluters of the environment. Humphrey and like-minded ecologists answer that these personal acts help build up a constituency for larger political acts. They point to the passage of the "Save the Bay" bill last spring and the defeat of the timber bill in Congress recently as two examples of the growing political support for legislation that preserves the environment. Moreover, Humphrey feels that if enough people use their power as consumers, they can affect corporate decisions. "There is no way they can make us consume," he insists. But he also admits that there is a gap between what Ecology Action can achieve now and what needs to be done; he foresees the group's becoming more political and hopes to recruit some graduate students doing basic research on environmental problems.

The third criticism extends to all environmentalists. Isn't the new interest in ecology diverting energy and resources from the difficult and frustrating problems of the inner city? And hasn't President Nixon been able to "co-opt" the movement by his rhetorical, if not material, identification with it?

As to the first question, Humphrey and most other ecologists insist that the "environment" must include Watts as well as the redwoods. "Anyone who doesn't still address himself to the old issues—housing, medicine, poverty—is not being honest," he said. "It would be a bad scene if money were siphoned off from a housing program to pay for a park somewhere so that middle-class people could have recreation." But many in the movement also share the urgency of Stephanie Mills, the editor of a new magazine on ecology called *Earth Times*: "It would be the ultimate cop-out to give all our money to the Black Panthers and then have them all die in twenty years because they couldn't drink the water." One thing that continues to bother people, however, is that any slowdown of the "growth economy" would inevitably be most disastrous to those on the bottom. Ecologists are in the uncomfortable position of telling poor people that affluence and material comfort are not good for them.

As for Nixon's "co-opting" of the movement, few activists take him seriously. "There is a fantastic gap between what men like Nixon and Henry Ford are saying and what they're doing," Humphrey said. "In any case, the President is talking about cleaning up some smoke and dirty water, but that's not what we're concerned with. We're concerned with a whole way of life."

All this does not fully explain the tremendous new interest in environmental issues. To some extent it's a fad, especially among politicians. "A lot of them are the same guys who wore Davy Crockett hats when they first came out," said Melissa Shorrock, a recent Russell Sage graduate who is editing the proceedings of an ecology conference. But to many people, it is a very serious matter. One reason for their seriousness is that environmental problems affect everyone. Some are moved toward involvement by a new piece of information or a personal experience. Kathy Radke, who, with her husband, Ted, operates a "life house" in their hometown, Martinez, described her own conversion: "I was pregnant at the time and I read about DDT and mothers' milk. I was planning to nurse the baby, and it really upset me. The dosage in mothers' milk is greater than in cows' milk!" Ken Cantor, a Ph.D. in biology who works at the Ecology Center, a combination bookstore and information clearinghouse in Berkeley, said, "The air pollution around here has been increasing radically from year to year. You're bombarded every day with the fact that you can't see across the Bay anymore. And once one thing like that gets people upset, they start looking at other things, and their concern broadens."

Peggy Datz, who fled a teaching job in Detroit and now also works at the Ecology Center, thinks the moon shot last summer helped stimulate interest. "I don't think a lot of people understood the concept of a finite life-support system before," she said. "You could see very clearly what the resources necessary for life were—they had them on their backs. You couldn't imagine a *deus ex machina* who would always be there." Others talk about seeing the earth photographed from the moon and getting a new sense of its terrible fragility.

Vietnam also helped in several ways. "We got a lot of people who were totally frustrated by the old Peace and Freedom, SDS kind of activity," Humphrey explained. "It's sad in a way, but we wouldn't have gotten such a start if so many people hadn't worried about the war for so many years and found themselves totally unable to get it stopped. There was a potential there for a new thrust. There really is only a limited attention span on any one issue, and all of a sudden here was another way to get it on, to make your concern known."

For others, Vietnam had nurtured a whole new political viewpoint. Steve Cotton, a Harvard law student on leave to work on the Environmental Teach-In April 22, explained, "Many people saw Vietnam as a tragic mistake in American foreign policy, but the more radical kids are saying that it was a natural outgrowth of a system that doesn't care about people, just about profits, about its own expansion and nothing else. There has been a lot of thinking about the system, where it's going and what the alternatives are.

Some of it is heavily ideological, but a lot is just a vague sense of unease, of disquiet, that the whole thing is rushing pell-mell in the wrong direction. Environment as the kids conceive it is an expression of that. They're not saying this is a sanitation job, that if we spend enough money we'll scrub it all clean. They don't buy Nixon's rhetoric that this is a mistake or an oversight. The state of the environment is just another symptom of society's corruption; it's what the system is all about."

Jim Hunt, who graduated from Bates College in Maine last June and is now performing his alternate service at Benvenue, agrees with Cotton. For Hunt, Vietnam was a "stepping-stone to ecology," an experience that not only taught him "the incredible amount of energy wasted by the system," but the potential power of grass-roots sentiment. Once he came to California, however, Hunt found that ecology was not just another issue to make speeches and hold rallies about. "It had a profound effect on my life-style," said the youth, a native of New Britain, Connecticut, who edited the newspaper at Bates. "I began to see ways I could purify my life. When I came here there was nothing in my middle-class background I was particularly against, but I began to see how a lot of things in my background could be very destructive—the love of gadgets, concern with speed and convenience. I had been troubled by some of these things, but I never really knew why, or that an alternative existed."

In other words, for some youths ecology is not only a political but a cultural concept, a new "way of life," as Humphrey puts it, a way of fitting all one's dissatisfactions and aspirations into a coherent structure. Like many similar movements, it also provides a community and a sense of purpose for young people who look at their future with an apprehension bordering on terror. The act of giving up an automobile, or even burying the garbage, imparts a certain sense of accomplishment, even righteousness.

One young man who found a home at Benvenue is Gregory Voelm, who graduated last spring from Antioch College in Yellow Springs, Ohio, and is also working out his conscientious-objector obligation. Soft-spoken yet fiercely articulate, he described what it was like to graduate from college in June, 1969: "We were the first protest graduating class. . . . I was frightened of what lay before us. We had demonstrated and marched and screamed trying to change things, but it had never been real. Then all of a sudden we had to be part of that mess. . . . Everywhere I went, all I saw was plastic and McDonald's hamburger stands. I had a feeling of an overwhelmingly hostile environment. I looked for adult models of how you could be happy, and it didn't look like you could. It was very freaky. I had the feeling that after graduation you dropped off the end of the world. Some of my friends went to Canada or Mexico, and others went to communes out in the country. Few of us considered beginning a career—it was just too much to handle. There was a great feeling of meaninglessness, a search for something to grab hold of, some unifying thing, and I found it. Ecology is a good metaphor; it gives a unity to experience.

"At first I thought recycling all that stuff was stupid, but when you do it you feel you are fitting into something, you're taking a positive step toward relating to your environment, and it feels good. What goes under the name of ecology is the answer to alienation. We're alienated from nature and alienated from our ability to relate to each other, to love. But to break down that alienation between the individual and his environment is really a radical thing. When you destroy part of the environment, you have to realize you're destroying part of yourself."

In some cases, the concept of ecology takes over a person's whole life. For several years, Keith Lampe was an activist against the war, counseling draft resistance; then he helped Jerry Rubin and Abbie Hoffman form the Yippies. After the Chicago convention—he carried a tennis racket all week on the theory that the police "would think anyone who played tennis had money and connections"—he moved west with his wife, Judy, and their small daughter, looking for new causes. Allen Ginsberg first interested Lampe in ecology, and several months later his friend Gary Snyder, another poet, dragged him to a conference held by the Sierra Club. "That really put me over the hump," recalled Lampe, who was wearing a bunch of plastic string beads around his neck and a little pigtail. "I realized that ecology would be my thing for a while."

Last spring, Lampe, who is in his late 30s, started an ecology newsletter called *Earth Read-Out*, which he distributes to interested people and underground newspapers. But recently even that has not been satisfying. "I'm leaving for Colorado soon to look for some land," he said, pacing up and down a kitchen that has a magnificent view of San Francisco Bay. "I have to get out of the typewriter thing and into reality. We take this population-food squeeze very seriously, and we're going to go out and grow more food than we can consume. My wife has a trust fund, and we're in a position where we can afford to buy some land, so that's what we think we ought to do." The conversation rambled, but every once in a while Lampe would look up and say, "It's amazing I could do that! Incredible! I'm going to be a farmer?"

"The great thing about ecology as a cause," writes Art Hoppe, the columnist for the *San Francisco Chronicle*, "is that everybody's guilty." And for people caught up in the cause, it means a lot of hard decisions. The Lampes, for example, decided to have a legal abortion recently. "Having only one child is to ecology what unilateral withdrawal used to be to Vietnam," he said with a laugh. "Having only two children is like favoring a negotiated settlement." (Indeed, it's reached the point in some circles where mothers are made to feel like criminals. "Jesse Unruh said that environment is the motherhood issue of 1970," remarked Ken Cantor during a discussion at the Ecology Center. "I guess he'll have to revise that; motherhood isn't very popular anymore." Peggy Datz replied, "Apple pie is still all right—as long as there are no cyclamates in it.")

Keith Lampe's decision to leave the city for rural life is not unusual. Thousands of young people across the West have fled urban centers in recent years and set up new communities in remote areas of Oregon, New Mexico, Colorado, and California. Their decisions flow from a current that is running very deep in American youth. It is a search for simplicity, for privacy, for meaningful work, for basic pleasures, for harmony with nature, for roots, for wholeness. In a world of piecemeal communities, they want personal communion; in a world of machines, they want magic; in a world of frozen foods and TV sets, they want to bake their own bread and make their own music, in a world where there is never enough time, they want to take time; in a world of computers and assembly lines, they want a place and a job that is their own; instead of concrete, they want trees; instead of money, they want joy; instead of status, they want peace. In a world of fragments, they want to be put back together.

Their search has shown itself in the furor over People's Park here in Berkeley—perhaps the first time many youths were able to create something entirely by themselves. It has shown itself in the phenomenal popularity of *The Whole Earth Catalog*—the best-selling book in both Berkeley and Cambridge—which contains innumerable suggestions on how to live off the land. And it has shown itself in the entire ecology movement, which in its highest sense is a search for the spiritual values buried by the advent of rationality and technology. "It is really a new religion," Peggy Datz said. "I went camping in the Sierras last summer and we were three days from the nearest road. It did fantastic things for my head. I had a really mystical feeling about being part of a total living community."

Yet as ecologists are groping for a new spirituality, their world is shadowed by their keen perception of impending doom. Everyone has his own scenario for how the world will end—hunger, suffocation, floods, ice. They are usually able to brush the knowledge from their minds, but sometimes it comes rushing back in a black, fearful wave. "I went to a party the other night, and I was watching people dance," said Ken Cantor. "All of a sudden I wondered what would be here in eighty years. I am beginning to cope with the idea of my own death, but this really hit me. Maybe no one will be dancing. Maybe no one will be here at all."

1970

Halfway Between Dropping In and Dropping Out

"Plant seeds, not bombs."

—Graffito in People's Park Annex.

Dan Siegel has been through it all. The peace marches, the sit-ins, the demonstrations, the rallies, the speeches, the busts. Two years ago, when he was student-body president at the University of California here in Berkeley, he was arrested for inciting to riot when he urged an audience to "seize" a plot of land called People's Park, and they did. It was only one of five times Siegel has been arrested. Once he sat in at the offices of Charles J. Hitch, the university president, and became one of the "Chicano Eleven," which is quite a feat for a Jewish boy from Long Island.

Today Dan Siegel is a lawyer, the holder of a prestigious Reginald Heber Smith Fellowship, working in a federally financed legal services program in Oakland (although the local bar is not overly delighted with his arrest record and is holding up his admittance). This spring he spent a great deal of time working for the April Coalition, an amalgam of radicals and liberals who ran four candidates for the Berkeley City Council. Three of them won.

This is not a story, however, about a young man who grew up, learned the foolishness of his ways, and worked within the system happily ever after. Dan Siegel has grown up; so have the other veterans of the "movement," the shock troops who filled the streets and the jails and the headlines of the sixties. That much was inevitable. But many of them, like Dan, are just as radical as ever, maybe more so. They have not slipped back into Crabgrassville, as their elders confidently predicted they would.

Instead, they are trying to create a new style of life halfway between dropping out and dropping in, a sort of Culture in Limbo that remains concerned with the system but is not part of it. "Splitting for the country" or "grooving on nature" is considered a cop-out. They are settling in for the long run. A whole range of new institutions has sprung up: medical clinics, schools, law firms, churches, businesses, and, most importantly, living groups. Taken together, these institutions are beginning to amount to a distinct alternative to straight society.

Berkeley, of course, is an unusual place, a bubbling caldron of social experiments that are often copied elsewhere. But outposts of the "alternative society," as one writer called it, show up everywhere. This counterculture feeds off the straight world, particularly through food stamps and unemployment compensation. Independence goes only so far. But the counterculture also embodies a different set of values. It stresses cooperation, not competition, which is one of the reasons why it needs financial help from outside.

The years of protest used up a lot of energy and a lot of hope. For so many it came to so little. And now in Berkeley, those who call themselves "revolutionaries" are not so interested in changing the world as in changing themselves, or their block, or their community. I saw Siegel the night of the Berkeley elections and he talked about their significance. All around us longhairs were cheering election returns, which is as strange as if they had been cheering football scores. "Electoral politics is just a tactic, but it represents a new maturity," he said. "People were not concerned with rhetoric and minor differences, and united in a struggle each could perceive had some merit. A lot of us started in the movement five or six years ago and went through the Pentagon and Chicago and People's Park, and now we realize that if a revolution is necessary it's going to take twenty years. You have to organize people around their basic concerns and needs. Just standing up and saying 'I'm a revolutionary' isn't enough."

One of the most striking things in Berkeley today is this new sense of perspective. It comes partly from reading Mao and Oriental philosophers who teach the virtues of patience, and partly from experience. My father once told me that the only good thing about growing old was that you live through history, and that is happening to the movement.

Of course, some of the things they are doing are hardly new. Communes have been around a long time, and the biggest new fad in town is potluck suppers, of all things. Energy spurts off in all directions and a lot of promising projects never get finished—or even started. Any list of "alternative institutions" is almost immediately obsolete. Moreover, the rhetoric is as egregious as ever. I could live very nicely without ever hearing "getting it together" or "power to the people" again; after a few days of constant exposure to the local lingo one's brain begins to feel like cornflakes that have been soaking in milk too long. Yet something is happening here. It's very tentative, and very fluid, but quite real.

"Dear Jesus, I would like to remind you that you are due."
—Graffito in bathroom of Free Church.

Dan Siegel lives in a "cooperative" called the Red Fox; most people here use the word "collective" but Dan thinks that implies too much group discipline. They got the name one morning reading the comic strip "Mark Trail," which said the red fox "was one of the few animals which actually grew in populated areas and managed to outsmart man."

The nine members of the Red Fox share a large wooden frame house in the "south campus" area of Berkeley—actually it's a block over the line into Oakland. So many hippies and radicals have settled in this older and slightly shabby neighborhood that in moments of exuberance residents call it the "liberated zone." There are about 100 similar communal living groups here at any one time. The Red Fox is rather unusual because it is so homogeneous: three of the members are lawyers, and three are law students. But many collectives combine living and work. The editors of *The Tribe*, an underground newspaper, live together; so do members of People's Architecture, a community planning and organizing group. Another version is the Channing Way 2000 Block. More than a dozen families have torn down the fences between their backyards and cooperate on such projects as day care and a community garden.

I went to the Red Fox for dinner one night. Upstairs, where most of the people sleep, Dan was going over a law brief with Barbara Dudley, another house member and a third-year law student at Boalt Hall in Berkeley. They joked about the phone being tapped—"We insist on complete security over the phone"—and about straight neighbors looking in the window to catch a glimpse of a joint.

Promptly at 6:30 we were called to dinner by Marty Fassler, another law student. It was Fassler's turn to cook and he produced a tasty salad, meat loaf, and noodles, with a special cheese sauce. The house was sparsely furnished in Student Modern, but comfortable and clean; the only touch of luxury was a stained-glass window in the dining room, a remnant of Berkeley's quieter, statelier past. Everything is organized, and someone is assigned to cook and clean up every night. Other jobs, like house treasurer, are also apportioned. It is all rather bureaucratic and bourgeois, but it is *their* bureaucracy, and that makes the difference. As a member of another collective told me, "If you live any other way, daily family life can be oppressive, the work of living is drudgery. But if you live collectively the spirit of revolutionary work is joyous and fun. It really is fun to cook for others—if you don't have to do it every day."

During dinner, Barbara remarked that in her graduating class of more than 200 at Boalt Hall only about 30 had ordered caps and gowns. As she described it, graduation seemed like some obscure ritual practiced by an almost extinct tribe. Another house member, a high school teacher named Jim LeCuyer, said he was being sued by the parents of one of his students and he was looking for a way to bring a countersuit. "She publicly accused me of being a Communist—is that slander?" he asked. "No," said Dan, laughing, "it's a compliment."

Dinner over, Barbara left for an evening lecture, and Marty Fassler got ready for a rehearsal of a guerrilla theater production he was doing with some other law students. Fassler is an intense bundle of energy who quit journalism when he decided he wanted to be "an activist rather than an observer." What was the guerrilla theater about? "I play a heavy, male-chauvinist, big-business judge and I hope it will demystify the law for the people watching, and for us, too. It's all a lie. The neutrality of the judge is a myth; the neutrality of the law is a myth." This is one of the articles of faith in the alternative society—there is no neutrality. As a poster in the Free Church puts it, "Which side are you on?" It's all a little uncomfortable for a reporter from, say, *The New York Times*.

> *"I hate myself."*
>
> —Graffito in the Free Church.

For the members of the Red Fox like Dan Siegel, communal living helps overcome the contradiction between their life and their work. Life and work are integrated into a "whole," another key word in the movement.

From whole grains to whole people, there is a tremendous desire to fuse together the fragments of modern life. "We criticize one another and give assistance to one another," he said. "There's a lot of knowledge here and people share things. There's also a lot of support for what you're doing, and that's very important. A lot of aspects of movement work can be very alienating."

Very alienating and very lonely. "It sounds kind of trite," said Dan, "but last year I'd work all day and have another meeting at 7:30. Usually I'd stop somewhere on Telegraph and have a quick and not very good dinner. It was kind of depressing. Here there is always dinner at 6:30, and usually there are ten or twelve people around. It's good companionship." A girl in another commune explained how they had started: "We got arrested together and no one wanted to go home alone anymore." Several of the girls had already known one another from a karate class.

But the value of a collective goes deeper. "For me it's like a home," Dan went on. "I have three younger brothers and my family is big and noisy and very close. That seems like a healthy way to live." Barbara, home from her lecture, added, "It's nice to be a family and to have a name, so someone doesn't say, 'That's Tom Hayden's house' or, 'That's Ralph Johansen's house.' It's like somebody saying 'Dan Siegel's girl friend'—you want to kill. More and more people in the movement are saying, 'Which collective—not which individual—will take care of thus and so.' I really like that. I like that form of identity, it's a place to belong." Home, family, belonging—the words tell a lot about the yearnings of the young.

Collective living is also an economic necessity. Since many people in the alternative society have given up the idea of a "career" in the traditional sense, and do not want to work full-time, the struggle for solvency is constant. The Red Fox is better off than most groups. Ralph Johansen, an older lawyer who owns the house, has an old mortgage, and monthly payments are only $230. Buying food in bulk and sharing many meals at home cuts costs further, and each member of the Red Fox pays only $65 a month for food and lodging. Most of them have to work only part-time and can devote the rest of their efforts to the movement.

Barbara works at a Legal Aid office and Marty does research for a law firm, and each earns about $50 a week. Dan's fellowship pays $10,000 for the year, but that is temporary. Like many radical lawyers, he plans to survive by taking an occasional draft or drug case. Parents are often willing to pay plenty to keep their children out of the army or jail. The standard fee for a draft case is $500, and a drug case can run from $200 to $1,000. (Dan estimated that most straight lawyers would charge $1,500 for similar services.) If a man can afford it, radical attorneys charge $200 to $300 for a habeas corpus petition involving the military, instead of the usual fee of $1,000.

Living levels vary. Many communes cannot afford even meat loaf. But there is a pervasive feeling in the movement that people do not want material rewards, except perhaps a good stereo and the chance to travel. "Things seem to come along and we're able to make enough," said Barbara. "I guess one of the distinguishing facts of our generation is that we never really think about money." A cliché, of course, but people are living that way.

The Red Fox and another group of lawyers, known as the North Street Wrecking Company, serve as the legal arm of the alternative society. For other services one can utilize other "counterinstitutions." Everyone reads *The Tribe* and listens to KSAN, a quasi-underground radio station; movies produced by Solidarity Films are shown at rallies; Barbara asked the Women's Collective at the Free Clinic for the name of a gynecologist; Dan took a course in photography at the Free University.

About 6,000 people in Berkeley now belong to "food conspiracies," groups that buy food directly from wholesalers. The Red Fox people admit they are too lazy to join a conspiracy, so they down their guilt and shop at the Co-op, once *the* radical store in Berkeley and now a pillar of the Establishment.

"Paranoia is heightened awareness."

—Graffito in Free Church.

In Berkeley today, personal relationships are as important as political strategy. There is an almost desperate search for new styles and forms of living, and here the battle is not against The Man but against men—the network of instincts and instructions that channels people into traditional patterns.

To many, the nuclear family is as obsolete as the Democratic National Committee. One reason is that political work places enormous strains on a couple; there is always another protest to plan, another leaflet to write, and the time left for each other dwindles away. Dan Siegel, like many radicals, got divorced when his former wife would no longer put up with his total commitment to politics. Children from these unions sometimes shuttle back and forth between their parents' diverging worlds, and it must be confusing, to say the least. I interviewed one radical who was caring for his year-old daughter for the day, and when she kept dropping her bottle he cajoled, "You've got to be more decisive, comrade." The guy's commune recently took care of four babies at once, and several had to sleep in dresser drawers.

Even couples who share political activities find that normality is a som e time thing. Red Fox members Jennie Rhine and her husband Barry Winograd recently decided, only half in jest, to set aside Tuesday nights for meetings between the two of them. (Berkeley radicals attend more meetings than presidential candidates; occasionally, Barbara Dudley concedes, she gets "met out" and has to flee. Many communes take R&R trips to the country just to get away from the hothouse atmosphere of Berkeley.)

Probably the strongest force tearing at traditional patterns is Women's Liberation. Endless debates discuss male chauvinism and sexism. "The real sexual revolution in Berkeley isn't people sleeping together; it's changing sexual roles," said the Reverend Richard Boylan of the Free Church. This goes far beyond men washing dishes and baby sitting although they do that. Much of the energy toward collective, as opposed to hierarchical, organizations flows from the women's movement. Some radicals even espouse the principle of "women's leadership," on the ground that women have been "less damaged" by society.

These currents of restlessness generated by the women's movement have a devastating effect on traditional family life. If women across America are questioning their roles, the effect is infinitely multiplied in a place like Berkeley. Virginia Harrison, a young mother of two sons, now separated from her husband, said, "Everyone I know is going through really big changes. They're trying to figure out ways to meet their own needs for emotional satisfaction and freedom and yet take care of the things they have to. It's very difficult. Everyone I know tried to keep themselves together and they all ended by breaking up. They've grown apart or something—they didn't seem to be able to hold things together. A lot might not have collapsed if they thought there were other ways of living."

Many people agree with Mrs. Harrison that "other ways of living" can help provide "emotional satisfaction and freedom." Dan Siegel put it this way: "In a lot of cases Women's Liberation is breaking up marriages, but a cooperative helps people deal with issues of male chauvinism within their relationships. In a house like this you're supported by others, and people find it easier to struggle with those issues."

Many people stay in couples, married or unmarried, even when they live in a collective. Women's Lib would probably insist everyone has been "socialized," but it seems that even radicals like to feel the security of a one-to-one relationship. Others are experimenting. Some houses actively discourage couples; one collective makes sure that a man and a woman who live together do not cook and clean up on the same night, so they are forced to "relate" to others in the house, and women and men often meet separately to discuss issues of concern.

A few are going beyond couples to group relationships. Four of the people who work together at People's Architecture—one married couple, a single man and a single woman—have started living as a family unit in one large room. The room was created by tearing down an inner wall, an act the group feels was symbolic as well as practical.

But ripping out walls is easier than ripping out the past. "I'm 27 years old," said Gary Russell, a former architecture student who is the guiding force behind People's Architecture. "For 25 of those years I was a pretty typical American. After 25 years it's hard to be something different."

All communes wrestle with the privacy problem. No matter how attractive group living can be, it cannot erase the human need to be alone. The People's Architecture house will have a room in the attic where anyone can go "and escape from the whole thing," but space is not the only problem. When a relationship turns sour, or one person sinks into a depression, communal living can be a strain. "Your urge for privacy is not always respected," said Barbara Dudley. "We all get into bad moods, and when you do, there are more people to brush against. When one couple has problems it lands on all of us. And with nine people living together, the odds are that one of them is going to be unhappy at any one time."

As the nuclear family reels under the attacks of Women's Lib, communal life eases two other major problems—housework and child care. Arrangements vary. The Red Fox has a set schedule for chores; at People's Architecture, "whoever has the energy gets the food." In most cases, individual women are freed from the daily burden of domesticity. Male radical superstars throughout Berkeley have traded in their soap boxes for soap powder.

Many communes also share responsibility for children. This kind of cooperation is particularly useful in a place like Berkeley, where many mothers lack mates, for one reason or another. In some ways it is an attempt to recreate the old extended family, where a grandmother or an aunt often lived within baby-sitting distance.

But communes remain artificial families, and not everyone appreciates the joys of child care. The Red Fox has gone through some "heavy" group sessions about children, and another commune I heard about is splitting over the issue. The three adults who "relate" to the 2-year-old in question, including his mother, are moving into one house where there are other children; the three other adults are moving into a childless commune. I asked Betty, a member of another collective who helped organize a nursery school called Blue Fairyland, to describe the effect of communal living on children. "The kids in communes are different from kids in nuclear families, but they're also different from each other," said Betty, who dropped out of several of the nation's finest colleges. "The kids from families have different life-styles and values; they're used to certain clothes, to doing certain things. Often it's basically a financial difference. The kids from communes are used to a looser, more fluid environment, and they're less dependent on their parents. But I've also noticed that it's good to have more than one kid in a commune. It confuses them to have too many authority figures around—or just too many adults."

Blue Fairyland started as a practical matter: The one child in Betty's commune had gotten to be a disturbing influence and needed companionship, and his parents were unhappy with the nursery school he was already in. But Blue Fairyland, and other schools like it, also reflect the movement's renewed interest in children. There is more talk here about day-care centers than abortion clinics, and everywhere I went in Berkeley I seemed to encounter a long-haired child eating an apple—organically grown, of course. Betty explained why: "We used to think we didn't have any time for children, and that there were too many white children anyway, but I think we're starting to relate more to reality. Child care is a need the community has and we're trying to serve it. Maybe the movement has become less abstract." The interest in children also reflects the sense of perspective I mentioned earlier, the understanding that people are in this for the long run. "More people want kids," said Betty; "they don't think the revolution will happen next year and they have time for it. Children are seen as a positive thing."

I visited Blue Fairyland one day to see what a "radical" nursery school was like, and encountered a shockingly normal tableau of organized chaos: making candles, feeding rabbits, reading stories, fighting over toys. The poster art runs to Mao rather than Martin Luther King, and several small signs proclaim, "Blue Fairyland Is Right On!" The school is run by dedicated radicals who conceive of it as something like a breeding ground for the revolution. "In most nursery schools kids are railroaded from the beginning," explained Betty; "everyone has to learn to read and write the same things. We try to emphasize sharing; we're trying to create a collective spirit rather than an individual trip."

That is hardly an original idea, and most middle-class playgrounds echo with the plaintive cries of mothers exhorting their offspring to "share." Moreover, one has limited options for dealing with 2-year-olds, but Blue Fairyland does try. Instead of the stress on individual achievement that is a feature of schools like Montessori, Blue Fairyland urges the children to work on things together, from drawing posters to preparing lunch. Some of the kids stay for dinner with the parent commune and occasionally a few sleep over, an attempt to decrease dependency on their own parents. The routine seems to have some effect. Fran Cahn, the wife of a graduate physics student, dropped by to pick up her daughter, and I asked her reactions. "Everybody really does work together; they learn to care for the child next to them rather than compete," said Mrs. Cahn, who ranks as one of the "straighter" mothers. "Just in the past week Deborah has started saying things like, 'Everybody has to do this,' and, 'Each one has to have one.' She was sitting at the table the other day and I gave her a big glass of milk and she was angry because I didn't give everyone else one."

Blue Fairyland also promotes political education. "We try to instill some kind of consciousness—which is our consciousness—that some people are really getting messed over, and we don't think that's right," Betty said. "One of the parents was arrested during the May Day demonstrations and we talked about that, and the kids knew Bobby [Seale] and Ericka [Huggins] had gotten out of jail, because I was back east when it happened, and they talked about it. I'd like to tie-dye some shirts one day with a women's symbol on them and talk to them about the women's movement. . . . We spend a lot of time looking for books that aren't racist or bourgeois or sexist, and it's not easy to find them. We had some books from China but they were too propagandistic. The little girls had aggressive sorts of roles, which was nice, but we need something more indigenous. We want to do something about the boys' identification with cowboys. It's amazing how much they've already absorbed about the cowboys being the good guys and the Indians the bad guys."

Not all the parents are wild about the political side of Blue Fairyland, and one mother told this story as an illustration: "We were taking a walk one day and one of the girls picked a flower. A guy from the school said she shouldn't pick the flower, and when she asked him why, he said, 'Because too many people are into a property thing.' That was kind of dumb. All it did was show his disapproval of her. He was half joking, but half not. He conveyed a lot of hostility in that one sentence."

> *"When the power of love overcomes the love of power, then there will be peace."*
>
> —Graffito in Free Church.

Marty Fassler talked about "demystifying" the law; eliminating the aura of secrecy and status which surrounds many professionals is a major aim of the movement. It is all part of giving people more control of their own lives. A prime example is medicine. One doctor, who has worked at many free clinics in the Bay area, put it this way: "Professionalism keeps patients totally at the mercy of the medical-industrial complex. They prescribe X drug, which costs 40 cents, when Y drug, which costs 5 cents, is just as good. The patient has no say over what the doctors do, and no information about his own body."

This doctor has trained every member of his collective in paramedical skills. (The collective is highly political and so concerned about "élitism" that it won't allow its name, or the names of its members, to be used; but anonymity is its own form of arrogance.) Some of the women, in particular, have taken the medical training seriously and function as part-time medics in the community. The doctor explained, "They come on my rounds with me—I had a home delivery last week and several women came along— that's the way knowledge gets transferred. I have confidence they can handle it because they are not out to compete; they just want to provide care to the people. If they don't know something they will call me: There's nothing to be gained by faking it and hurting a patient. Doctors constantly bluff their way when they don't know things."

"How can you free me, when you can't free yourself."
                                                             —Graffito in Free Church.

Probably the oldest "alternative institution" in Berkeley is the Free Church. It was started in the summer of 1967 by the Reverend Richard York, a young Episcopal minister, who saw that established social service agencies could not begin to handle the itinerant flower children who swamped the Bay area. That was a generation ago, maybe several generations, but the Free Church still functions as a catchall friend and counselor to the street people of Berkeley. Formal worship, featuring spontaneous sermons by the congregation, is only a small part of its work. The main project—which was one of the first in the country—is "Switchboard," a telephone service that people call for advice on everything from curing V.D. to hitchhiking to Seattle. Other services include a coffeehouse, crash pad referrals, a place to check backpacks, a mail drop, a message center, and a job exchange.

I was greeted one morning by Mr. York's assistant, the Reverend Richard Boylan, a married Roman Catholic priest who also studies sociology. A scruffy dungaree jacket passed for clerical garb. Father Boylan said the church's clientele had changed considerably over the years. "It's not just the summer groovies anymore," he said; "there's now a permanent population on the road. A lot of them have dropped out of school and just aren't tied to any cycle. We're an axis point between Mexico and British Columbia, and we see a lot of traffic."

As an open and visible place, the Free Church has suffered more than most institutions from a growing Berkeley phenomenon—the rip-off. The door is constantly pried open and packs stored in the church are rifled. A mimeograph machine had to be moved to a safer place. A group of motorcycle "bikers" took to hanging around and hassling the longhairs, and it got so bad the church had to close for a few days. The trick worked, and the bikers went elsewhere for amusement, but the problem is symptomatic. A rise in heroin addiction has led to a rise in street crime, and the police practice of using long-haired infiltrators has only aggravated a certain innate suspiciousness. "Clothes and hair styles are no guarantee of a mind set," Boylan said. "The willingness of people to trust others has been truncated by bad experiences."

I asked Boylan how he felt about these rip-offs, since the Free Church objects to violence against people, but does not condemn violence against property. "You have to understand our policy in context," he said. "With the violence of genocide and hunger in this world, it's hard to preach against such minor episodes as the political bombings we've had. But our objection to the violence against the Free Church is that it was done by people who should consider themselves brothers. If it had been a John Birch, crypto-Klan group we might have expected it, but we didn't expect it from these guys."

Boylan feels kids come to the Free Church partly out of nostalgia for religion, partly because the ministers cannot be compelled to testify in court, partly because many are looking for a slightly older security figure (Boylan is 31). "They don't like dealing with bureaucrats," he went on; "they don't like to make appointments and they don't like to deal with people who remind them of their parents, with their straight clothing and straight admonitions."

The Free Church is interesting not only for those who use it, but also for those who run it. Clearly people on both sides of the Switchboard benefit. As we talked, several volunteers who man the switchboard phones pulled up chairs. Jim, 24, gets unemployment compensation and lives in a van, a common practice the city is trying to abolish. "I was on a personal trip, doing a lot of drifting, but I was getting nothing out of it," he said. "I was really going nowhere; I was as hung up as the people who come in here for help. Working here has been beautiful—it really calmed me down a lot; it's made me feel like I live here, like I'm part of the community." On another level, Jim is looking for the same thing Dan Siegel is—a place to belong, useful work. One of the good things about the alternative society is that someone can be useful without having the seal of academic approval stamped on his forehead.

"This is the dawning of the Age of Aquarius—and the sunset of corporate state Fascism."
—Graffito in Free Church.

Politics in Berkeley spans the spectrum from apocalyptic radicalism to rampant indifference. A few collectives meet every day to debate the finer points of Kim Il Sung and Mao, the prophets of collectivization. Many other groups are not nearly so disciplined, but do believe in the ultimate necessity of a socialist revolution, and they see "alternative institutions" as building blocks toward a larger political goal. Dan Siegel put it this way: "Our idea of 'serving the people' flows from the notion of providing services in the context of organizing the community behind our leadership. This is Mao's notion and the Panthers' notion; that's how they use their breakfast program. I think the mistake is made by some that they provide services without a political program. Then all you do is substitute for the welfare department; you don't mobilize people for social change."

On the other hand, most of the regulars at the Free Church would agree with Joan Goldstein, a Switchboard volunteer, who said, "I'm not into politics, it's more of a people thing." Richard Boylan can really explode at the mention of the "heavy" politicos. "In Berkeley you could drown in leaflets and bull," he fumed. "The Trotskyites never served a person a meal in their lives; they just give you a leaflet. . . . I've had it up to here."

As people have withdrawn into their own communities, they inevitably have cut their ties with other groups. When they say "serve the people," they usually mean each other, the rest of the counterculture. For all the talk about the "poor blacks in Oakland," the Berkeley radicals have little contact with them, or any blacks, for that matter.

This operates on both personal and political levels. In personal terms, it is very difficult for blacks and whites to share the intimacy of communal living, and I don't know one collective in Berkeley that is integrated. ("We'd like to be integrated," Dan Siegel says, "but I can't imagine a black who shares our goals who would want to live here.")

These problems also affect politics. With each ethnic or racial group wanting to run its own show, cooperation often degenerates into mutual ego-tripping; moreover, blacks and whites tend to differ on political goals. But distrust between the races goes even further. "Blacks don't really think whites are poor," says a black journalist. "They feel the whites can always go back, they can always fall back into the other thing, while a black can't. The young whites have also put themselves in competition with blacks for housing, for jobs, for welfare, for lots of things. Go down to the Goodwill, you see old blacks and young whites. The whites could afford new Levi's, but they want the old ones, the kind the blacks used to get. As for jobs, blacks used to get the kind of jobs the white kids want now. But the whites do them better; they're better educated, and they don't make so many mistakes, and they get the jobs."

"You are the unwilling, led by the unqualified, doing the impossible, for the ungrateful. Power to the people."

—A "message from a brother in Canada" addressed to "G.I.s/deserters" on the Free Church bulletin board.

"This all could be a fantasy," said a member of a political collective with long ties to the movement. "Economics is the Achilles' heel of any alternative institution. At this point we just can't support masses of people—we're scuffling and scraping to stay alive. We can't develop an alternative economy, and we could get co-opted by the need for funding."

Contrary to some popular notions, few members of the counterculture seem to get money from home. There are, of course, a few youthful dilettantes who "are supported by Mom and Dad while they do their hippie number," as Richard Boylan put it, but the older group is largely self-supporting. However, many people do get unemployment compensation; a few, usually women with children, get welfare; and just about everybody who qualifies gets food stamps. As Richard Boylan said, "Food stamps are one of the few chances where The Man has opened himself to exploitation and people feel it's almost their patriotic duty to exploit The Man when they can." The Man may now be somewhat harder to exploit, however. On July 1 the Nixon Administration instituted new rules on food stamps aimed directly at communes. The rule prohibits people who are not related from applying for stamps as a group, although many individuals will probably still qualify.

Few people work full-time. Those who do are usually professionals—teachers, doctors, lawyers—and they also devote a lot of time to free clinics and the like. But almost everyone has to work occasionally. The better-known radicals can make money speaking or writing. A few can survive by selling handicrafts. Some still deal in drugs, and a certain small element specializes in petty thievery, or "instant socialism," as it is called. But most people just pick up odd jobs, and try to make the most of the money that is available. For instance, a proposal to create a "Free Credit Union" urges the community to "recycle money." The idea is to use the deposits in the credit union to finance projects like an automobile-repair cooperative.

A number of stores and services have already sprung up outside the economic mainstream. One of the first was the Leopold Stokowski Memorial Service Pavilion—known as Leopold's—a discount record store. It was started two years ago by students at the university in what amounted to a large closet; today it is a sprawling place selling records as much as $2 below competitors.

How does Leopold's sell so low? Salaries are pegged at $2 an hour. The cheap counters came from Goodwill, the record racks were "whanged together" out of scrap lumber. Most important, profit is low. Fifty percent of what there is goes back to Students of Berkeley, Inc., the managing corporation, which has used the money to open five other shops, including a clothing store and an artists' supply shop called The Dirty Rainbow. The other 50 percent is donated to community projects—a child care center, the Black Panther breakfast program, the Free Clinic.

Down from Leopold's on Telegraph, a sign in the window of a health foods restaurant says, "Love is Service Done." There is a great flowering of handicrafts in the counterculture, some of it not very good, but most of it an earnest attempt to avoid the folding, spindling, and mutilation that radicals feel is the inevitable result of most forms of gainful employment. Farther down the street, I noticed a storefront with the sign "Resistance Repair." On the front window was taped a handwritten note that read, "Resistance Repair exists as an alternative to the numerous rip-off repair shops in the community. We will do righteous repair for fair prices. . . . There is nothing magic about electronics and you should not have to pay sorcerers' prices to get your music going again." Inside the door, on a shaky card table, was a can of tobacco, some cigarette papers, and the invitation, "roll one."

The name "Resistance Repair" is only partly a play on the electronic term; the shop has political implications for Joe Campbell, the amiable proprietor. "Take the basic analogy of the body politic," he said, "of all parts of the community working in concert together, everybody doing things that are mutually beneficial. Then people have a symbiotic relationship, not a parasitic relationship." But Campbell also values competence, and he still burns at the thought of the "brother" who recently fixed his car so badly it broke down within days. "It is just not true that I can do anything I want, that the only thing holding me back is the ugly old Establishment," he said. "The fact is that people have talents. It doesn't take a large intelligence to know that despite a guy's hair and the jargon he uses, the world will still be full of idiots."

True enough. But it is also true that here in Berkeley, rhetoric is being put into practice. Instead of just talking about "self-determination" and "controlling one's own life," people are working on new ways to do that, ways to fill needs, to make money, to organize personal lives. They are looking beyond the next demonstration, or the next semester. They know that changing society is a long process, and that it begins at home. Gradually they are overcoming the idea, as one girl put it, that "life is a spectator sport." There are few models, and the conditioning runs very deep. But people really are beginning to build a community based on cooperation, not competition, on serving others rather than oneself. That could be a hell of a lot more revolutionary than smashing windows on Telegraph Avenue.

1971

TOP OF THE HEAP: THE POLITICAL ARENA

Ronald Reagan easily won reelection as governor in 1970 but decided not to seek a third term four years later. He remains a favorite among Republican conservatives and by 1974 was touring the country, scouting out potential support for another run at the presidency in 1976. He remains a smooth performer with the same old crinkly-eyed grin he once used to sell light bulbs. But without the "mess in Berkeley" and other demons to frighten his constituency, I think his effectiveness might diminish. He remains, above all, the ultimate triumph of image over substance. In five years he was the least spontaneous and most carefully programmed person I ever interviewed. I was so mad when I left his office that I dropped my tape recorder on the marble floor of the capital. Tom Bradley, in contrast, represents the triumph of substance over image, a man whose dogged energy and persistence made up for a poor public personality.

Ronald Reagan Is Giving 'em Heck

Labor Day, 1970. Ronald Wilson Reagan, former sports announcer and movie star, former "bleeding heart" Democrat, now governor of California, was going campaigning. The press had been waiting for several minutes when he bounced onto the bus, waved out the window to a pair of white-haired "young ladies," handed his notes—neatly printed on white cards—to an aide, and settled into a front seat. Then the bus pulled slowly away, headed for the Orange County Fairgrounds and the annual picnic of Local 324 of the Retail Clerks International Association, AFL-CIO. It passed little stucco bungalows with aging Fords in the driveways, women in bermuda shorts raking the grass and kids in T-shirts riding bicycles, American flags flapping in a soft breeze and freeways carpeting the sun-charred landscape with wall-to-wall concrete. It passed something called "Movieland of the Air" and the General Steam Corporation, Dover Shores Veterinary Hospital, and the Happy Land Pre-School. As it approached the fairgrounds one of the Governor's companions remarked that working people did not like to go to Labor Day picnics any more. Reagan flicked at the subject like a frog at a fly, "You youngsters probably don't remember," he said to the middle-aged labor leaders sitting around him, "but when I was young, golf was a sissy, rich man's game. So were boating and skiing and horseback riding. Today they're weekend sports for the working man; he doesn't have to go to Labor Day picnics."

The labor moguls nodded silently as the bus stopped and Reagan climbed down. He was dressed in a rather stiffly casual manner: black, pleated trousers hitched well above his imperceptible stomach, immaculate white suede shoes, a white sports shirt, open to reveal a well-tanned chest slightly mottled with his 59 years. Deep lines fanned out from his eyes; giving the impression of a perpetual half-squint. His jagged smile, revealing an uneven row of bottom teeth, glowed warmly. He was obviously fit, although slightly less bulky than usual, without the padded suit shoulders he favors. After greeting the leaders of the retail clerks, Reagan stepped gingerly into the crowd, a sea of $2.95 plaid shirts, white-rimmed sun glasses, flowered-print dresses covering bosoms still clearly supported by Maidenform, drippy cones of crushed ice, Instamatic cameras, and silver hair.

"Hi, how are you?" the Governor repeated as he pushed slowly ahead, grabbing hands and signing his name. "Hi, how are you?" A man with a lot of c's and z's on his name tag asked about a proposed abortion law. "If they liberalize it all the way, you bet I won't sign it," came the answer. Someone handed Reagan a flag, then a yellow teddy bear. The gifts were quickly passed back to his covey of youthful aides, most of whom looked like slightly weathered student-body presidents, all thinning hair and thickening officiousness. (The teddy bear was treated like a time bomb; no one knew what to do with it. When the bus was leaving hours later the aides were still handing the grinning yellow toy to one another, trying to get rid of it.)

As the crowd flowed around Reagan, it was obvious that they were not interested in seeing just another politician, or even another governor. They wanted to see a star. "I remember your pictures, Ron," called one man. A mother nudged her daughter as she strained for a better look: "He used to be in the movies." A woman with a huge Unruh button, advertising Reagan's opponent, pushed through for an autograph. Why? "For my kids," she said sheepishly. "How come you never get old?" gushed another admirer. "You just get better-looking."

Ronald Reagan is getting old, but he still looks pretty good to a lot of Californians. As he enters his campaign for a second four-year term in Sacramento, his vibrant self-confidence seems entirely justified. Any incumbent bears the scars of unfulfilled promise and unavoidable boredom, and the White Knight of 1966 is beginning to rust in spots. But the polls continue to give him a consistent margin of about ten points over Democrat Jess Unruh, former speaker of the state legislature. Most experts would be surprised if he wins by less than a million votes, the margin by which he defeated former Governor Edmund G. Brown in his first try for public office four years ago.

It was altogether fitting that Reagan should open his campaign at a Labor Day picnic, the traditional hunting grounds for Democratic votes. The Governor won about 25 or 30 percent of the labor vote in 1966, and that helped provide his margin of victory in a state that still has a majority of registered Democrats. In California, as in many states, the labor vote remains crucial, the celebrated "Great Silent Majority" torn between its Democratic past and apparently Republican future.

As they sat there in the simmering Orange County heat, the retail clerks were obviously ripe for Reagan's plucking. They are scrambling to pay the taxes on those stucco boxes and the repairs on those '65 automobiles, and welfare is an affront. They are almost as weary of the war as they are of peace marches, but they do not want to see America "lose face." They want a good education for their kids, but they are appalled at narcotics in the high schools, demonstrations in the colleges, and sex just about everywhere. They are not poor, at least not the way their parents might have been poor; some do play golf or go boating. But they are certainly not rich, and probably not even very secure. They are not miserable, but they are not very happy, either, and they are confused by the "eggheads" who tell them the values they were taught to believe in do not hold anymore. They are basically decent people, but they have a capacity for hate when the neat patterns of their lives are disrupted. When you look at them you have a feeling you've seen them before: yelling at the kids integrating the high schools of Little Rock or protesting public housing in Queens or throwing rocks at Martin Luther King in Cicero.

After Reagan finally disappeared behind the stage of a large amphitheater, the leader of the retail clerks' union, a pudgy, graying fellow in a two-tone, mustard-colored shirt, led the pledge of allegiance "to the flag of our great country." Then he announced expansively, "First we'll have a few speeches, then a puppet show, and then the highlight of our day, the drawing for some wonderful door prizes." The first speaker was the only Democratic candidate to brave the wilds of Orange County, State Senator Alfred Alquist, who is running for lieutenant governor. Having been relegated to a rank of importance somewhat below that of the puppet show, Alquist could not stir up much enthusiasm. Even his dire warning that "the handwriting is on the wall," that unemployment and inflation were both rising under the Republicans, did not have much impact. He was like a bumbling comedian trying to fill the time before the burlesque queen was ready.

Finally he finished and Reagan was on. "Hey, Ronnie," yelled the crowd, "Hey, Ronnie, baby." The Governor began by reciting his own union credentials—six terms as president of the Screen Actors Guild—and presenting a scroll to the union for its humanitarian work in local hospitals. It was important, he went on, to recognize "labor's partnership in the free-enterprise system," especially on Labor Day. "It's kind of wonderful, in our troubled times, to stand up and speak about something so traditional. It seems like so often today that the world we know is coming unglued." From that note he shifted easily into his standard jokes, which he delivers with impeccable timing. "I've got a new way to stop smog," he announced, "stop burning down the schools." And then: "The young people want three political parties, one in power, one out of power, and one marching on Sacramento." For some reason he left out one of his favorites: "I had a nightmare last night; I dreamed I owned a Laundromat in Berkeley."

The main topic of the speech was welfare, and the main message was clear: You, the taxpayer, are getting stuck. "Welfare," Reagan declared, "is the taxpayer's greatest domestic expense, and it is increasing in cost faster than our revenues can keep pace." One reason is fraud: 16 percent of the families receiving Aid for Dependent Children cheated last year, at a cost of $59 million. More important, he said, "I am also convinced there is a sizable percentage of people who have taken advantage of loopholes in the thousands of overlapping federal regulations to augment their incomes at your expense." Then he recited a few horrible examples: an unmarried girl who got $400 for an abortion despite her parents' income, a social worker making $13,700 who received aid under the A.D.C. program, a citizen owning a $30,000 home who was eligible for free surplus food. These situations, he thundered, are made possible by "self-seeking politicians" who urge organized welfare groups to "make poverty a profession." And the courts have not helped. When the Supreme Court nullified California's one-year residency requirement for welfare it cost the state $95 million a year. The phrases spurted out: "able-bodied malingerers . . . special-inter-est groups . . . massive tax drain. . . ."

When it was over, the crowd swarmed around Reagan again. A Chicano youth edged his way forward and yelled, "Why don't you do something to help the people in East Los Angeles [the largest Mexican-American barrio]?" The Governor looked up, but his eyes registered no recognition. He turned quickly to an autograph seeker. "I should never have learned to make anything but an X," he quipped. A lady in bell-bottom jeans rushed up and shouted: "Give 'em hell, Governor."

Governor Reagan is giving them hell, or, as he would say, heck. (In public, Reagan blushes when he uses a word as strong as "damn"; in private, he tells off-color stories with great relish.) His whole style is suited to attack, to criticism. But he has been governor for three and a half years, and that presents problems. He has to find reasons outside his administration for all the trouble. Spiraling welfare costs are thus the work of the "professional poor," the courts, the federal bureaucracy. Campus unrest is caused by "revolutionaries" determined to "tear down the system" and administrators who "appease" them. But Reagan must still run on his record, and I went to Sacramento one day to talk to him about his tenure.

I saw Reagan in his office, a richly paneled room with old hunting prints and bulletproof windows. He has a reputation for being a very difficult man to interview, and many capital reporters no longer bother. ("It's just like hearing the same record over and over again," said one. "I don't think he knows how to be candid.") When I checked the notes of my own interview, I found that most of what he said had come practically word-for-word from old speeches.

Ronald Reagan takes an essentially negative approach to government. He has said many times that his major goal is "cutting the cost of government. This should be the top priority of every administration." And this is probably the most significant impact he has made on California. After he took office, he was faced with such a huge budget deficit that he had to ask for the largest tax increase in state history (an increase that conveniently produced enough surplus to permit a tax rebate in time for the election this year). But ever since, he has been slashing away at the government with great gusto. When I asked what accomplishment he was proudest of, he said, "We're a growing state—got a million more people than we had when I started—and that had been the excuse for years and years for the increase in the size of the state government. Better than 5,000 employees were added to the state payroll every year. Well, we've been here three and a half years and there are fewer employees than when we started."

The major issue in the state is, and has been since Reagan started campaigning against the "mess in Berkeley" in 1966, education. After his election, the governor set the tone for his administration when he engineered the firing of Clark Kerr, the president of the University of California, and announced that the state should not "subsidize intellectual curiosity." This prompted the *Los Angeles Times*, which had supported his candidacy, to declare that, "an anti-intellectual political reactionary now

governs California and is determined to bring higher-education growth to a
grinding halt." To many observers, the last three years have borne out the
Times's prediction. As student unrest spread from Berkeley to the university's other eight campuses, Reagan escalated his attacks. He says occasionally that students have some "legitimate" gripes, particularly the size of
classes and the inaccessibility of professors. But in general he has denied the
validity of student complaints. Young people are "indoctrinated" by
left-wing professors, he insists, and "march only to disrupt." In heated
moments his rhetoric would make President Nixon's epithet "bums" sound
positively charitable. He has called students "brats," "freaks," and "cow-
ardly fascists," and last spring, in discussing order on campus, he said, "If it
takes a bloodbath, let's get it over with. No more appeasement." Later he
said the remark was a "figure of speech" and that anyone who took it
seriously was "neurotic." Within a few days, four students were shot at Kent
State.

    Despite the opposition of many California liberals, Reagan's stand on
campus disruption is extremely popular. One of his chief campaign
strategists put it this way: "Campus unrest is an issue between Reagan and
the people, with nobody in between. They understand what he's saying.
Reagan is a polarizing politician, much more than Nixon. With Nixon, there
are all shades of gray, but that's not the way Reagan operates—he lays it out
there. This campus-unrest issue is really bugging a lot of people. Hell, they
didn't go to college, but they want their kids to go, and they're paying for
the state system. And it just outrages them to see a building burned down.
They have no way of really understanding the legitimate student complaints
because they never went to college and they have no understanding of what
happens on a college campus. The first reaction on every poll I can show
you is, 'Throw the s.o.b.s out.'"

    But education in California is more than a political issue. Many people
fear Reagan is destroying the university. He has consistently cut its budget
requests by about 20 percent, and construction funds have been slashed
even deeper. Moreover, his attacks on the university have helped create a
climate in which the legislature found it popular to exempt professors from a
5 percent pay raise granted all other state employees. University president
Charles J. Hitch, commenting on his budget for next year, said, "The first
thing these cuts mean is that our students will get a short-changed

education—not only next year, but as the effects of this action take hold and deplete the university for many years after that." He held out the possibility that some qualified students would have to be turned away—something California vowed would never happen.

As Reagan has gained control of the Board of Regents, he has exerted more influence over the university. At his urging, the regents last year took away from the nine chancellors the final power to appoint faculty. Last spring they used that power to delay the promotion of two radical professors, and more such cases are expected. Also last spring the Governor led the fight against Angela Davis, the young black Communist who was appointed acting assistant professor of philosophy at U.C.L.A. The regents finally fired Miss Davis, even though the courts had said that she could not be dismissed for her political beliefs. (Several weeks later Miss Davis was linked to the shoot-out in which a judge was killed in a San Rafael courtroom; she fled, but was arrested in a New York motel ten days ago.) The regents also vowed a crackdown on student newspapers and ordered the chancellors to prepare rules that would prohibit "sociopolitical advocacy" and "the dissemination of lewd, obscene articles and photographs" by student journalists. Faculty morale is plummeting. Established teachers are leaving, good young ones are hesitant to come. "Crisis" is too mild a word to describe the situation.

The decline of the university is undoubtedly hastened by the tactics of those who feel that throwing a rock through a window is a valid expression of political belief. Reagan and the radicals need and use each other. The violent student minority gives the Governor a chance to vent his moral outrage and avoid the deeper problems bothering students. And Reagan's rhetoric and actions and those of the police reinforce the radicals' contention that California is on the brink of fascism, enabling them to gather wide support on campus. The only ones who lose are those in the middle.

Reagan knows who his constituents are. He placed top priority this year on a tax-reform bill that would have lowered property taxes for the 65 percent of the population who own homes. The reduction would have been financed mainly by an increased sales tax—a regressive levy that hits the poor hardest. (The bill was blocked by Democratic legislators who insisted—against Reagan's adamant opposition—that a tax increase be used to aid education.) At the same time, Reagan endorsed a bill that increased the take for racetrack owners and reduced the state's share of track revenues. He also advocated a higher tax on public power companies, saying they have an unfair advantage over private power, and a reduction of the state's business-inventory tax. Business, he told an Anaheim audience, "is already being sand-bagged by the federal government." If its taxes are raised too much it would be like "killing the goose that lays the golden egg."

When he opened his campaign, Reagan listed the issues this way: "taxes and tax relief; the size and cost of government; the continuing effort to cut those costs; the state's role in helping to finance and provide the best education for our children; the progress we've made in getting tougher laws and tougher judges to protect the citizen, his family, and property; the work being done to protect the magical environment of California; the programs to build and expand the California economy so there are jobs and job opportunities for our people. . . ." Not one word about poverty, slums, disease, discrimination, job training, or justice. Listening to Ronald Reagan, it is possible to imagine that blacks or Chicanos or Indians do not really exist in California—except as welfare chiselers or threats to "family and property." He has always maintained that racial integration is a "desirable result," but he opposes open-housing legislation and the busing of school children. Last winter, in talking about the integration of minority groups, he said, "As we bring them up to where they have the economic means to follow the trend to the suburbs and to move and disperse from some of these communities, we are going to find that this problem to a large extent solves itself."

In many ways, this is the essence of Reagan's appeal. He holds out the hope that all those troublesome problems that make the evening news so unpleasant will solve themselves. "For many years now," he said in his inaugural address, "you and I have been shushed like children and been told there are no simple answers to the complex problems which are beyond our comprehension. Well, the truth is, there are simple answers." In fact, he implies, many of those problems do not even exist. Students are unhappy not because of an insane war or distorted national priorities but because they are "indoctrinated." Taxes go up not because society has a responsibility to the underprivileged, but because people are cheating on welfare. A liberal Republican politician explained it this way: "What the people really want is for all this turmoil to go away, and they go wild about a man who promises to do everything to dispel that turmoil. What the Great Silent Majority wants most of all is silence. They don't want to get involved, they want things the way they used to be. As a politician, Reagan is a great psychiatrist. He puts the voter on the couch and says soothingly, 'You're great, why don't they appreciate you?' He's like a medicine man with his little bottle of elixir that will make everything go away—those fuzzy-wuzzy blacks staring at you on the 11 o'clock news and those professors who keep saying how smart they are and how dumb you are. He's a boy with his finger in the dike, holding back the future."

But Reagan is even more subtle than that. He gives people a reason to feel good about their lives. In a recent speech to the state chamber of commerce he said, "We have been picked at, sworn at, rioted against, and downgraded until we have a built-in guilt complex, and this has been compounded by the accusations of our sons and daughters who pride themselves on 'telling it like it is.' Well, I have news for them—in a thousand social-science courses they have been informed 'the way it is *not*'. . . . As for our generation, I will make no apology. No people in all history paid a higher price for freedom. And no people have done so much to advance the dignity of man. . . . We are called materialistic. Maybe so. . . . But our materialism has made our children the biggest, tallest, most handsome, and intelligent generation of Americans yet. They will live longer with fewer illnesses, learn more, see more of the world, and have more successes in realizing their personal dreams and ambitions than any other people in any other period of our history—because of our 'materialism.' "

Reagan understands the spiritual values of his people—thrift, hard work, caution, security. He also understands that they are patriotic, that they believe their country has a mission and that through that mission they will somehow transcend their limited lives. "Manifest destiny" is one of the most basic ideas in American history, and seldom has it been stated in a purer form than when Ronald Reagan said recently, "I think on our side is civilization and on the other side is the law of the jungle. . . . We all have to recognize that this country has been handed the responsibility, greater than any nation in all history, to preserve some 6,000 years of civilization against the barbarians."

That statement was not concocted for political effect. It reflects, as much as anything he has ever said, Reagan's view of the world. "You know," one of his aides once told me, "Ronnie really does believe in good and evil."

And he believes in his role as a defender of the good. "The trouble with Reagan," said one politician, "is that he can't decide whether he was born in a log cabin or a manger." The Governor's finely honed sense of the apocalyptic comes bursting through in his campaign rhetoric. In talking about welfare abuses to a luncheon at the Elks Club in Napa, he said, "We should all clearly understand the stakes in this economic and social 'Battle of Armageddon.' What we are fighting for is the survival of our system."

Reagan's obvious sincerity is one of his greatest political assets. One of his campaign organizers said recently, "I'm not really concerned that the campaign will be decided on issues. It will be decided on image. If we can get people to believe that Ron is still trying to put forth a point of view, that he's still trying to get things done, we'll win with no trouble. He's just a straight guy trying to do a job." A week later the California Poll, conducted by Mervin Field, affirmed that view. What the voters liked most about Reagan was not what he said but how he said it. Thirty percent of those questioned by Field said Reagan's strongest point was among the following: "speaks his mind, honest, sincere, straightforward, decisive." The most important substantive issue, campus unrest, was mentioned by only 19 percent of the respondents.

This image of sincerity comes across with great power, particularly on TV. Thus Reagan's strategy is similar to Nixon's in 1968: Reach the voter, as one aide said, through as few "sieves" as possible. That means a large budget for packaged television ads. And it means grabbing free TV time whenever possible (except to debate Unruh). Bill Boyarsky, the Associated Press's former bureau chief in Sacramento and the author of a book on Reagan, has said, "If we pen-and-pencil reporters catch him at the airport alone, we get no story. But if the TV cameras are there, he turns it on, and he talks right to the camera. That's why you see him on TV so much, because he's provocative and he goes places where TV covers things."

The most damaging thing to a candidate of this sort is a critical analyst—a "sieve" that filters his message. Reagan likes television because he can communicate directly with the people, but also because TV newsmen seldom have the time or the expertise to interpret what he is saying. Like Vice President Agnew, Reagan has conducted a campaign in California to discredit the writing press, which does have the capacity for criticism. At almost every stop he will say something like, "I don't mean to imply that these reporters don't write the truth, but . . ." Writers who are critical of the Governor often find themselves isolated by the staff. One correspondent recently received a letter from Paul Beck, the Governor's press secretary, who informed him that he would no longer receive any official cooperation in covering the campaign.

Reagan is, of course, a professional TV performer (for several years before his first gubernatorial campaign, he was the host of the television show "Death Valley Days," a job that he concedes was like "subsidized retirement"). But expertise alone does not explain his success. The main reason he communicates so well with his people is that he genuinely shares so many of their values and outlooks. His official campaign biography has been doctored a bit—his first marriage to actress Jane Wyman, their two children, and their divorce have been expunged from the record—but that was hardly necessary. "He is the personification of the American dream," said one assistant. "At a time when everything is in such disarray, people want to know that nice guys don't always finish last."

One of the strongest influences in his life is his wife, Nancy, described in her official biography as "a dedicated wife and mother." The sketch omits the fact that Mrs. Reagan, the daughter of a prominent and conservative neurosurgeon in Chicago, was a movie actress before turning to the joys of domesticity. No matter. Nancy Reagan is as stern a guardian of public morality as her husband, maybe more stern. She believes, for example, that an abortion is "committing murder." When an interviewer recently asked her about a woman who has no choice about having a baby she replied, "But she does have a choice. It starts with a movement of the head, either yes or no. This cheap, easy thing they say—that I can do whatever I want sexually and not take responsibility—I don't agree with that at all." Women's Lib? "Ridiculous," said Mrs. Reagan, using one of her husband's favorite words. "They're going to end up being unhappy women."

The Reagans have simple tastes. Their greatest joy is horseback riding, which they do as often as possible in the Malibu hills. (They once owned a ranch in the area, which they recently sold to 20th Century Fox, but they've retained the right to keep horses there. The ranch is only a short drive from their home in Pacific Palisades, where they stay on weekends.) After dinner they often watch television. One day riding in the campaign bus I asked Reagan what shows he liked. His reply: "I'm not able to get out riding as often as I used to, so even if a show is lousy, I like it if it has plenty of horses and outdoor scenes. Some of them are made on the Fox ranch, and I can pick out trails I made fifteen years ago."

The Reagans' 17-year-old daughter, Patti, who has been away at boarding school, entered Ohio University this fall, but when the kids—Patti and her 12-year-old brother, Skipper—are around, the family likes to go out to the movies or screen one at home. "I call up my friends at the studios to see if a film is all right for the kids," Reagan said, "but so many of them are rated X these days my friends have to say no."

Reagan and his wife are both ardent foes of film frankness. "A kiss is only beautiful to the people doing it," he said. "It's pretty ugly to someone watching it." Two of his recent favorites were *Patton* and *Butch Cassidy and the Sundance Kid*. "Patton was so totally honest, nothing contrived, it really happened," Reagan explained. Then with a frown he added, "I've never understood the avant-garde person who likes the most abstract painting and says 'Use your head,' and then justifies going to the bathroom in the street because it's 'realism.'"

Reagan is also a man of great personal charm. He is smooth and self-possessed, but not too smooth; his speech is flecked with enough slurred words and homey expressions to make him seem human, approachable. Total strangers just naturally call him "Ronnie." It is the "aw, shucks" school of politics, and it works—well, like a charm. For instance, in recalling his days as host of the "General Electric TV Theater," Reagan mentions his opposite number at Westinghouse by calling himself "the Betty Furness of G.E." The audiences roar at the line. They don't rip off his cufflinks or muss his hair, they just like him. "Delivery is half of the game," said one of Reagan's confidants. "Agnew is a little too harsh. Barry Goldwater was a little too feisty; he laid down a challenge every time he spoke. Ron comes across as reasonable. In 1966 he said the same things Barry said in 1964, but he said them in a reasonable manner."

In 1966 Reagan called himself a "citizen politician," and in announcing his bid for reelection he said he was "just a citizen temporarily in public service." That may be so, but few observers of California politics doubt that he has become a highly competent politician, managed by the best professionals around.

He was first urged to run for public office by a group of conservative millionaires, including the late Cy Rubel of Union Oil; Holmes Tuttle, a Ford dealer and finance chairman of Reagan's current campaign; Henry

Salvatori, who made his money in oil exploration; Leonard Firestone of the rubber company; and Taft Schreiber, vice president of the Music Corporation of America and Reagan's first theatrical agent. It is difficult to judge the continuing influence of these men, dubbed by the press his "kitchen cabinet." They did, for example, band together with about a dozen others to buy a house for Reagan when Nancy decided the Executive Mansion in Sacramento was a "fire-trap." (Reagan pays $1,200 a month rent.) They can usually talk to the Governor when they want to, but they do not seem to have much power. "All they really get is recognition," said one assistant. "They go to the Governor's house for dinner once in a while; their wives love that stuff."

    At campaign time, at least, the most important influence on Reagan is Spencer-Roberts, the political-management team that has revolutionized the business of winning elections. Squirreled away in a nondescript office building in downtown Los Angeles, with a Norman Rockwell drawing of Ronald Reagan in the foyer, Stu Spencer maps the basic strategy of the campaign. (Bill Roberts is working full-time on the reelection campaign of Senator George Murphy.) A rough-talking, short-haired cynic with tattoos on his arm, Spencer will not talk for attribution, but his basic mode of operation is well known. The key is information. Every night a team of telephone operators calls a selected sample of voters and asks them a series of questions. The results of this procedure, called "tracking," are fed into a computer. The computer then prints out, in considerable detail, what the people of California are thinking. At the beginning of the campaign, Spencer could gauge within a week or ten days the impact his candidate was having. If more money is invested, the lead time can be cut to twenty-four hours.

    The Reagan people insist that the main criterion for selecting a campaign issue is the Governor's feeling about it; what the voters want to hear, as revealed by the tracking, is only secondary. But they admit that there is a remarkable correlation between the Governor's impulses and the results of the surveys. When pressed, they cannot think of a discrepancy. To the Governor's more bitter critics, this means that he is "completely programmed," a man without a mind of his own. The Governor himself will occasionally say something like, "I'm in the hands of people who . . ." This is partly true, but it ignores the fact that Reagan's thinking meshes so well with that of his constituents. He does not need a computer to tell him that people are upset about campus violence or pornography; he is, too.

The best example of switching signals because of the tracking surveys was the conservation issue. Last year voters started identifying the environment as a major concern, and Reagan jumped on the bandwagon. "But you know," said one adviser, "the polls show a direct correlation between interest in the environment and the smog season. When the air clears up they forget about it. That shows you something about the electorate."

As the campaign accelerates, Reagan is in an excellent political position. He has thrown a blanket of unity over the Republicans that covers—some would say smothers—just about everyone. Even former Senator Thomas Kuchel, whom Reagan helped depose in 1968, recently endorsed him (while refusing to endorse Senator Murphy). As one lady at a fund-raising party told me, "He is everything to everyone." A moderate like Kuchel responds to his apparent reasonableness and flexibility, as exemplified by the conservation issue and his willingness, after years of staunch opposition, to endorse the withholding of state income taxes. The *Los Angeles Times*, a traditionally Republican paper, also endorsed him again, saying, "The great majority of Californians are people of the center—moderate, reasonable people who want pragmatic solutions to real problems. The Governor's conduct in office has shown his growing awareness of these realities and a growing flexibility in meeting them." At the same time, the right remains mollified by his adamant stand on such issues as school busing. After his renomination, for instance, he was asked to comment on George Wallace's campaign for governor of Alabama. He hemmed and hawed and finally muttered, "Well, let's just say I wouldn't have campaigned that way." Hardly a devastating critique.

In contrast, Jess Unruh has split his party, or rather, he has failed to heal the gaping wounds of the past. As speaker of the assembly for many years, "Big Daddy" Unruh was an extremely powerful man who made many lasting enemies. In particular, he fought bitterly with former Governor Pat Brown, and this year some of Brown's friends and money raisers are sitting the election out or openly backing Reagan.

Since his association with Robert Kennedy in 1968, however, Unruh seems to have undergone a conversion—he is, for instance, strongly against the war. But many of the liberals he despised for so long remain highly suspicious. As he moved from the back rooms of Sacramento to the TV screen, Unruh shed about 100 pounds, got his teeth fixed, and polished up his delivery, though he remains a rather dull speaker, with little humor or charisma. And like many Democrats this year, he has found money about as scarce as a welfare recipient at a Reagan rally. (Reagan has had no trouble raising a budget that his advisers put at $1.5 million, a figure some observers feel is too small.)

Unruh has no plans to buy TV time. Instead, he is counting on free coverage, and that has forced him into some blundering attempts at the dramatic. During the first week of the campaign he led a troupe of newsmen to the mansion of Henry Salvatori, Reagan's best-known millionaire friend, to charge that the Governor's tax-reform proposal would have saved Salvatori almost $5,000. The figures were right, but, unfortunately for Unruh, Salvatori and his wife were home. They rushed outside and denounced him—as the cameras rolled—for invading private property. "We earned our money," shouted Mrs. Salvatori, who has a heart condition.

Unruh's real problem, of course, is Reagan. "Our main frustration," said one Democratic official, "is getting Reagan to come to grips with an issue so we can draw clear distinctions between our policy and his. Reagan is so vague and so glib that he makes the issue whether he's a good guy or not. It's awfully difficult to present a clear choice to the voters."

Reagan is clearly weak on two issues. The first is education. There are signs that people are beginning to realize that it is *their* kids who are attending second-rate schools and suffering because the state will not increase its contribution to local school districts. At the last minute, Reagan found some more money for schools in the budget, and he has promised to deal with the problem next year. Meanwhile, Los Angeles schools had to cut a period out of the class day this year because of the financial squeeze.

More important is the economy. California's unemployment, fueled by cutbacks in the aerospace industry, is a full percentage point above the national average. And even Reagan's advisers admit, "Every poll shows that the voters think the Democrats are better at handling the economy." For the time being, the advisers point out, unemployment has affected relatively few people, and they are confident they can ride out the storm. But if things get bad, they say, "We'll just start attacking Nixon, that's all we can do."

On the other side, the Democrats concede that rising unemployment and inflation are their only real hope, even though Reagan is hardly to blame for economic ills. "If there's something close to a depression, Jess has a chance," said one party official. Another Democrat commented, "It's all a question of which fears you play on—the fear of an economic disaster or the fear of the kids and the blacks."

Assuming that Reagan does win again, where does he go from there? A recent national column said that he was deliberately staking out a position to the right of Nixon, using the welfare issue, in the hope that the President would falter by 1972 and be vulnerable to a challenge. In 1976, the reasoning goes, Reagan would be 65, too old to run.

It is doubtful that Reagan would be quite so calculating. But, though he knows as well as anyone that Nixon is an odds-on bet to run again in '72, the dream of national office that flared briefly in 1968 has not died completely. There are plenty of men around Reagan who still wonder, "What if something should happen . . ." Reagan says he is not one of them. He insists that he loves California and would never leave. But he was willing to run in 1968, and most observers believe he could be prevailed upon to take another grab at the brass ring. Since 1968, of course, there's been another factor: Spiro Agnew. To a significant extent, the Vice President has usurped Reagan's potential national constituency; the Governor seems to get few out-of-state speaking invitations these days. If something should happen to Nixon, it is questionable whether Reagan could beat Agnew for the nomination, assuming Agnew wanted it.

The other possibility is for Reagan to run for the Senate in 1974 against the incumbent, Alan Cranston. The Senate would suit Reagan's preference for speech-making over administration, and by that time his children would be older, freeing him for more travel. But it is no secret that Robert Finch is hungering to take on Cranston and would probably have Nixon's blessing. When he was elected lieutenant governor of California in 1966, Finch ran ahead of Reagan, and the outcome of a primary fight is by no means certain.

Meanwhile, Ronald Reagan is still a hero to California's millions, chief executive of the nation's largest state—no small achievement in itself. "This is quite a place to be," he told an interviewer recently, and he undoubtedly meant it. But maybe Reagan's greatest role is neither George Gipp nor governor of California, but the Lone Ranger, riding in on his white horse, solving the problem in time for the cereal commercial and leaving a silver bullet behind. One can almost hear them, standing in the yard of their stucco bungalow, talking in hushed tones as the stranger rides into the distance.

"Who was that masked man?"

"Don't you know? That was Ronald Reagan."

1970

Tom Bradley—A Mayor Who Happens To Be Black

Los Angeles

The San Fernando Valley is probably the best example of the spectacular suburban growth that has blanketed the "sunbelt" states of the West and the South since the war. Thirty years ago it was an isolated area of orange groves and truck farms, untouched by the freeways that have since slashed through the Hollywood Hills, binding the valley in their concrete grasp to the fortunes of the Los Angeles metropolis. Today more than 1 million people live in this northwestern section of the city, dwelling in comfortable, if unoriginal, homes, shopping at convenient, if impersonal, malls, eating at fast, if indistinguishable, restaurants that have finally created, not a melting-pot culture, but a frying-pan culture. A Big Mac is a Big Mac is a Big Mac.

The relentlessly middle-class denizens of this valley tend to work in the service businesses and modern industries—such as electronics and computers—that provide the economic underpinning for suburbia. But while many of them make enough to get a taste of affluence—maybe a camper or a boat—they seldom erase that tinge of insecurity that can become badly inflamed, like a sore tooth, in times of inflation or unemployment. Except for a few small pockets, the valley is mainly white, and in 1969 the people here panicked at the prospect of Los Angeles's electing a black man, City Councilman Thomas Bradley, as mayor. Sam Yorty, then a two-term incumbent running for reelection, nurtured those fears with the devotion of a mother tending her baby, and Bradley was snowed under. Last spring the two men met in a rematch, and then, four years later, times had changed. Many valley dwellers still did not like Bradley, but the hard edge of panic had subsided, and faced with the choice of a "black or a buffoon," as one analyst put it, large numbers just stayed home. As a result, Bradley got half the white votes cast city-wide, and scored a smashing victory in a city that is only 18 percent black.

As Bradley marked his first six months in office at the beginning of the year, I went to the valley to see what the people were saying and feeling about their new mayor. Out of more than two dozen interviewed at random, only a few viewed him negatively. One of them, Mike Sellheim, an installer of burglar alarms, said the Mayor had "not done a damned thing." He had voted for Yorty because Yorty was white, but now he was confused. "I'm prejudiced in a way, and in a way I'm not," said Sellheim. "If he does his job properly, it wouldn't make any difference what color he is. But I was brought up in a white society, and I don't know. It's hard on him, the fact that he's black. I wonder if he'll favoritize the blacks, and not us." But a more typical comment came from Arnold Zweig, an insurance executive who also voted against Bradley: "I think he's trying; I feel he's a respectable and honest person who's doing the right thing, in general."

Except for Mike Sellheim, not one person now thought that Bradley's race was a drawback. "The fact that he was black bothered me for a while, but not anymore," admitted Alfred Lipschitz, a technical writer. "We're all brought up with certain prejudices, but once the guy's in office and shows what kind of a person he is, it becomes a thing of the past. It's like when Kennedy was running for President. A lot of people thought his being Catholic was an awful thing, but that's another thing that's gone away. People are realizing how inconsequential these things are." Something seems to be happening in Los Angeles. The rages and passions of the nineteen-sixties have cooled. No one is saying, "We shall overcome," or "Burn, baby, burn," or "Off the pig." But out there among the freeways and patios and carports of the real heartland of America, people are saying that a man should be judged by ability, not color. To most people, he is a mayor who happens to be black. "In this sense, I think we've attained what we've always looked for, a color-blind electorate," one labor leader said.

In another sense, Bradley's race is still very important. To many, he is a symbol of success. "People are happy to see a colored—a black man—mayor of a big city," said Lois Rowe, who did not vote for the Mayor. "They're proud of it; it shows we have made some headway." Nowhere is that felt more keenly than on the other side of the mountains from the San Fernando Valley, in the black districts of South Central Los Angeles that voted more than 9 to 1 for Tom Bradley. "It gives hope for our children that color doesn't matter," Lucy Green, a barber, said. "Whatever background they come from, rich or poor, they can make it."

Tom Bradley could not agree more. He is 56 years old, a middle-aged, middle-class man who has never lost faith in democratic, peaceful progress. He is possessed of a quality almost as rare these days as chastity—patience. As bad as things might seem, he knows they are better than they once were. He has played by the rules, and has won. He has been called an Uncle Tom and a tool of "The Man," but he spent twenty-one years as a policeman, and he feels he has learned something. In 1969 he apologized to an interviewer for sounding "trite," and then said, "During my years on the police force, I learned that hostility breeds hostility. I saw that every man was looking for some kind of warmth, whether he would admit it or not. People, all people, are looking for respect, for human dignity. This is something we all nourish. I have faith in this element of human nature, faith that there is an underlying decency in every man."

If Tom Bradley does sound trite occasionally, after a while you realize he generally means what he says. In this age of "doing your thing," he *does* believe in such "old-fashioned" virtues as toil, even sacrifice. His aides worry that President Nixon has given the work ethic a bad name, but the Mayor's faith remains undaunted. "All this didn't fall into my lap," he said simply. "It took hard work and a long, bitter struggle."

That struggle began in Calvert, Texas, where Tom was born the second of six children to Lee and Crenner Bradley, field hands on a cotton plantation. He was 7 when the family joined the migration westward, seized by the elemental hope that things would be better "out there." But once in Los Angeles, his father jumped from job to job—waiter, steward, porter— and after a year or so the Bradleys split up. Tom's mother started doing "day work" as a domestic, and by age 9 the youngster was helping out with a paper route. Somehow, even then, Tom had developed an iron core of determination. When it came time for high school, he deliberately left the poverty and pathology of his old neighborhood and entered a largely white school, thus setting a pattern that would recur frequently in his life. He realized athletics was the only way he could finance an education, and he perfected skills in football and track that won him a scholarship to U.C.L.A.

Jobs were scarce for young blacks in 1940, even for those with college degrees, and civil service offered one of the few opportunities to get ahead. The police department was still largely segregated, but when things loosened up, Bradley rose to lieutenant, the highest rank reached by a black until that time.

He might have been seething inside, but Bradley's reaction to the racial snubs was to find some practical way around them. When he bought a house in 1950 in the white neighborhood of Leimert Park, he had a white friend negotiate the purchase. "Using a third party was the way it was done," he explained. "Getting mad wouldn't have gotten us our house any faster."

Frustrated by the limits of police work, Bradley decided to go to law school at night, and in 1961 he retired from the force to open a law practice. But some white businessmen who had met him during his police days urged him to get involved in politics, and in 1963 he became the first black elected to the City Council, representing a racially mixed district. In 1969 he was largely an unknown when he ran for mayor, and Yorty adroitly manipulated that ignorance to convince people that militants would "take over" the city if Bradley won. At a time when black students were marching out of college buildings, guns drawn, when the Watts riots were still a vivid memory, the anxieties and prejudices that were festering in the tract homes of the San Fernando Valley seemed justified to many whites.

As Bradley has noted about himself, he often gets rebuffed the first time he tries something, but that seldom dissuades him. The day after his galling defeat, he started running again. For the next several years he moved around the city, showing people that he did not, in fact, have horns on his head and a Molotov cocktail in his pocket, a task made easier with the disappearance of the rioting and demonstrations. Moreover, Los Angeles is a special city. Despite the problems, racial tensions are palpably lower than in a place like New York. The small bungalows of Watts are just not as menacing as the tenements of Harlem, and they are farther from white neighborhoods. White people here don't imagine every black as a potential mugger—if only because neither whites nor blacks often walk anywhere. The city has never developed much of a militant black leadership and, since blacks account for less than 20 percent of the population anyway, whites generally do not feel as threatened as they do in a city like Detroit, where blacks approach a majority.

As the 1973 campaign approached, Bradley received sizable financial support from a group of younger liberals, many of whom had been drawn into politics by the civil-rights and antiwar movements. Probably the best example was Max Palevsky, who made a fortune in the computer industry and contributed about $200,000 of it to the Bradley cause. And with that kind of war chest, Bradley launched an expensive TV campaign about six months before the election. In addition to conveying the moderate-responsible image, "we also wanted to show very early that Tom Bradley was black," explained David Garth, the New York-based political consultant who designed the media campaign. "We wanted people to get any kind of racial animosity out early." By election time, many people just did not believe the inevitable Yorty propaganda.

Tom Bradley is quite obviously black, and proud, but his quiet, almost dull demeanor does not frighten people. A flamboyant black—a Jesse Jackson or a Bobby Seale—might excite his supporters, but scare off everybody else. Bradley is more like Senator Edward Brooke of Massachusetts; he has the capacity to reassure people in a way that is particularly useful in the current climate of suspiciousness toward politicians of all colors. As Natalie Marks, a salesgirl in the valley, put it: "You just can't believe anybody anymore, but I don't think Bradley is out for himself. I think he's really working for the people."

One of the most frequent criticisms of him is that he is too buttoned-up, an unexciting plodder with a charisma quotient approaching Calvin Coolidge's. I went to see him one day in his City Hall office and, after years of watching him in action, I still noticed the contradictions. He is 6-foot-4, has the thick shoulders, neck, and hands of the powerful football player he once was, yet his smile is thin, unsure, a bit embarrassed, often a tentative stab at a jollity. His aides considered it a victory when they got him to swear occasionally during the campaign; and he would no sooner wear an Afro than a dress. He acknowledges the criticisms made of him: "A lot of people have said to me, 'You know, you're not as flamboyant as some people think a black man ought to be and you are too deliberate.' And I say, 'I have no intention of changing. Maybe you would call me deliberate, like a Sherman tank is deliberate. But it gets the job done.' " As one shrewd politician observed, "Bradley has adopted the mannerisms of a 1940s civil servant. His appearance isn't as strong as the blacks of the sixties and seventies, the militancy isn't there. But he is a very, very strong man, very much in control of his emotions." Some other politicians see him as a man of limited imagination and intelligence and worry about whether he is really up to the job. Though David Garth, who has handled more than forty candidates, says of Bradley: "He's among the brightest."

It is still too early to make definitive judgments about his performance as mayor but certain impressions do begin to form. The *Los Angeles Times* said that his "biggest accomplishment" during his first half-year was "his emergence as an activist mayor," but that style has been tempered with an innate sense of caution. His frugality is already entering political folklore; his press secretary, Bob Kholos, recounts the time several staff members brought him back some chicken soup for lunch. When the Mayor looked at the plastic container the soup was in, he beamed and said, "It's reusable." In his first months, Bradley sliced more than $10 million from the budget he had inherited. C. Erwin Piper, the city's administrative officer for twelve years, finds Bradley more conservative fiscally than Yorty: "It surprised the hell out of me; I rather expected that he would not be so conservative. But as he said to me, 'Let's make a buck squeak every time we spend one.'"

Some think Bradley has been too cautious about the selection of a staff. There was some obligatory talk after the election about a "national talent search," but the Mayor wound up selecting mainly young, local people who had worked for him on the City Council or the campaign. Several people close to Bradley told me, in critical terms, about the brilliant graduate of Harvard Law School who had worked for Mayor Lindsay in New York and now wanted to come to Los Angeles. But Bradley would not even interview him for a job.

The mention of John Lindsay brings up some interesting comparisons. Lindsay took office during the first blaze of concern over the "urban crisis." He stocked his administration with Ivy Leaguers, the best and the brightest of the urban wars, whose arrogance led them to promise victory in the Holy Crusade against poverty and decay. But in the end Lindsay's legions suffered the same disappointments as their counterparts in the Pentagon. Bradley takes a much more modest approach. One political strategist said, "As a black, he's probably sick and tired of politicians coming and saying, tomorrow will be Shangri-La. He's not about to make the same kind of empty promises."

Bradley chose as his chief idea and research person a 26-year-old named Norm Emerson, who might not have a distinguished academic background but who had worked as a city planner and legislative aide in Sacramento. As Manuel Aragon, a deputy mayor, puts it, "We're not ideologues; we're not high-wire intellectuals. But we're very practical; we have a lot of experience being resourceful and solving problems." Aragon, a Mexican-American, worked several years as a fruit picker and attended three colleges before winning a degree; he has run a business and the Los Angeles poverty program; he can talk to farm workers in Spanish about their working conditions, and then put on a board-room accent and chat with business executives about profit margins. Aragon says the staff is thin in spots, mainly because the City Council has not appropriated enough money to hire enough people. (It does not appear to "favoritize" blacks; on a list of twenty-eight top appointments I counted five blacks, four Chicanos, and two Asians.) On the other hand, Bradley had to do so much for himself for so long that he has yet to master the art of delegating responsibility; it is hard to run a city when you still pick up your laundry and make your own plane reservations.

Sam Yorty had plenty of time to make plane reservations, since he always argued that the mayor's office had little power and then proceeded to act that way. In fact, Los Angeles does have a governmental system that was heavily influenced by the reforms of the Progressive era, particularly the negative notion that if no one had much power, no one could do much damage. Officially, the city charter mandates a "weak mayor, strong council" set-up. The mayor controls only about sixty jobs, and the rest of the payroll is so dominated by civil service that even major department heads can be removed only for cause. During the campaign, however, Bradley contended that the mayor could do a lot more if he wanted to, and since July he has been trying to prove his case. He shows up at so many places around town you half expect him to wave to you from a garbage truck.

One of his most successful tactics has been to visit different neighborhoods and spend the day listening to local problems. He also invited citizens to come to City Hall and vent their grievances, and, while this was done partly for public-relations value, people seem to feel that they have an accessible and active mayor. Out in the valley they kept saying that Bradley "cared" about the city, and Larry Bees, a graphic designer, said, "He seems more concerned with the average person. He gives the definite impression that he's looking for solutions; he's not up for sale, in other words." This activity also continues his strategy of making people comfortable with the idea of a black mayor. Bradley has been mayor for six months and "nothing terrible has happened," as Stephen Reinhardt, one of his advisers, put it, and some former opponents even see him now as an insurance policy against racial violence. Other people agree with Jim Wyatt, a technical writer: "Bradley looks at himself as a chance to prove a black man can be a good mayor, and he's putting out twice as hard as anybody else would. He wants to be a good example for his people and he's beating his brains out to be great."

Bradley *is* working hard, and, although he has had his frustrations, he has made a significant impact in a number of areas. As a ten-year alumnus, he has been able to improve relations with the City Council. And he has made inroads with the business and banker power sources downtown, which had long viewed him with suspicion, enlisting their aid with such problems as rapid transit and fuel supply.

Rapid transit is a perennial topic out here in the Car Capital of the Western World. During the campaign Bradley promised he would break ground within eighteen months for a new system; now he admits that figure is unrealistic, but a real start has been made, which is more than Yorty accomplished in twelve years. And in the meantime, the city is experimenting with computer-run car pools and something called dial-a-ride, a cross between taxi and bus service designed mainly for older people.

Bradley's style of personal persuasion and public pressure came to the fore during Los Angeles's recent encounter with the energy crisis. The municipal power company had contracted to buy much of its oil directly from the Middle East, and when the embargo was clamped on, the city faced a deficit of almost 50 percent in its energy supply. Bradley went on TV and radio, bluntly warning of the danger and urging people to conserve fuel voluntarily. But he was out of town, attending a League of Cities meeting in Puerto Rico, when the Department of Water and Power proposed a number of mandatory conservation measures, including a limit of fifty hours a week on all commercial and industrial establishments. Immediately cries of outrage from the business community bombarded City Hall, and for a day or so the administration seemed confused. But then Bradley called the office and helped arrange for a special citizens' committee headed by a department-store executive to study the problem. Bradley does have a tendency to name "blue-ribbon committees" and "*ad hoc* task forces" at the drop of an interoffice memo, but in this case the group worked night and day for a week and hammered out a compromise that provided for a 10 percent power cut for residential and commercial users and a 20 percent cut for industry.

By this time Bradley was back in town and he appeared before the City Council to urge it to accept the compromise. When by midafternoon it still had not, he strode into the council meeting, announced he was going to Washington that night to seek more fuel for the city, and allowed as how it would be nice if the legislators took some action before he left. A few councilmen yelped as they felt their arms twisting in the mayor's grip, but within hours the new ordinance had been passed unanimously. Bradley then appeared for the third time, thanked the council, and caught the red-eye special for the East. Now under the theory of the squeaky wheel getting the oil, Los Angeles, along with some other cities pleading special problems, has been promised special consideration on heating-fuel allotments and, in the event of rationing, gasoline. Most participants praised the Mayor's performance. "The guy does his homework," said Dan Waters, general manager of the Central City Association and a former campaign aide to Richard Nixon. "That doesn't mean we always agree on approaches and procedures, but we find he has a very open mind; he wants all the help he can get in solving the city's problems."

Sam Yorty seemed to care little about many pressing city problems— poverty, for example, or police relations with minority groups. He was a friend of big business, a man who believed that all growth was good, and if you asked him about his proudest achievements, he would mention the burgeoning skyline or the new convention center. To listen to Sam Yorty, Watts could have been in Kalamazoo. Since Bradley is determined not to step on too many toes, he has moved slowly in these sensitive areas, but changes are detectable. Take crime and police policy, which became major issues in the campaign. Unlike many white liberals, the ex-cop met the problem head on, and told me at the time, "The black community cares more about crime than any area of the city. Those who describe themselves as liberals see the problem as one of root causes, and want to hear more discussion of that. But it's a real crisis now and we have to deal with it now."

As mayor, Bradley retained Police Chief Edward Davis, whose right-wing fulminations frequently offended the town's civil libertarians. But then he appointed a police commission—the five-man body that oversees the department—headed by William Norris, a downtown lawyer with solid liberal credentials. The vice president is Sam Williams, one of the best-known blacks in the city's legal Establishment.

The commission has displayed the same mixture of assertiveness and caution that marks Bradley's own methods. Quietly it has questioned police recruiting practices that tend to eliminate candidates who might have smoked marijuana or marched in an antiwar demonstration. "My major concern is that the department is too homogeneous," said Norris, who wants to run for state attorney general. "They all tend to look alike and act alike. I want to see some people with long hair on the force because there are a lot of people in this city with long hair." Out on the street, the commission has pressured the department into spending less time and manpower on such "victimless" crimes as homosexuality. Police in the Hollywood division have even invited gay leaders to ride around in squad cars, in order to learn more about police procedures and establish better communication. The sweetness-and-light policy has extended to Chief Davis's attending an ACLU dinner, which to some here is almost like Goebbels's attending a Hadassah card party.

The planning commission, to take another example, has traditionally been a rubber stamp for developers seeking code variances to jam a few more houses into tracts with names like Crestwood Lakes and Oakridge Estates. Today the city, which now has 2.8 million people, is zoned for a capacity of 10 million, but the Bradley commission wants to cut the limit back to 4 million, and has already reduced the zoning in several sections, including Westwood, the lovely home of U.C.L.A., which is now threatened by a glut of high-rise construction.

Under Yorty, the Model Cities program was so badly run that Washington cut $7.5 million from the city's grant. Bradley placed a high priority on revamping the operation, and now there is a good chance the money will be restored. In a proposal to the council, Bradley has recommended that the new money be used mainly for child-care facilities and services for the elderly; another large chunk would be used to rehabilitate more than 1000 homes that have been repossessed by the federal government in poverty districts. But in this area, as in many others, the city cannot do much without massive federal aid. "This program," conceded Deputy Mayor Aragon, "is a long way from having sufficient scope to really affect the fundamental problems of a city the size of L.A."

So far Bradley has been fortunate. He has not had to face the kinds of issues, like a teachers' strike, or a battle over low-income housing in a middle-class neighborhood, that pitted blacks against whites during Lindsay's tenure in New York. Probably he never will have to face them. But even if it comes to a crunch, Bradley would seem to have a tremendous advantage over someone like Lindsay, who was always perceived, at least, as something of an élitist. As Larry Bees, the graphic designer, put it, Bradley identifies with the "average" people in this city, of any color, and they are beginning to identify with him, to feel that their mayor, who lives in the same small frame house he bought twenty years ago on his policeman's salary, understands their problems. They tend to agree with Irma Gross, a white salesclerk in the valley, who told me, "I feel he's one of us." Salesgirls or taxi drivers or schoolteachers in New York did not think they belonged to the same group as John and Mary Lindsay.

Yet Bradley is black; he has been shaped by different forces than Irma Gross or John Lindsay, and when I looked for the source of his tremendous determination, the roots led back to race. "As a white man, it's something you can't understand," said Bill Elkins, a boyhood friend of Bradley's and now one of his top aides. "There's something in the black experience that produces a driving, motivating force in many young blacks to achieve. They feel a need to disprove all the myths of racism." Bradley once told Robert Kistler of the *Los Angeles Times*, "All my life I've had to be better and smarter and tougher than the next man. If I hadn't, I wouldn't have made it as far as I have."

After the election, however, Bradley seemed to relax a bit. Smiles and jokes came easier, and at his inaugural he startled the crowd by proclaiming: "I is de mayor." A small thing, but very revealing. When I asked him recently to explain the remark, he gave a brief glimpse into what it must have been like to be a black at Poly High and U.C.L.A., in the police department and Leimert Park. He said he felt "a kind of looseness that I had never known before, the ability, the security to say that kind of thing over a radio or TV where the whole world is going to hear it. . . . I think that I have always been pretty disciplined about what I would say and what I would do. I think unconsciously I would be very careful so as not to make a mistake that could be used against me sometime in the future. And now having won, there's no worry. You don't have to think about that."

There have been costs. The need to be tough, to avoid mistakes has impaired Bradley's personal life. His golf clubs have been gathering dust for ten years, and apart from an occasional football game—which usually turns into a campaign event—he seldom indulges in personal pleasures. For Tom Bradley, said his aide Phil Depoian, relaxation is working in a sweater instead of a coat and tie.

Bradley's wife and two daughters, now in their late 20s, have had to do without a husband and father most of the time. "You know," Ethel Bradley said during the 1969 campaign, "that man went to law school eighteen years ago and I haven't seen him since." She has built her own world around her own interests—the Los Angeles Dodgers and a spectacular flower garden— and when Tom finally does come home, she is there. One daughter is a schoolteacher, the other a beautician and secretary who has had occasional brushes with the law over possession of marijuana. They, too, lead their own lives, and one gets the feeling that being a parent has not been a major part of Tom Bradley's life.

He has clearly decided that the price of being a public figure is worth it. Today, Tom Bradley is a recognized power in the Democratic party, the most likely heir to John Lindsay as a spokesman for American cities. A few of his more ardent admirers whisper about a possible vice-presidential nomination someday, and "Teddy and Tom" bumper stickers sprouted briefly after the election. But Bradley really loves Los Angeles in the way only a parent can love a gangly adolescent, and whatever happens in his political future, one thing is certain: He is de mayor!

1974

WHAT'S GOING ON HERE?

When I was writing about pornography in 1970 I took my wife to several "hard core" films showing sexual intercourse. At the time you could only find them in a few big cities, and they were strictly stag operations. The proprietor of one theater in Hollywood was so flustered to see a woman, he made her sit in a special chair in a corner of the room. Today, *Deep Throat* and *The Devil in Miss Jones* are practically considered family entertainment. The attack on pornography continues unabated, however, and recent rulings from the Nixon Supreme Court have slowed the tide of legalization described in "Pornography Has Taken Off." But the basic point—that people are voting with their wallets—remains valid.

In a similar way, health foods have become more common than they were just a few years ago. The magic word for advertising copywriters used to be "golden"; today it is "natural." I half expect to hear about "natural artificial flavoring" one of these days.

Venereal disease is still spreading, but public attitudes have improved, and the state legislature passed a bill allowing drugstores to display prophylactics openly.

You don't hear much about the "youth culture" these days, and maybe one explanation came from the prisoner of war who saw his country for the first time in six years and exclaimed: "The hippies have won!" The drug scene might have diminished, communes might be a bit passé, but flower power lives, even without a *Life* photographer around. These movements ebb and flow, and today the media cliché is the students who worry about grades and security. But they have not gone back to the fifties. They can't—not after the acid in San Francisco and the communes in Magic Valley. Nor can some of their parents. They probably did not know it, but many couples who are splitting today, or opting out of the "rat race," started down that road the day the first be-in happened in Golden Gate Park.

Pornography Has Taken Off

Los Angeles

Pornography has become big business in America. In a nation founded by Puritans, there has developed a huge and often shadowy industry devoted to the exploitation of sex. Using the techniques of modern business, from mass production to mass distribution, the pornography industry makes a variety of books, magazines, movies, records, photographs, and "sexual devices." Its customers are millions of Americans every week.

There appear to be two main reasons for this explosion of erotica. The Supreme Court has, over the last decade, deemed most pornography legal. Only so-called hard core pornography, or obscenity, is considered illegal, although local interpretations vary. "Obscenity," says Stanley Fleishman of Los Angeles, one of the nation's best-known lawyers in the field, "is a matter of geography."

More important, the sexual revolution in America—and around the world—has made people more tolerant. Public opinion polls still say that more than three-quarters of the population want stricter laws against pornography. But the pressure to suppress erotica has waned considerably in the era of the mini-skirt and the coed college dormitory.

The annual volume of the pornography business is difficult to estimate. Some observers have said $2 billion; most experts put the figure at closer to $500 million. But what is not disputable is the industry's tremendous recent growth.

Five years ago about 90 theaters around the country showed "sexploitation" movies or "skin flicks." Now there are more than 600, and the number is growing weekly. Some have abandoned seedy downtown areas for the suburbs; many are clean and respectable looking, with admission prices as high as $5 in big cities. But these theaters are not limited to metropolitan areas. "Skin houses" have opened recently in cities as varied as Litchfield, Massachusetts; Augusta, Georgia, and Girard, Ohio.

"Adult bookstores" have enjoyed a similar prosperity. Only 9 such

⊙

stores existed in Los Angeles several years ago, most of them on Main Street, which is similar to New York's 42nd Street. Today, there are more than 90 bookstores here catering to sex, and 20 of them are in the suburban San Fernando Valley. Six new stores have opened in Houston in the last year. Atlanta has more than a dozen, and New York, which along with Los Angeles produces almost all the pornography in the country, now has more than 200.

Probably the fastest segment of the pornography business is mail order. While several large companies dominate the market, more than 500 operators offer through the mail material ranging from color film to artificial sex organs. Last year the Post Office Department in Washington received 232,070 complaints from people who had received unsolicited advertising for pornography. The total was up almost 100,000 from two years ago.

When the mail-order business started several years ago, sellers used specialized lists to solicit customers. Then some enterprising operators in Los Angeles started taking names at random out of phone books. At the same time, the ads started to include pictures of the merchandise. The most explicit material is still available only in major cities. In San Francisco, for instance, which has twenty-five sex-oriented movie theaters, several have recently started to show detailed films of actual oral and genital copulation. In St. Louis, stores openly display magazines showing female genitalia in such detail that they look like gynecological textbooks. Many stores are selling a book with Danish photographs that portray several techniques of sexual intercourse. The price of the book is $4.75.

There are still towns, of course, where *Playboy* magazine is considered dirty. One recent issue was confiscated in Concord, New Hampshire. But in most medium-sized cities, that is, with more than 100,000 population, a knowledgeable buyer can find films and magazines showing frontal nudity.

In bigger cities, the most popular purveyor of pornography is the "adult bookstore," a veritable supermarket of erotica for every taste and price range. Most of them are dingy storefronts, with the windows painted black or covered with wrapping paper for privacy. Inside, the books and magazines are arranged on crude racks according to subject matter: heterosexual, homosexual, lesbian, bondage and flagellations, bestiality, and foot fetishism. Films and sexual devices are often displayed near the cashier, who will sometimes provide such illegal material as stag films on request. A popular attraction in many stores is the "arcades," a collection of jukebox-like machines that for a quarter show a film that lasts about a minute.

The cardinal rule in an adult bookstore seems to be silence. Patrons tend to stand as far away from one another as possible while perusing the merchandise. Any untoward movement and they start like frightened deer. The only sound, as one observer in Madison, Wisconsin, put it, "is the jingle of the cash register."

Why is pornography good business? Who buys it and why? The answers cannot be precise, but there is general agreement within the industry that the bulk of its customers are middle-class, middle-aged men and white-collar and blue-collar workers.

Hyman's Book Store in Des Moines, Iowa, reports that its most consistent customers are the doctors, lawyers, and dentists from nearby office buildings. The owner of the Monument Square Smoke Shop in Portland, Maine, said, "My customers include all kinds, but there are plenty of businessmen who come in and carry out the books in their briefcases."

Few buyers of pornography like to talk about it. "I enjoy it," is virtually the universal reason given for buying it. But the issue is more complex. "Most of the buyers are lonely, frustrated men who use this to stimulate themselves," said one bookstore owner. A theater owner from Long Island said, "Basically, we are all voyeurs."

Pornography is not used only for solitary gratification. "Many guys come in here and say they want something that will turn their wives on," said a book dealer in Hollywood. "Sometimes they're rather pathetic. 'What can I do?,' they ask me. 'Why won't she respond to me?' But I also get some sophisticated couples who want to know what's happening. I had a girl the other day who came in and bought two magazines for her husband as a present."

Just about every producer agrees that young people make very poor customers. "Kids today look on sex as a participant sport, not a spectator sport," said David Friedman, a major sex movie producer. "If a kid wants to see a naked woman, he tells his girl friend to take her clothes off. He doesn't have to see my movies. When they do come, they come to laugh. They think it's camp."

Some producers fear that when the younger generation grows up, the markets for pornography will diminish. But others are not so sure. "These kids will get old, too," said one with a chuckle. "When they get to be 40 they'll do less acting and more looking."

How does a pornographer get started in the business? In the early 1950s, for example, Bill Hambling was publishing science fiction magazines in Chicago. His friend, Hugh Hefner, tried to borrow money from him to start a magazine called *Playboy*. "Hef," Bill Hambling said sagely, "you can't sell sex to the American people."

Several years later, Mr. Hambling reevaluated his judgment. He brought out a magazine called *Rogue*, which included, among other things, a foldout, color photograph of an undressed young lady. Soon he branched out into book publishing. Today, Mr. Hambling is the president of Greenleaf Classics of San Diego, and he can laugh at the chance he missed to own part of *Playboy*. Greenleaf publishes thirty-six new paperback titles every month, with a print run of 30,000 a title, or a total of 1 million books. Almost every one has a single subject: sex.

Sex publishers do not talk readily about economics but the average book costs about 25 cents to produce. If it carries a cover price of $2 the publisher sells it to the distributor for $1.

Mr. Hambling's office is in a plush new building the company owns and is decorated with modern art. The publisher dresses sharply, drives a new car, and greets people with a direct manner that is almost military in its crispness.

"When I first started, we published a book about Harry Truman and the Prendergast machine," Mr. Hambling recalls. "I thought it was great, and I set up a $10,000 advertising budget. The book lost $40,000. A few years later, we did a big book about Vietnam, with an introduction by Senator Fulbright. It laid the biggest egg of the year. But when we brought out *Candy*, people were lined up to buy it. I was as stupid as any publisher who thinks he can create a market. I can't make you want to read anything—all I can do as a publisher is exploit your need. I've never lost money on a sex book—that should be some indication of what the public wants."

The movie business is similar. Dozens of general theaters, faltering under the impact of television, have switched to sexual fare. The change is often dramatic. Leroy Griffith, a theater owner in Miami, said, "I built a brand new theater and played *The Sound of Music*, and I lost money. I switched to an adult policy, and the first week I made $4,000.

Pornography is a highly competitive and specialized industry. Take the magazine field, for example. The heart of the business is the photography, and editors must constantly keep up to date or risk losing their share of the market. "At first we tried to put out things we thought were in good taste," one editor said. "Then I saw what the others were doing, and it made our stuff look like *Mother Goose*. I thought they couldn't get away with it, but my salesmen came in and said we were getting returns from all over the country. So we had to keep up. You can't make a living selling buggy whips."

One marked change in the pornography business is the girls who pose for the photographs. According to officials in New Orleans, once a center for illicit pornography, most models twenty years ago were prostitutes. Today, the girls are different. They are usually wanderers in a big city, lost and penniless, who may sleep with many men but seldom accept money for this. That is particularly true in Los Angeles, where many young people are attracted by the warm weather, the glamour of Hollywood or the promise of a "hippie" life-style.

"The simple and most important reason is that they're looking for bread," said the manager of an agency that specializes in nude models. "If they have a rent payment due, and they need decent money fast, this is one of the few legal ways they can get it. A girl doesn't need references or skills—just a good body—and she can get the money right away. Most of the girls who come in here are too lazy to hold down a regular job. This is easy money—$50 a day—and they have no inhibitions about taking their clothes off. A few are rebelling against their parents, or the Puritan ethic, but not many."

The book business is somewhat different. While magazines are still vying for explicitness, there are few descriptions of sex acts that have not been written about many times. Thus, the premium is placed on originality. There is a joke around the industry that the man who can dream up a new fetish will strike it rich.

Several years ago the booming segment of the market was books about homosexuals. Little had been written about the subject before, and homosexuals bought nearly everything that came out, no matter how badly done. Now the market has leveled off. The best-selling stories today involve wife swapping, with a hint of group sex and bisexuality. Greenleaf has a whole line devoted to the subject.

Certain topics have always sold well, however, including stories about nurses and stewardesses. "Most men take a plane and here's this pretty girl who's very nice to him, and his fantasies start whirling," explained one writer.

The pay for sex novels is usually very low, about 1 or 2 cents a word. Thus, for a typical 50,000-word manuscript, a writer might get from $500 to $1,000. Nevertheless, publishers receive ten times as many manuscripts as they can use. They come from out-of-work television and movie writers, teachers, insurance salesmen, aspiring novelists who need rent money while they do their "serious" work. Only about 10 percent of the authors write sex books full-time.

One who did—until he switched to mysteries last year—was Victor Banis, the author of more than 100 steamy paperbacks over the last five years. Mr. Banis, who grew up on a farm in Ohio, was working as a government clerk in 1964 when he decided to try writing full-time. He recalled, "I had done a lot of writing in school, and I gave myself a year to make it. I took the approach of being a commercial writer. I wanted to make money at it, and sex books seemed a good way to do that." He worked on a strict schedule: $100 a day. If he is getting $700 for a book, he works a week, but he has done some in three days. He does not even retype his first draft. "Once you learn the basic formula, it's easy," he said. "The best example is the confession novel: sin, suffer, repent. Most sex books were confession stories, but now they're getting a little wilder." One thing that doesn't sell is humor. "The editors think humor takes the sex out of a book," he said.

Most people in the pornography industry admit that most of the books they publish are junk. Many editors do not even read the stories, especially if they know the writer's work. The major changes made in most manuscripts involve spelling and punctuation.

Nevertheless, the sex books have sold so well that many of the major publishing houses are copying the style. "When Irving Wallace's new book came out," said a large publisher, "one of our editors cracked, 'That's formula number 6 we abandoned four years ago.'"

Competition from the legitimate industry is even fiercer in movie making. The line between the "sexploitation" movies and some "major" films has blurred beyond recognition.

The "sexploitation" or "nudie" industry started about ten years ago with *The Immoral Mr. Teas*, a movie about a man who finds a pair of eyeglasses that allow him to see through clothing. The director, Russ Meyer, a former Army combat photographer, invested $24,000 and grossed more than $1 million.

Mr. Teas started a rash of low-budget, poor-quality films with plots out of *True Romances* and as much skin as possible. Around the industry, large breasts are known familiarly as "ticket sellers," and sell they did. The average producer could at least double his money on most pictures with little trouble.

The "nudie" films are facing tough competition. The major studios often show as much skin as they do and sometimes more. So independent filmmakers have started making movies that include close-ups of male and female genitalia and some sex play. They do not have even the pretense of a plot. Mostly shot in 16-millimeter, these films are shown publicly in several big cities and are spreading rapidly.

Despite the competition from legitimate publishers and movie studios, the pornography business is thriving more than ever. The police here have some evidence that the Mafia thinks the business is good enough to be a target of muscling-in. But most pornographers are independent entrepreneurs who started with very little and built up huge businesses. "Some people say we're part of the communist conspiracy," joked one movie maker, "but we're really classic American capitalists."

The basic law governing pornography was enunciated by the Supreme Court in the Roth case of 1957. In that case, the Court ruled that obscenity was not protected by the First Amendment guarantee of freedom of speech. But the Court went on to define obscenity in this manner: To be obscene, the Court said, the material, taken as a whole, must appeal primarily to the prurient interest, must go significantly beyond accepted community standards, and must be utterly without redeeming social value.

Applying this test, the Court has gradually widened the definition of material that is not obscene. The process has been accelerated by publishers and filmmakers who constantly bring test cases on franker and franker material. In addition, the courts have established numerous procedural safeguards to protect pornographers from police harassment.

As a result, the police across the country have complained that these rules seriously hamper their ability to control pornography. Donald Shidell of the Los Angeles police department vice squad said, "The courts have created so much utter chaos and so many restrictions that they have almost legalized obscenity." Many legal experts agree with Mr. Shidell and say that the Supreme Court is moving toward standards under which virtually anything will be permitted for adults. The Court has upheld laws, however, that prohibit the sale of pornography to minors. It has also said that "pandering," or advertisements that promote material as obscene, can be held against a defendant.

The most controversial legal area today involves the burgeoning mail-order business. Citizens receiving unsolicited advertisements have inundated the post office with complaints, and 200 bills have been introduced in Congress to curb the flow of unwanted erotica.

According to public opinion polls, the nation continues to be adamantly opposed to pornography. A recent Gallup Poll reported that 85 percent of the people want stricter laws regarding mail-order solicitation, and 76 percent want tighter restrictions on street sales. Organized groups such as Citizens for Decent Literature continue to denounce the spread of "smut," and politicians regularly take up the cause—particularly at election time.

But perhaps the most telling expression of public opinion is recorded by the cash register. "If the public practiced what it preached, we would be out of business tomorrow," said Paul Mart, a noted "sexploitation" filmmaker.

A major question that remains unanswered about pornography is its effect on people. To its opponents, it "erodes the moral fiber" of the country and can lead to sexual assaults and similar crimes. Most scientists in the field agree that no conclusive evidence is available. But the research that has been done indicates that pornography seldom leads to criminal acts and might even be helpful in some cases. In some California hospitals, pornography is being used on a highly experimental basis to treat sex offenders. And some psychiatrists think that it can be useful in everyday life.

In any case, the trend in America today is toward allowing individuals to decide for themselves what they should read and see. President Nixon tacitly admitted this last spring when he sent a message to Congress on obscenity. "When indecent books no longer find a market," the President said, "when pornographic films can no longer draw an audience, when obscene plays open to empty houses, then the tide will turn. Government can maintain the dikes against obscenity, but only people can turn back the tide."

On that basis, the people show little inclination to turn back the tide—or the clock.

1970

The Health Food Boom

Los Angeles

There was the DDT scare and the cyclamate scare, the cranberry scare and the tuna fish scare. Robert Choate said there was not enough nutrition in cereal, and Ralph Nader said there was too much fat in hot dogs. Members of the counterculture said anything their parents ate must be bad.

Over the last few years these seeds have been fertilized by publicity and watered by a general concern for the deteriorating environment. Now they have blossomed into a verdant and rapidly growing industry—health food. The health food business, of course, is not new, but traditionally it catered to a select group of faddists who mixed their meals in blenders and guzzled carrot juice. Today middle-class, Establishment mothers are munching organic figs and giving their kids wheat germ as snacks.

Experts estimate that the number of health food stores in the country has doubled in three years, from 1,200 to 2,500. In California alone, three new stores open every week. And some big supermarkets and department stores have already opened health food sections or are exploring the idea.

The boom has centered in California and New York, but New Orleans, for example, now has twelve stores, four of which opened in the last year. Kahan & Lessin Co., one of the biggest distributors in the country, has doubled its sales volume in three years to $12 million annually. Most individual stores report a similar growth. In fact, the biggest problem facing the industry today is not selling but buying. There is just not enough merchandise to go around. Recently, a store owner in Los Angeles placed orders for seventy-eight different products, including thirteen kinds of herb tea, that went unfilled.

The enormous demand and the lack of supply has led to abuses. Bruno Corigliano, who recently became manager of a store here called Naturway, said, "When I took over they had 'organic' signs on everything. That's impossible because I know people just don't grow organic cauliflower and broccoli. Another produce guy started sending me stuff he said was organic and I got suspicious. I took a razor blade and started scraping an apple, and all the spray came off."

"There is nothing mysterious about health foods," added Mr. Corigliano, who was formerly an insurance underwriter. "It's just the natural food with nothing put into it or taken out of it." This means no preservatives or additives, no bleaches or dyes or sprays. "We guarantee spoilage," joked a New York market owner.

The staples in any health food store include whole grains and breads, unrefined sugar and unbleached flour, a bewildering array of tea and honey, dried fruits and nuts, pure juices, special cookies and candies, fertile eggs, raw milk, peas, yogurt, peanut butter that is all peanuts, and jam that is all jam.

Some carry chickens that have been allowed to run around and scratch for their own food. Meat is scarce, but a few stores offer such products as frankfurters made from cows that are not given hormone injections. More stores are trying to stock organic fruits and vegetables, meaning they are grown with no synthetic fertilizers or pesticides. But almost all organic produce is raised in California, and this is the only state where it is available regularly.

One section is usually devoted to hundreds of vitamins and minerals, enzymes and elements, protein potions to make you strong and herb concoctions to make you regular. Here there is a pill for every ill, a powder for every problem—all available without a prescription.

Many of the outlets are typical Mom and Pop operations, but some of the newer ones are indistinguishable from modern supermarkets, all enamel and plastic and fluorescent lights. Those catering to the hip culture often look like the store in Madison, Wisconsin, that was described as "a combination of a storefront Zen Buddhist chapel and an old-fashioned grocery with its wares stored in wooden barrels."

What they all have in common is high prices. A survey conducted in Berkeley by a University of California nutritionist estimated that the local stores charged 150 to 250 percent more than regular markets. Most prices are not that inflated, but one store here was selling organic tomatoes for 95 cents a pound recently; nonorganic tomatoes in the next bin were 59 cents. Eggs in Manhattan cost 60 to 75 cents in regular stores and $1.19 in health food markets.

The main reason for the price differential is that health foods require special handling and are produced in smaller quantities. Individual stores can buy only in small lots, particularly since the lack of preservatives makes many items highly perishable. And because they have a small volume, the stores have to make more on each item. Moreover, distributors will sometimes charge a health food store more because they assume the store can charge a higher price.

There has also been a sharp increase in the number of health food restaurants. Los Angeles has at least a dozen, including the Discovery Inn, H.E.L.P. Unlimited, and the Taming of the Stew. In Boston, a young entrepreneur sells health foods from three carts attached to bicycles, and at nearby Brandeis University the student cafeteria now has a special health food line.

Patrons of health food stores and restaurants fall into three broad groups: sickly, often older, people; youthful members of the counterculture; and the better-educated middle class. Each has its own reasons.

The sickly types have tried many doctors and had little success. Some have read books and decided they could cure themselves. A typical comment came from Mrs. Vivian Ellsworth, who was shopping at Full O'Life, a store in Burbank: "Two years ago this July, I had the virus flu and pneumonia. I got out of bed a bag of bones. I had a really bad time. I went to the doctor twice a week for shots, but they cost $14 apiece, and they weren't doing me a bit of good. I passed this store, and I decided to come in and look around and see what I could do for myself. I went out with $90 worth of stuff. In one month I had snapped out of it, and in three months I felt beautiful," she said.

Store owners are prohibited from prescribing remedies for a particular ailment, but the distinction between prescribing and suggesting is a fine one. Many proprietors got into the business after "curing" their own illnesses and strongly imply that what worked for them could work for anyone. Often they say that a program of food supplements "can't hurt" or tell a worried customer that "you have nothing to lose."

Younger patrons of health food stores scorn this approach as "looking for health in a bottle." For them, health foods are part of a broader change that involves the return to simpler, more natural ways of living. Instead of getting high blood pressure, they just "get high on nature."

Jake Blum, a 24-year-old cook in a health food restaurant in Cambridge, Massachusetts, gave this explanation for organic eating: "It has to do with God and a concern for the planet. The environment is really screwed up. We are trying to eat in a way that is in harmony with the environment.

The food itself is the only thing that explains it. Most people who aren't familiar with it are amazed at how good it is. It's really involved in the total cycle, from putting the seed into the earth to putting organic garbage back into the earth. We have some of the most beautiful garbage in town—it has no chemicals."

Young people often feel the prices in regular stores are too high and sometimes form cooperatives to buy their own. In St. Louis, for instance, soybeans sold for 69 cents per half-pound in one store. But a group of vegetarians went to rural Illinois and bought 50 pounds for $5.

While many are quite serious about health foods, some young people go along because it is the thing to do, another fad in the endless search for something that gives meaning to their lives. Mr. Corigliano at Naturway recently hired a salesgirl who "was so natural she refused to wear a bra or shoes to work." But then, he added wryly, "I found her one day eating a chocolate bar and a Coke."

The third group has neither a medical nor a mystical motive: Its members just worry about polluted food, in the same way that they worry about polluted air and water. Max Folsom, an advertising photographer shopping at Naturway in Hollywood, explained, "Once you get involved and start reading about it, it's kind of scary to realize what you're eating." A middle-aged shopper at The Good Earth, a Manhattan market, said, "I thought I should do something for my grandchildren. Maybe it helped."

Professional nutritionists generally approve of the new trend. "The more interest in nutrition the happier I am," said Dr. Doris Calloway, professor of nutrition at the University of California at Berkeley. But they also have some doubts. Dr. Kathleen Harris, a nutritionist at the University of Southern California, thinks that health foods are largely beside the point. "The biggest nutritional problem in this country is overeating," she said. "The most important thing is a balanced diet, and if you know what you are doing you can often find the same food benefits shopping at a supermarket."

The main point nutritionists make is that consumers should become more informed about nutrition and demand better products. Dr. Calloway put it this way: "The food industry is like anyone else in the marketplace— they design a product that will sell. What housewives have been willing to pay for is convenience. They also want it to look good. Orange juice should be orange, even if it comes from a yellow orange, and they don't want the liquid and the solid separated in anything they buy. Each preference makes the processor change his product to meet the demand of the market. By the same token, if manufacturers were convinced that an informed purchasing public was going to give top priority to nutrition, they'd change. It's up to the housewife, or whoever does the buying. They have to be informed."

1971

The VD Pandemic

Los Angeles

The Los Angeles Free Clinic is a small, rather shabby building wedged between a Chicken Delight ("We Deliver") and an appliance store ("Quality Merchandise—Best Service"). Across Fairfax Avenue stands a mammoth, grayish brown structure, the West Coast headquarters of CBS. About 5:30 the young people start crowding into the narrow alley alongside the clinic, waiting to sign in for treatment. They include well-scrubbed college students and scruffy street kids, both sexes, all colors, as young as 15 and as old as 35. Despite the diversity, they have two things in common: They need medical help, and they can't, or won't, get it anywhere else. Many just cannot afford a private doctor; others cannot afford to have their parents find out what's wrong with them. That could be almost anything: pregnancy, hepatitis, various infections and fears, tired blood and tired brains, maybe just the flu or a bad cold. More than 25 percent have VD, venereal disease.

What passes for interior decoration at the Free Clinic is a brightly colored mixture of the psychedelic and the scientific. One poster shows two bodies whirling in a sea of purple; another, giving the symptoms for VD, advises women: "If a guy you balled has it, come for treatment. If not treated, germs will spread up causing great pain and inability to have kids." One night recently, two boys and a girl from a local high school were chatting in a corner of the cramped waiting room. ("I had him for chemistry. . . . I used to go to a lot of dances at AZA. . . .") The girl, who wore her name on a gold chain around her neck, needed birth control pills, and was getting anxious about the time. She did not want her parents to start wondering where she was. "Have you ever tried being honest with them?" gibed one of the boys. "Yes," she answered, a little grimly, "it doesn't work." The second fellow was tall and curly haired, radiating what used to be called "boyish charm." He said his name was Greg, and we asked him if he ever had VD. "I'm in the process," he replied sheepishly. Was he concerned about getting it? "No, I never really thought about it. I got it, and I'll take care of it. It's a big pain, but I'll make sure it doesn't go too far." Was he surprised? "This thing shocked me," Greg admitted. "I knew the people I was with pretty well, and I didn't think they had it. I really can't figure out who I got it from. I guess I had a bad stereotype of the person who has VD—that's why I was shocked. I thought the only one who got it was a girl or a guy who balled an awful lot without any real feeling about it—someone who didn't take care of his body. I guess if I can get it, anybody can."

Greg is hardly overstating the case. Anybody can get VD, and more and more people are. The United States today is in the midst of a monstrous epidemic. Within the last year the American Social Health Association, a private organization that studies such matters, labeled the VD outbreak a "pandemic," an epidemic of "unusual extent and severity." According to the association, VD has reached such proportions only twice before in the last fifty-three years: after World War I and toward the end of World War II, before penicillin came into wide use. Robert R. Lugar, an advisor to the Los Angeles County Health Department, described the situation this way: "If you pose the question, where is VD, the answer is: everywhere. My God, if there's anything in this world today we can't stop it's VD. VD is strictly on wheels today. It's no more possible to restrict the spread of VD than it is to keep the flies in one room of your house."

The phrase "venereal disease" comes from Venus, the goddess of love, and refers to maladies that are almost always transmitted by sexual contact. (Some infections, such as vaginitis, can be caught in a variety of ways, including sexual intercourse, but they are not included here.) There are at least five types, but only two are important, gonorrhea and syphilis. Gonorrhea, commonly known as "the clap," is milder and much more prevalent. In the fiscal year ending last June, 624,000 cases of gonorrhea were reported nationwide, a jump of 9 percent over the previous year and 130 percent over 1963. That figure exceeds the number of all other communicable diseases combined. The year before, California alone reported about 105,000 cases; in comparison, there were 10,000 cases of hepatitis, 6,000 of mumps, and 4,000 of tuberculosis. A random sampling of 164,000 women at both public and private clinics revealed that 1 in 10 had gonorrhea, usually without knowing it. Syphilis is a far more serious disease. Last year it increased nationally by 15.6 percent to 23,500 reported cases.

But reported cases are merely the tip of the iceberg. About four cases are treated for every one reported to public health authorities. When you add the victims who did not seek treatment, that means about 4 million Americans contracted venereal disease last year. Syphilis, in particular, can linger for years, and it is estimated that at least 500,000 people have undiagnosed cases.

Does it matter? Public health officials say yes. Most cases of VD do not cause long-term complications. But if 10 to 12 percent do—the estimate of the American Social Health Association—that is still a lot of people. When it goes untreated, syphilis can cause insanity, paralysis, blindness, heart disease, sterility, and death. The Communicable Disease Center in Atlanta reports that in 1968, 9,600 patients were hospitalized with syphilitic insanity, at a cost to the taxpayers of $41 million. Unchecked gonorrhea causes more sterility in both sexes than any other disease, and also produces a painful form of arthritis. In women, it can lead to such problems as pelvic infections and tubular pregnancy, which occurs when the fallopian tubes are blocked by scar tissue and the fertilized egg cannot reach the uterus. In men, gonorrhea can scar the urethra, making urination painful and difficult. This can also result from repeated cases, even if they are cured.

Venereal disease is a national problem, although it is concentrated in larger cities and industrial states. Alaska and Georgia have the highest rates of gonorrhea, but both figures are considered a function of reporting. California is third, just ahead of Illinois, and makes a good case study. California agencies, particularly the Los Angeles County Health Department, have made special efforts to control the diseases, and their experience tells a lot about the problems involved. It should be stressed, however, that VD is not just another kooky California phenomenon. The city with the highest VD rate is San Francisco, but the top ten include Atlanta, Washington, D.C., Newark, Cleveland, and Chicago.

Who gets VD? Mainly those who are sexually active, of course, and that means the young. Nationally, about half the cases of gonorrhea occur in people under 25, although the California figure approaches 70 percent. Los Angeles officials estimate that 1 in every 10 teen-agers here will get VD this year; by the time they leave high school, 1 in 5 will have had it. If present trends continue, the rate will be 1 in 2 by 1980.

The Free Clinic is a good place to find these youngsters. Here they will talk openly about a disease that often causes as much embarrassment as pain. (The University of Wisconsin found the subject so difficult that it installed a computer this year to answer students' questions about VD.) For example there was Bushy, 18 years old, a runaway from Kansas City, and the proud possessor of his third case of gonorrhea. "I'm one of the experts," he declared. "I get it about once a year; it's one of the chances you have to take these days."

Jeff, 24, had his first case since coming back from Vietnam five years ago, and he was "pissed off." As he explained, "I've been pretty careful; I thought I was smart. I try to trust my judgment on who I bed down with, but sometimes it doesn't work out. I guess I'm mad mainly at myself, though. Whoever I play around with I expect to be playing around too—I'm one of the boys like she's one of the girls. This is the first time in five years; I guess that's not too bad."

Carol squeezed onto a crowded couch, trying to read a magazine. She was 22, very pretty, and a little uneasy. "Things haven't been normal, so I'm playing it safe," she said. "I'm not really worried though; I've always been going with one guy." Suppose the guy had gotten it somewhere else and given it to her? "I never thought about that one," she said.

As with most diseases, the poor and the racial minorities also suffer high rates of infection. But the problem is hardly limited to the ghetto. "I got in trouble once for saying that VD was the leading communicable disease in Southeast L.A., the black area," said Mr. Lugar, the county health advisor. "But the same is true in Bel-Air." In fact, the spread of VD to chic neighborhoods like Bel-Air is finally forcing the public to pay some attention. Dr. Geoffrey Simmons, a young physician who works in several VD clinics, put it this way: "It's just like drugs. Drugs were in the black community two or three decades ago and nobody gave a damn because it was the black community. As soon as it got into the white community all hell came loose and now we have programs to help. Well, there's almost a parallel with VD. When it was in the black areas, and the poor areas, nothing was done. Of course, there were other factors, too—nobody likes to talk about VD. But now that it's significantly into the white middle-class community it's become talked about a little bit, and they're trying to do something about it."

VD can turn up just about anywhere. A gynecologist in a posh residential neighborhood of Los Angeles recalled one patient recently, the wife of a man who earned about $20,000 from his own catering business. She was having an affair, she told the doctor, the man had contracted VD, and she was worried that she had caught it. "She wanted treatment—immediately," said the doctor. "She wanted to be sure she was cured before she had sex with her husband."

Vernon Mitchell, an employee of a large aerospace firm, got interested in the problem several years ago when his friends started turning up with the disease. He organized the Committee to Eradicate Syphilis, which runs a "hotline" to answer questions, and Mr. Mitchell described a typical evening: "I had two calls last night, one from the Hilton Hotel and one from the Ambassador Hotel, both traveling types here on a school project or something. I had one from a man who had been in the East who had never cheated on his wife in twenty-five years and just this once he did. He hadn't had sex with his wife so we told him to talk about headaches so that he didn't have to play the role of the complete husband until he could be treated. Quite frequently we handle it where the marriage is saved, this is one of our services. This is an area where it's imperative that a private physician be brought in. If the wife has been infected the doctor can bring her in, say, for a physical, and treat her for a low-grade kidney infection."

The causes, and the cures, of the VD epidemic are varied and complex. They involve behavior patterns, scientific problems, and probably most important, public attitudes. For even now, despite our self-proclaimed and well-publicized "liberation" in sexual matters, venereal disease remains clouded in myth and taboo. Dr. Theodor Rosebury, in his new book *Microbes and Morals*, put it this way: "VD is shameful. . . . Nice People don't talk about the whole subject, or if they do, it is with mincing and blushing or with a phony solicitude, under which finger-shaking is more plainly visible than the Nice People can imagine." Or as the Los Angeles Health Department said in a recent publication, "One of the reasons for the continued existence of gonorrhea and syphilis is the widespread belief that decent people don't acquire the disease, decent people don't talk about the disease, and decent people shouldn't do anything about those who do become infected."

Syphilis and gonorrhea present somewhat different problems, but certain generalities can be made about them. For instance, both diseases are apparently being spread by the "sexual revolution." Some researchers do not think anything more is happening now than thirty years ago, but most doctors who treat VD feel that increased sexual activity, particularly "indiscriminate" activity, contributes to the epidemic. One of the favorite examples among VD people is the San Francisco man who recently contracted gonorrhea after a brief liaison with a stewardess in the bathroom of a jetliner 30,000 feet above Kansas. Dr. Simmons also cites the "new morality" and explains why: "I think it exists and I think it is significant. I work at the Free Clinic and I have for two years. Girls are coming and getting birth control pills who are 14, 15, 16 years old—and lots of them are getting them. These girls aren't taking them for menstrual cramps, they're taking them to ball—and they admit it freely. When I went to high school, which was not that long ago, talk about sex was not that common. Most females I went to high school with, unless I was sheltered, didn't engage for fear of pregnancy. But when you have the pill you're not afraid of becoming pregnant. The fact that you can get an abortion now adds on to this new morality. It's quite open; it's just like eating a meal to them. They want to screw, they want to have fun. They're upset when they have VD, not so much because they have VD, but because they have to abstain for two or four weeks."

Sex is probably most "indiscriminate" in the homosexual community. About 40 percent of the new syphilis cases come from homosexual encounters, although the gonorrhea figure is much lower. Treatment is still hampered by the reluctance of some homosexuals to name their "contacts," and many doctors just do not think to check for infection of the anus, a common homosexual malady. But partly as a result of educational campaigns by homosexual groups, more are seeking help. One of the patients at the Free Clinic was a male hustler named Gerry, who shrugged off his infection as an "occupational hazard."

A second major cause of the epidemic is the birth control pill. Not only are people free from the fear of pregnancy, but they dispense with that traditional, if inconvenient means of contraception, the condom, or "rubber." Condoms were originally designed to prevent VD, and remain the most effective prophylactic method—90 percent sure against syphilis, close to 100 percent against gonorrhea. Moreover, many doctors believe that the pill actually changes the chemical "milieu" of the vaginal area from acidic, which tends to kill germs, to alkaline, which does not. According to one estimate, about 20 to 30 percent of the women who are exposed to gonorrhea, and are not on the pill, actually catch it. Among women who take the pills, the infection rate is over 90 percent.

When you talk about scientific and technical causes, there are important differences between syphilis and gonorrhea. Syphilis is carried by tiny organisms called spirochetes, and is virtually always transmitted by physical contact. The old canard about toilet seats and door handles is a convenient, but untenable, excuse. (What other disease do you even need an excuse for?) The disease first appears as a lesion or sore where the spirochete entered the body. This is usually in the genital area, but could also be around the mouth. The lesion is painless, appears between ten and ninety days after infection, and goes away without treatment. Two to six months later the second stage appears, in the form of a rash, sores, falling hair, or fever. These signs, too, disappear without treatment. But years later, the spirochetes can invade and destroy vital organs, causing blindness and other disabilities already mentioned.

Thus it is quite possible to have syphilis and not know it, which is one reason why there are one-half million undiagnosed cases. This "silent" character of the disease is a major obstacle in controlling it. Fortunately, there is an accurate blood test for syphilis, and many cases are detected that way. In addition, since the disease has such a long incubation period, public health authorities are able to use the "case finding" method of control. This involves tracing down all known sexual partners of an infected person, and getting them treated before they spread the disease to others.

Gonorrhea, which is caused by gonococcus bacteria, is also transmitted by sexual contact, but there the similarities end. In the male the symptoms are obvious: a burning pain when urinating, and a discharge of pus. But 80 percent of the females who get gonorrhea have no visible symptoms. As a result, there is a huge "reservoir" of infected women, an estimated 60,000 in Los Angeles County alone, who spread the disease without knowing it. "If you could sum up our problem in one word it would be 'female,'" said Robert Lugar. "How great that reservoir is, is only now beginning to come to light." (To make matters worse, 10 percent of all males are also asymptomatic.)

Moreover, there is no screening process comparable to the blood test for syphilis. Taking a vaginal smear and growing a culture from it is time-consuming, expensive, and only about 60- to 80-percent accurate. Even if you could detect gonorrhea easily, the incubation period is so short—about three days—that the case-finding method is all but useless. "Tracing gonorrhea," lamented one doctor, "is like trying to trace the common cold."

If that isn't enough, some strains of VD are developing considerable resistance to the main drugs used for treatment, particularly penicillin. The dosage given today is 48 times what doctors prescribed twenty years ago, and still, a certain number of cases defy normal treatment. The resistance problem seems to be aggravated by the importation of new and hardier strains from Southeast Asia. Indeed, VD must rank close to heroin addicts on Vietnam's list of exports.

Right now there is a debate raging over proper treatment of VD. Some doctors, including Dr. Walter Smartt, head of VD control in Los Angeles County, have abandoned penicillin, which is injected directly into the patient, in favor of orally administered drugs, particularly tetracycline. Dr. Smartt claims he gets a 10-percent higher "cure rate" with Vibramycine, the drug used in Los Angeles. But the United States Public Health Service still maintains that penicillin is the "drug of choice." In fact, Dr. Robert J. Brown, until recently chief of the VD branch of the Center for Disease Control, blames the oral drugs for contributing to the epidemic. "Practicing physicians," insists Dr. Brown, "are not giving adequate amounts of antibiotics to cure the disease, and are not properly informed as to the best method of managing gonorrhea." With oral drugs, the level of "patient error" is high—patients lose pills, forgot to take them, give them to friends They think they are cured, but they're not, and the infection spreads. The real point is that even the professionals do not agree. Not enough is known about the diseases to resolve the squabbles, and no one is willing to spend the money to find out.

This leads to the whole question of public attitudes. Not only is VD considered "shameful" and something "decent people shouldn't talk about," but there is still a widespread belief that VD is caused by sex itself, and that anybody who contracts it "gets what he deserves." Probably the classic statement of a classically wrong-headed position came from Dr. Max Rafferty, the former superintendent of California schools, who said, "The only way to stop VD and illegitimate pregnancy is to label them as sins and crimes and mete out appropriate punishment. Illicit premarital sex is a crime against God and man."

These views have a devastating impact. Most doctors agree with Dr. Rosebury that at least in regard to syphilis, "we could solve the problem if we really wanted to." But apparently we do not really want to. Syphilis was a scourge in this country until penicillin was discovered. The rates dropped swiftly after that, and in the mid-fifties health authorities relaxed, thinking the disease was headed the way of the dodo bird. But as soon as control efforts eased, the rates jumped again. In 1962, after the surgeon general called attention to the renewed problem, the federal government put about $7 million a year into syphilis control, mainly to pay case finders. In the last two years, federal funds have held steady, and even dropped in some cases; in a time of inflation, this has produced havoc. At the peak, Washington was financing more than 600 case finders; today it pays only about 450. A few years ago, health authorities were tracking down 98 percent of the syphilis cases; today they can reach only about 50 percent. Thus, after a steady decline, syphilis rates leaped 8 percent in fiscal 1970 and 15.6 percent last year.

Scott Winders, a drug company executive who heads the California VD Task Force, spoke for many when he said, "We've had a cop-out by the federal government and, frankly, if they don't get off the dime we're going to have syphilis in epidemic proportions." The states are no better. Each one gets a block federal grant to use for health services, and few rank VD higher than hangnails in setting their priorities. "VD is just not a popular disease; it never has been," explained Dr. Warren A. Ketterer, head of VD control for California. "A tremendous number of people moralize about it. They think that if you stop sex, you'll stop VD. That's true, but you never think of stopping TB by stopping breathing. . . . We could have controlled VD fifty years ago if we tried. But we never had a president with VD who said, 'Let's go on a VD campaign.' It's not an honor to have VD. People don't realize what it costs society. If they realized it cost $1 billion a year to treat VD, they might do something."

Every doctor emphasizes the importance of his specialty. Working on a popular, or at least a critical, disease, means more research money and more attention, and the VD people do not shrink from self-promotion. Many resent, almost petulantly, the publicity that was given to polio, and is now focused on drugs. Dr. Smartt, the VD chief here, noted that all county health departments took a budget cut this year. "Of course," he snapped, with a mixture of bitterness and pride, "I was the only one with an epidemic." And like members of all subcultures VD people delight in recounting the famous members of their group. (Some of the best-known victims: Henry VIII, Pope Leo X, Job, Keats, and Woodrow Wilson, who died from syphilis.)

Moreover, when it comes to setting health priorities, VD just cannot compete with, say, cancer or heart disease. In most diagnosed cases, cure is relatively simple; fatalities are rare (although doctors like to speculate how many "heart failures" are really syphilis). Yet as one doctor said, "It is the only disease I know of where we have a known cure and yet still have an increasing incidence."

Government money is not the only victim of public ignorance and indifference. Another serious problem is education. Only two-thirds of the nation's schools teach anything at all about VD, and much of the information they dispense is incomplete or inaccurate. The subject makes parents and educators so nervous that many publishers just omit the subject from standard health texts. This is in the face of the fact that the rate of infection is rising faster in the 15- to 19-year-old group than in any other.

California is probably the best example of timidity triumphant. Two years ago, the legislature passed a bill sponsored by John Schmitz, a member of the John Birch Society and now a congressman. The bill declared that before a school could offer a course on sex education, parents had to be notified and given a chance to withdraw their children from the class. The procedure involved so much cost and confusion that many schools dropped the whole thing. Despite the pleas of health authorities that VD should be discussed under the heading of disease, not sex, school officials were "running scared," according to Mrs. Mabel S. Rickett, a specialist in VD education. "Teachers now feel they can't talk about sexual organs, and therefore they can't talk about VD. Everyone's afraid that the kids will ask embarrassing questions, or that the teachers will be quoted out of context," Mrs. Rickett explained.

In schools that do offer sex education, only about 2 percent of the parents actually take their kids out of class. But that small minority wields enormous power. This year, the legislature passed a bill that merely clarified the distinction between sex education and VD education, so schools would feel free to talk about the disease. But Governor Ronald Reagan, bowing to conservative pressures, vetoed the bill.

VD people all say the same thing: "We can't alter behavior. We have to give the kids information so they can make their own decisions more intelligently." But that is precisely what the opponents of sex and VD education cannot accept—children making their own decisions. They want to impose a moral code, a code that denounces VD as a "sin and a crime," to quote Dr. Rafferty.

The subject is so sensitive that even in schools with VD education, instructors are not allowed to talk about prevention. The same is true in county health clinics. Some parents are petrified that if their kids know how to prevent VD, they will have one less reason not to have sex; and both school and health officials are petrified that some parent will start hollering. Now the VD figures indicate that Junior is having plenty of sex anyway—without the proper information. Sermons ranting against the "epidemic of immorality," as one minister called it, fall on ears deafened by peer group pressure, if not by Creedence Clearwater Revival. In fact, our discussions at the Free Clinic indicate that if youngsters know something about VD, they tend to be more selective in choosing sex partners. Even Bushy, the 18-year-old runaway, said, "If someone's really funky, I'm not going to chance it."

But reason often crumbles in the face of righteous indignation, to say nothing of fear and confusion. It is not easy being a parent at a time when 15-year-old girls are chunking down birth control pills like one-a-day vitamins. We have friends in the neighborhood who think smoking and drinking are cardinal sins. Their 13-year-old daughter tells us that about half of her friends have VD, and that her best friend "screwed ten guys last summer." Even allowing for exaggeration, how is that mother going to relate her upbringing in the rural South to what her daughter is facing in Malibu, California in 1971?

If the reaction to VD in some quarters is indignation, in others it is indifference, which also contributes to the problem. Disinterest is practically epidemic among doctors. By law they are required to report every case of VD, so health authorities can track down the patient's contacts. But only 12 to 17 percent of all privately treated cases get reported. Some physicians are afraid to violate confidentiality, some are afraid to lose a patient, and many are just lazy. (In fairness, it should be noted that there are not enough case finders now to trace even the small fraction of cases that get reported.) The Committee to Eradicate Syphilis opened a free clinic to treat VD, but now it is closed most of the time because few doctors would volunteer to keep it open. Dr. Smartt described their attitude this way: "The medical profession sees VD as no problem, so I can't get their support. The private physician feels that since he has good treatment, this disease has been eliminated. You schedule a meeting on VD for private physicians, but they won't come. They figure, 'I know how to treat that disease; what do I want to go listen to that nut in the health department for?' Private medicine isn't interested; it couldn't care less; it doesn't give a damn."

A lot of the people who get VD don't give a damn, either. At the Free Clinic Dr. Michael Talbot, who is not much older than some of his patients, described the situation this way: "There are people we see many times, and there are people who we find have had the disease many times. People aren't afraid of it anymore; it's like a cold. It's not that serious; it can be treated. They view it as a part of living, a part of growing up."

One clinic official likened this attitude to "thinking the best means of birth control is abortion." Bill Greenburg, the clinic's medical director, added, "Some kids are proud they've had the clap ten times. That's the main reason why we started a health education unit here." Now every night a nurse talks to the kids in the waiting room. She tells them that many people don't know they have VD, that complications can be serious, that babies with congenital syphilis can be born blind, deformed, or dead. Does it do any good? "Not really," concedes Dr. Talbot. "Most people don't have very much foresight. Look at adults who drink and smoke. They know something about lung cancer and emphysema and cirrhosis, but it really doesn't have much effect. So it's hard to expect kids to have that kind of foresight."

"It's terrifying," said one clinic nurse, "to realize we see the more intelligent ones; we don't know what's out on the street." But since the educational programs in the schools are so poor, even some clinic patients remain ignorant. The night we were there, two black youngsters heard the nurse's talk and realized, for the first time, why the boy had had trouble urinating for four months. Another youth, who knew the symptoms, didn't realize that gonorrhea could cause sterility until he read the poster on the waiting room wall.

In some areas, lack of information helps breed the notion that the masculine thing to do is "tough it out" and not seek treatment. Unfortunately, some of those he-men are going to find it tough to urinate for the rest of their lives. Another storehouse of misinformation is the popular literature on sex. Doctors are driven crazy by such books as *The Sensuous Woman*, which blithely advises, "As unpleasant as venereal disease and crabs and unwanted pregnancies can be, the risks aren't adequate to deprive yourself of a wonderful sex life. The chances of these calamities descending on you are slight. . . . So relax and make love."

Even knowledgeable people don't get exercised. To many, as Dr. Talbot said, VD is like a cold. "Nobody really sweats it," Bushy said. "Just about everybody I know has had it; it's a big joke with us." Tom, 29, was at the Free Clinic with his girlfriend, Susan. "If you know what to do about it,

you don't worry, like anything else," he said. "You just go get it fixed."
Susan, a soft and gentle girl of 22, wasn't worried either. "Truthfully," she
said, "I wouldn't ball anybody I didn't know was clean. I don't ball anybody
but him and my friends." But since even "friends" sometimes don't know
they have VD, the waiting room was full of people who were confident they
could never catch it.

Given these attitudes, can anything be done to control VD? If the
money were available, researchers could probably find a cheap and easy
screening test for gonorrhea; some progress, in fact, has already been made.
Better drugs could be produced that don't build up resistance in the VD
organisms. Doctors could learn more about why some patients suffer
long-term complications and others don't. More case finders could be hired.
But as everyone in the field agrees, "you don't treat a disease out of
existence." Walter Smartt fumes, "I say to hell with treatment. Treatment
disgusts me—it's the cause of the present epidemic. We are too complacent.
All we're doing is treating, treating, treating, and we cannot get rid of the
epidemic that way. If this epidemic is ever reduced it'll be because
somebody has guts enough to do what we did for pregnancy."

In other words, prevention. There are ways to prevent VD now. The
best, of course, is abstinence, but that is hardly a likely possibility. Washing
before and after intercourse and urinating as soon as possible both help kill
the germs. Then there are prophylactic devices. A vaginal gel called
Progonasyl has been around for years but has never been fully tested. (A
group of prostitutes in Nevada is now trying the substance as part of a study
by the State Bureau of Preventive Medicine.) The "pro kit" used by the
armed forces during World War II—a device used to inject a disinfectant
into the penis—is probably too annoying and inconvenient. Some doctors
place their hope in the condom, but others think that is unrealistic. Mr.
Lugar, the health advisor here, insisted: "It's been demonstrated over and
over again that the promiscuous individual will not use a condom. When it
comes to such a mechanical approach, sex just loses its flavor." Out of the
dozens of youngsters we interviewed, not more than one or two would
consider using a prophylactic. "It kind of takes the fun out of it, to stop in
the middle and put on your good old prophylactic," said Bushy. "It's a little
awkward at times, you know." Awkward and, these days, insulting. If a girl
is on the pill, the only reason to use a condom is to prevent VD, and some

people are likely to resent the implication, no matter which partner makes the suggestion.

Despite these drawbacks, VD specialists say that the public should at least have the information about disease prevention. Today, with the schools and county health departments so touchy, people are not learning much of anything.

That leaves two other possibilities. One is a vaccine. One of the leading researchers in the field is Dr. James N. Miller of the University of California at Los Angeles. The scientific and financial obstacles are enormous, but Dr. Miller now predicts a syphilis vaccine within five years. Public acceptance is another problem. If people won't allow their kids to read about VD, will they allow them to be inoculated against it? On the gloomier side, a gonorrhea vaccine seems almost impossible at this point.

The other possibility is a pill taken regularly to suppress infection. In a recent study, Dr. Smartt had a group of highly promiscuous individuals take Vibramycine pills before having sex. In over 5,000 sexual contacts, claims Dr. Smartt, only two cases of VD were contracted. The procedure, however, is expensive and dangerous. Some people are allergic to antibiotics, and widespread use of any drug would cause a certain number of adverse reactions. Moreover, no one knows what the regular ingestion of antibiotics would do to the body's normal defense system against disease. Suffice it to say, popping a pill before play is a long way off.

The outlook, then, is not very promising, particularly for gonorrhea. Some things can be done. But today there is not enough public support for treatment, research, or education. Just from an economic standpoint, that doesn't make sense. We spend $41 million a year just to care for syphilitic insanity; the total cost of VD, from absenteeism, lost income, and the like, might reach $1 billion annually, according to one estimate. Yet the total federal outlay comes to less than $10 million. The cost in human suffering is also rising: more sterility, more blindness, more babies born deformed from congenital syphilis. One thing is certain: VD will continue to spread as long as it is considered dirty and shameful, something nice people don't talk about, a "just punishment" instead of a crippling disease.

1971
(*with Cokie Roberts*)

Beyond Psychedelic Drugs

San Francisco

"I got bored with acid," said Bill Esson as he lounged in a back room of the Haight-Ashbury Free Clinic. "Like anything else, it was an experience, but you can only experience so much on acid. As time went on it wasn't as good for me, and like, I had other things to do."

About five years ago the country became aware of "acid," or LSD, a chemical that most scientists agree can alter human consciousness. Since then, one million people have tried LSD or similar "psychedelics" such as mescaline, according to Dr. Joel Fort, a drug expert and the author of *The Pleasure Seekers*. The number continues to grow, particularly among teen-agers.

But many people, like Bill Esson, have taken the LSD trip and then gotten off. The market is so slow that here in Haight-Ashbury, once the center of the psychedelic movement, the price of one "hit" has dropped from $1.50 to 30 cents.

Thus there is now developing a post-drug culture, embracing thousands of former users whose experiences with mind-changing chemicals have permanently shaped their lives.

The mind is like a canvas, and the psychedelic drug draws a different pattern on each one. For some it has led to mental breakdown or harder drugs, for others to self-awareness or self-delusion, meditation or yoga, dropping out on the rat race or dropping in on social responsibility.

Bill Esson, who is in his 20s, manages the Free Clinic. He still smokes marijuana about as often, he says, as the average businessman drinks Scotch. But he drops acid only occasionally, and sometimes accidentally. (One evening recently, dinner at the house he shares with six other young people featured "electric iced tea," laced with LSD.)

Nevertheless, his experience with acid has left its mark. His hair now flows to his shoulders around his thin, sharp-featured face. But the big change was inside. As Mr. Esson put it, "Acid made me wonder a little more and wander around a little more. The whole idea that you have to be something by a certain age or you'll be nobody—that's all gone now. The important thing is to find happiness with life."

Why are people like Bill Esson giving up psychedelic drugs? And what is more important, how have the drugs affected them?

One reason for the disillusionment with psychedelics is that most of them are illegal. For instance, Dr. Richard Alpert, who did some of the earliest LSD experiments with Dr. Timothy Leary at Harvard, abandoned drugs, became a Hindu mystic, and changed his name to Baba Ram Dass. "I don't want to break the law," he explained recently, "since that leads to fear and paranoia."

Another problem is that some users have experienced "bummers" or "bad trips"—severe panic reactions to the effects of the drug. Even advocates of LSD admit that users, usually ones with a prior tendency to mental instability, have been thrown into permanent psychotic states.

A third reason for psychedelics being abandoned, is fear of physical harm. Recent studies at the University of California at Los Angeles and elsewhere have failed to produce any evidence that LSD causes brain damage or malformed children. But many people still worry about earlier studies that indicated such damage was possible.

The main reason people stop using LSD appears to be the nature of the acid trip itself. On one level, the drug vastly enhances one's sensory perceptions: colors often appear more vivid, sounds more lyrical, people more beautiful. But as Bill Esson said, the experience can get boring. "How many times can you see the Grand Canyon?" asked Dr. William McGlothlin, a psychologist at U.C.L.A.

"Dope got to be all that was going on," a former user explained. "All we talked about were prices, where the next shipment was coming from, who got busted. Dope is a very finite topic. It isn't at the heart of anything, it's just stuff."

On another level, many people who have taken acid feel it can produce profound insights into the "unity of all living things" and offer new perspectives on life and values. But those insights also have limits. Stewart Brand, who now publishes the *Whole Earth Catalog*, was a close friend of Ken Kesey, the novelist, in the days when Mr. Kesey was a leading proselytizer for psychedelics. About two years ago Mr. Kesey announced that people should go "beyond acid" and even staged an "acid graduation" ceremony for his followers here in San Francisco.

"As Kesey said, we used LSD to get through a door and into a room we were interested in," Mr. Brand said recently. "But if we kept taking it, we were just going back and forth through the door—we weren't exploring the room."

Another common effect of LSD is passivity and listlessness, and some users feared the drug was taking them in that direction. John Daley, a recent college graduate who now works at The Community Project, a program for high school youths in Berkeley, said, "Drugs seemed to demand that I become totally disengaged from society and try to create a utopia, but I couldn't abandon the problems I saw all around me. I felt it was important to try to change nitty-gritty issues."

Whatever reasons people have for giving up psychedelic drugs, most of them have been touched by the experience, often quite deeply. As John Finlator, deputy director of the Federal Bureau of Narcotics and Dangerous Drugs has put it, LSD "is the most powerful and probably the most dangerous drug known to man."

But it is difficult to isolate its effect. If someone "drops" acid, he probably already has certain feelings of rebellion and adventure. And as Dr. David E. Smith, director of the Haight-Ashbury Free Clinic, said, acid heads "have to be alienated enough to disbelieve what the Establishment says about the drug."

Moreover, many users, particularly young ones, become part of a psychedelic subculture or counterculture as it has been called. And this subculture has as much of an effect on many youngsters as the drug itself. One of the primary reasons they take drugs in the first place, it has become clear from interviews, is to become a part of the culture.

"The beauty of the underground world," said Dr. Paul Rosenberg, a psychologist in Los Angeles, "is that for many people, this is the first time they have ever really been part of anything."

Despite the difficulty of identifying the precise impact of psychedelics, it is possible to sketch out some of the broad areas of the post-drug culture. The range is wide, from the disturbed teeny popper to the detached mystic, from the rural communard to the urban activist.

People use different phrases to describe the LSD experience: "It erases old cultural forms . . . scrambles your circuits . . . suspends constancies . . . alters belief systems . . . puts you in touch with yourself." In other words, after taking acid a person is often faced with new and troubling choices about himself and his life. And in some cases this leads a user to take more dangerous drugs.

"One result of the psychedelic experience is real confusion," reported Dr. Smith. "We see that a lot here, particularly among young people. LSD tears down the ego, and these kids can become very vulnerable. They come in here and say, 'I took too much acid so I took heroin or speed to get my head straight.' "

A second post-drug trip is dropping out. Most experts believe the drug can only expand and reinforce feelings of rebellion, not create them. Dr. Fort has said, "The real cause is the alienating character of our society itself. Repressive family life, meaningless schools, pointless jobs, bigotry, wars, and intolerance everywhere: that's what people are reacting against when they drop out."

LSD plays a role. It helps make many "straight" jobs seem meaningless. "My first reaction," said one veteran user, "was to feel sorry for all those people running around so frantically."

And by making people more aware of natural beauty, the drug can also move them to abandon urban life and flee to the country. As Stewart Brand put it, "Drugs sensitize you to a lot of things that city life just steps on."

In many rural communities, however, drugs are not very popular. "In the country you don't need drugs to go to sleep, you're just tired from working," said one youth. And a girl who was living in the Oregon woods with her husband and baby said, "Up here it's a natural high."

Some dropouts have become health food faddists and vegetarians, although that is often required by the price of meat. But if a devotion to "natural foods" precludes LSD, a synthetic chemical, it seldom rules out marijuana. "God grew grass," one youth said as he passed a pipe in a Haight-Ashbury apartment.

A third broad segment of former LSD users have turned to religion, particularly variations of Buddhism, Hinduism, and other Eastern faiths. The head of the Student International Meditation Society has estimated that at least one-half its members are former drug users.

One girl started to meditate because she felt "despair" at needing drugs to attain a religious feeling. And many former users agree with William Burroughs, the novelist, who has said, "Anything that can be accomplished by chemical means can also be accomplished by other means, given sufficient knowledge of the process involved."

Thus some former acid heads have adopted yoga or meditation or similar practices that they feel enable them to recreate the "high" of an acid trip anytime they wish. Moreover, advocates of Eastern religions and psychedelic drugs often share a number of beliefs. Both usually expound a pantheistic view that everything in the universe is God. And both usually "place a premium on the cultivation of an inner psychic state," according to Thomas Robbins of the University of North Carolina.

In a recent study of the Meher Baba cult, who follow the teachings of a Hindu mystic, Mr. Robbins said that many "Baba-heads" turned to religion because it allowed them to live a more normal and productive life, without the legal and social ostracism often imposed on the drug user.

Probably the best example of an LSD user who turned to religion is Baba Ram Dass, formerly Dr. Richard Alpert. In a recent article in *Playboy* magazine he explains his conversion this way. "I think LSD is making itself obsolete. All acid does is show you the possibility of another type of consciousness and give you hope. But your own impurities keep bringing you down. It's a yo-yo phenomenon—getting high and coming down. After a while you dig that if you want to stay high, you have to work on yourself."

Former acid heads have also streamed into a variety of pseudo- or quasi-religions, including Scientology, Satanism, various encounter groups and sensitivity training schools, and a wide range of occult cults. Their practices also duplicate certain elements of the psychedelic trip. As Dr. Rosenberg put it, "Under drugs you feel meanings you can't explain—meaning comes out of the walls. People also experience synchronicity in reality."

But while some former LSD users drop out or take up new religious practices, a significant number "drop in" to greater social awareness and a sense of responsibility. "Under drugs people often get a view of what life ought to be like," said Dr. Smith, "and in some cases that turns them into militant activists."

"A great many people discovered that no drug ever rebuilt a school," said Dr. Fort. "Nobody improved his family life or his neighborhood while he was on a trip. Drugs just don't change reality."

"A lot of significant ideas and fantasies came into focus during my drug experience," Stewart Brand, whose *Whole Earth Catalog* is a handbook of "self education" among the underground. "I recognized a lot of connections, both internal and external, that I had successfully blocked out. Once you admit those connections it leads right into a sense of responsibility.

"The acid graduation was a real responsibility builder. It's where Lois and I decided to get married. I have my diploma out there in the office, it's a little signpost of something that's behind me."

Rudy Schleim works with Bill Esson at the Haight-Ashbury Free Clinic, a medical service that treats thousands of patients a year, ranging from pregnant middle-class teeny-boppers to ghetto youths hooked on heroin.

He described his experience this way, "I was a lab technician in Cleveland when I started dropping acid. I was really into the military–industrial complex. But that's a useless way of life to me now. The key thing is social awareness. People around here are concerned about other people; they're not in it for the bucks. You have to care more about your brother than you do about the bucks."

Psychedelic drugs change little things, too. Many users feel they become more sensitive to music, or to art. William Burroughs has said that "under the influence of mescaline, I have had the experience of fully seeing a painting for the first time."

One couple—she is a nurse, he is a college professor—stopped taking acid about a year ago because they feared its physical effects. But their outlook will never be quite the same. "We live a strange life," said the nurse. "We both have pretty straight jobs and we carry it off well, but we live in two worlds. We play the middle-class thing during the week and then drop out on weekends.

"We like money and we buy things and we go skiing, but my husband isn't out to be king of his university, and I'm not out to be the greatest nurse in the world—it just doesn't matter.

"Another thing is that we just cannot tolerate cocktail parties. We used to go to those big faculty things—it was a big social climbing thing to do—but we don't do that any more."

For only a few people psychedelic drugs produce the religious or sexual ecstasies preached about by their more ardent advocates—or the psychotic traumas warned about by their detractors. But in the words of Dr. McClothlin of U.C.L.A., the drugs do "shake you up." They do not give any answers, but they ask a lot of questions. As Dr. Rosenberg put it, "After taking acid, a lot of people look at the society and say, 'what the hell is going on?' "

1970

Yearning for the Simple Life

Cave Junction, Oregon

Richard, or Big Tree, as he is sometimes called, was working as a chemist for a mining company several years ago. He lived in a sumptuous Hollywood apartment and drove a Jaguar. Then his work took him to a beautiful little valley in southern Oregon. "I fell in love with this place," he said recently, motioning toward a sweep of golden fields and blue-green hills. "I came home and said we had to live here. We had to get away from all those cliff-dwellers and get back to the earth."

"We realized everything we were doing was ridiculous," said his wife, Little Tree, a former dancer. "We never saw each other; we were working all the time. Finally we decided that what we really wanted was to work on our own land and enjoy each other and the children."

About eighteen months ago, the Trees moved to Oregon. They bought several acres of rocky ground and began building a house with stones hauled up from a nearby river. Still unfinished, the house has one large room furnished with two mattresses. A pantry in the back contains mainly government surplus food. There is no electricity or running water.

The family also has a horse, a few chickens, a 3-month-old daughter named Lotus Tree, and a deep contentment. "We had to get everything off our backs," said Big Tree, a towering man about 30 years old, who wore hair to his shoulders and a pair of dirty jeans. "Then we had to decide what we wanted to put back—what was valid."

The Trees are among several hundred young people who fled the cities of California to live in the area many call "Magic Valley." They ask a visitor not to disclose its exact location because they are wary of curiosity-seekers and others who could shatter their fragile tranquility.

Some of them, especially during the summer, are conventional "hippies," younger dropouts with a preference for drugs and impermanent relationships to places and other people. A number are "making the circuit" of hippie communities and stay in one place only a few weeks.

But others, like the Trees, are older and more stable. They have often held responsible jobs. Magic Valley has everything from professors to lawyers to psychologists. Usually they are married with children and want to settle down. They sometimes cringe at the description "hippie," but they have not come up with a substitute.

Magic Valley is just one of dozens of retreats where young people have set up communities of their own. Most of them are in warmer places such as New Mexico, Arizona, and California, but a few have sprung up in Colorado, Pennsylvania, New England, and the Middle West. Other communities have been started in cities from Hollywood to Philadelphia but have not yet made the move to the country.

These communities represent a new, and perhaps more durable, phase of the "hippie" movement which started several years ago, with the flower children of San Francisco's Haight-Ashbury and New York's East Village.

They represent a basic revolt against the life-styles of most Americans —a flight from the impersonality, the pressure, the chaos, and the pollution of city life, as well as from the "hassle" of police crackdowns on marijuana and increasingly violent and "uptight" political movements.

What these revolutionaries are seeking is a reduction of life to essentials, to the simple things they can understand and hold onto in a time of turmoil. "We lost the connection with the land in the cities," said Jack, a blond refugee from Berkeley now living in Oregon. "We were not part of anything, we had no roots." A youth living near Placitas, New Mexico, added, "We want to go back to the ways of our fathers."

Many of the communities have had trouble with the local authorities. Rita Satterfield, a black woman who tried to help establish a commune in Clayton, Georgia, said that local vigilantes had shot up their house and broken all their windows. Hippies have been beaten and one girl raped near Taos, New Mexico.

"Policemen and others in the lower middle class resent people who are different from them," explained a priest who has worked with hippies in the Chicago area. "The crime of these people is that they are young."

While there are many similarities in these communities, there are also significant differences. In Magic Valley, for instance, some people have decided to live in communes, pooling their resources and their labor for the benefit of the group. One such commune has been started on a 16-acre farm, where about six permanent residents and more than a dozen summer visitors work in the nude tending fields of corn, beans, peppers, tomatoes, and strawberries.

Peter, a social science student at Berkeley and a self-taught agricultural expert, said he had lived in a commune in California and, for several years, has been looking for land to start a cooperative farm. "One thing we all share is that we were involved in some form of political action before," added Jack, an antiwar activist during his Berkeley days. "We also shared a disillusionment with it. We were tired of always being on the defensive, always complaining and tearing things down. We wanted to build something positive."

Bruce and Susie, on the other hand, have never been very political. As Susie put it, "A lot of people have decided that the best thing for the world is to be happy themselves." The couple has been footloose for several years, living all over the West for short stretches. They now occupy an old yellow school bus parked on land owned by a professor at Portland State College.

"All my father ever talked about was his job," said Bruce, who spends most of his time playing his guitar and swimming in the community swimming hole. "That job was his life, but the only interest he had in it was monetary; he didn't enjoy himself. As soon as I realized that you didn't need money to live, I decided I didn't want to stay tied down to a job."

"We tried living in sort of a commune but it didn't work," added Susie, as she breast-fed her baby in the back of the school bus. "Everyone has his own trip and it got real touchy at times. Besides, I don't think two women can work in the same kitchen without fighting. And if you have your own place no one can take it away from you."

Unlike some of the others, Bruce and Susie have kept contact with their parents. "Bruce's parents came and camped out with us for awhile; they're really groovy," said Susie, a gentle-eyed girl with a soft smile. "My mother has been harder. She just wants us to be happy, but she doesn't realize that her happy is different from our happy." As Susie talked, Sandy, a visitor from California, cooked the midday meal over an open fire, since they had run out of gas for their portable stove. The main dish was a panful of government surplus powdered eggs spiced up with an onion.

Larry and Clara live a few hundred yards away in a house they built with their own hands. They carefully saved their money before they came, but like many of the families, they now realize they will have to work at least part-time to survive. (Some also get money or such useful gifts as a water pump from their parents.) Clara earned $6 selling pottery buttons, and Larry is a proficient woodworker. They hope that a small gift shop recently opened to sell things made by the hippies will give them a regular income.

Many people in the community have adopted a rather eclectic religiosity. Their talk is sprinkled with words like "God" and "Jesus" and "karma." Some meditate regularly, or practice yoga, or follow the dietary codes of Zen Buddhism, eating mainly grains and no meat. Somewhere, they lost the ideas of their fathers—the work ethic, faith in progress. They are passive people, with an almost mystical belief that "what happens is meant to happen." Susie spoke for many of the colonists when she said, "Faith in people and faith in God is the same thing, although some people aren't ready to call it God. But everything is God, and everything is good."

If the community has a motto, it is a line from the Beatles' song, "I'll Get By With a Little Help From My Friends." They often help deliver each other's babies by natural childbirth. When Little Tree was sick recently, two women took turns nursing her baby. Whenever a house is to be built, everyone pitches in.

Like many colonies, Magic Valley has encountered serious problems with local townspeople. Several shooting incidents have been reported and a "free store" set up as a community trading post was burned down. Several dozen hippies have been arrested on narcotics charges and forced to leave the community.

Some town residents formed a "betterment association" and threatened to boycott any merchants who traded with hippies. Signs reading "We Do Not Solicit Hippie Patronage" have appeared in many store windows. One merchant who resisted the campaign had his windows broken, and paint was smeared on his building.

The campaign against the hippies has divided the townspeople. "The way to make a mess stink is to stir it," said Mrs. Eileen McLean, a member of one of the oldest families in the valley. "The hippies wouldn't bother anybody if they were just left alone."

"I don't like it," added Emil Paraino, a real estate broker. "It has happened before—whites against Negroes, Germans against Jews. They forget there are individuals in those groups. But people get so biased they are no longer reasonable. Something must be bothering them inside themselves for them to preach so much hate."

Nevertheless, the hippies have survived. They predict that many of their number will leave when the novelty wears off or when the weather and the isolation grow colder with approaching winter. Some will stay, but even those feel they are only beginning their quest. As Big Tree put it one day, pointing to his baby daughter, "We're waiting for these kids to talk so we can find out the next step. We're waiting for instructions."

1969

THE VIETNAM WAR:
TO FIGHT OR NOT TO FIGHT

As Vietnam has faded out of the news and out of our
minds, it is easy to forget the thousands of young men
who are still paying for their decision to resist the draft or
desert the army. Getting probation from a sympathetic
judge—in effect, amnesty—is still largely a matter of
chance. Many exiles would like to come home, but they
risk severe penalties if they do.

Michael Heck flirted briefly with the antiwar
movement but apparently decided to withdraw from the
limelight and return to school. I saw Captain Harry
Jenkins about a year after his return from captivity, and
his adjustment has gone well. Professionally he was
approved for a sea command and was scheduled to take
charge of a helicopter carrier in the fall of 1974.
Personally he has relaxed some of his more rigid ideas
but he was still stunned to hear his 16-year-old daughter
and 14-year-old son casually discuss rape. Like many
former prisoners he deplores Watergate and feels that
President Nixon is being criticized unfairly. He still
cannot accept the idea that his commander-in-chief
might have been wrong.

The Draft Resisters

Los Angeles

Two years ago, Alan Kent was drafted. Halfway through his physical examination at the Oakland induction center, he decided that he did not want to join the army. During the lunch break, he went across the street to a draft counseling center, and the man on duty advised him to resist induction. Later that afternoon, just before his physical examination was over, Mr. Kent handed his papers to another draftee and walked out of the induction center.

Eventually, he was convicted of violating the Selective Service Act. But instead of going to federal prison, he was placed on probation and ordered to do work of "national importance" for two years. Today, Mr. Kent, now 23 years old, spends at least twenty hours a week as a volunteer at Bridge Over Troubled Waters, a drug rehabilitation program in Berkeley. The volunteer work fulfills the terms of his probation while he holds a steady job at a steel fabricating plant.

His case is one example of how the federal judiciary in recent months has gradually but dramatically reversed its policies in the handling of draft cases. A growing number of judges are, in effect, defying draft boards and federal prosecutors and granting amnesty to draft resisters, on the condition that they perform the kind of public service required of conscientious objectors.

The question of amnesty for draft resisters has become a political issue in this presidential election year. The Democratic Platform Committee has approved a plank that states "our firm intention to declare an amnesty, on an appropriate basis, when the fighting has ceased and our troops and prisoners have returned."

President Nixon told an interviewer in January, "I, for one, would be very liberal with regard to amnesty, but not while there are Americans in Vietnam fighting to serve their country and defend their country, and not while POWs are held by North Vietnam. After that we will consider it, but it would have to be on a basis of their paying the price, of course, that anyone should pay for violating the law."

The price being paid in the federal courts changed sharply between 1967, when only 10.4 percent of those convicted in draft cases received probation while the rest went to jail, and 1971, when 62.7 percent received probation. The percentage of defendants who were convicted dropped from 75.1 to 34.8 during the same period. And draft counselors have become so astute that, according to some estimates, 90 percent of the young men who resist induction never even get to court.

The most sweeping changes have occurred in the major metropolitan areas, such as New York, Chicago, San Francisco, and Los Angeles. In Kentucky, most judges continue to mete out five-year sentences, and last summer, the United States Court of Appeals for the Sixth Circuit, in Cleveland, criticized one district judge for his "mechanical sentencing" procedures.

Many judges still give jail terms to militant leaders of the draft resistance movement and to defendants who appear insincere or frivolous. And even in California, a few judges insist on sending all resisters to prison. As a result, the whole process is a little like Russian roulette. In Los Angeles, if a defendant appears before Judge Harry Pregerson or Judge A. Andrew Hauk, he is likely to receive probation. But if the federal magistrate randomly assigns the case to Judge Charles H. Carr or Judge Manuel L. Real, the same young man could well receive a three-year prison sentence.

Judge Hauk, one of the first judges to grant probation, reflected the views of many of his colleagues when he said, "The gross disparity in sentencing can't be justified." But as Robert M. Latta, chief probation officer for central California, put it, "The law doesn't always change as fast as public attitudes, and that puts the courts in a very difficult position."

In general, however, the trend is clearly toward more liberal practices. A survey of judges, lawyers, and probation officers in a dozen states points to the following reasons:

1. Public attitudes toward the Vietnam war and the draft have shifted drastically. Judge Fred M. Winner of Denver said that his own views did not influence his decisions but added, "I am, however, cognizant that the public's views on the war have changed, and I take that into consideration."

2. Judges have decided that many draft boards are too cursory or too strict in refusing applications for conscientious objector status. They have also been deeply impressed with the intelligence and sincerity of many of

the defendants who come before them. Judge Richard C. Freeman of Atlanta recently placed a young man on probation—in essence, giving him a judicial C.O.—and declared, "I refuse to adopt the position that I've got to abide by the outcome of the draft-board hearing."

3. Some defendants were going to jail only because their religion prohibited them from volunteering for two years of public service work. But judges found that many of them, particularly Jehovah's Witnesses, would perform two years of service if ordered to do so as a condition of probation.

4. Many judges and probation officers are increasingly reluctant to send any defendants to prison, whatever their offense, and expose them to a "school for crime" and homosexual attacks. In addition, Judge Hauk said that probation was far cheaper, since it kept a man out of prison and his family off welfare and allowed him to earn money and pay taxes.

Thus, 650 young men, like Alan Kent, were sentenced to probation in 1971. The only problem is finding jobs for all of them, since traditional employers, such as hospitals, often cannot accept any more.

Some have found work at various community service and antipoverty agencies, Alcoholics Anonymous, and the Salvation Army. One is a volunteer fireman. David Malament does community relations work for the Washington Square Methodist Church in Greenwich Village. Henry Rangel is a production assistant at KCET, the educational TV station in Los Angeles.

Alan Kent's story is fairly typical. The son of an estimator for the metal shop where he now works, Alan dropped out of junior college and "bummed around" for awhile until his draft board reclassified him 1-A. He thought about going to Canada, but as he put it recently, "I really couldn't handle that at all; it seemed like running away."

Gradually, his views about military service crystallized. "I didn't like the way the war was going," he recalled. "I couldn't see myself getting shot up for that; it would really be dumb. I like to treat other people the way I like to be treated. I just didn't want to go into the army and be part of a machine I didn't have any control over."

Like many young men, he never got around to filing a conscientious objector application until it was too late, according to Selective Service rules. But when he went to trial, he got a sympathetic judge. "I basically just convinced him that I was a C.O.," he said. By that time, he was working, and the judge allowed him to keep his job if he did volunteer work in his off hours.

At Bridge Over Troubled Waters, Alan drives a truck on errands, joins therapy groups at the program's rehabilitation center, and lends an "open ear" to people's problems.

His wife has also gotten involved, and as Jack Goldberg, the director of Bridge, put it, "We don't think we're doing something for him. We look at the whole thing as a tremendous asset to the program."

Sometimes, probation can be a turning point in a young man's life. Jerry Polcer, 23, of La Grange Park, Illinois, was a dock worker before he was convicted and ordered to serve as a psychiatric orderly in a hospital. The job was so interesting it has proved to be a "blessing in disguise," said Mr. Polcer. When his service is through, he hopes to go back to school and earn a degree as a social worker or registered nurse.

Many judges feel that probation should "sting" a bit, and things are not always easy for these young men. Ted James, 21, works at a neighborhood center in San Francisco organizing activities for juvenile delinquents. He is not allowed to travel outside northern California without permission, and filing his monthly probation report usually leaves him depressed for days. "I never did anything to deserve this sort of treatment," he said. "I wonder if you have to pay your dues if you believe in something, like Martin Luther King. Probation doesn't stop me from doing what I want, but it's always in the back of my head, and that's a bummer."

Ed Shubin was one of the first defendants to receive probation here in Los Angeles, and he was sentenced to five years of alternative service, which ends next March. At first, he took a military leave from his job as an apprentice sheet-metal worker, but after he decided to resist induction, the union refused to take him back. After he was convicted, he found a job at Los Angeles County-University of Southern California Medical Center and took home $135 every two weeks, less than half his previous pay.

He tried holding a second job in a meat-packing plant, partly because he owed his lawyer $1,000, but he was too exhausted to keep it. Now 28 and married, he has been trying to buy a house for several years but still cannot afford it.

Would he refuse induction again? "I think I would," he said as he sipped coffee in the hospital's cafeteria. Then he paused. "I don't know; it would be a hard decision."

1972

Two Pilots, Two Wars

Los Angeles

On February 17, Captain Harry Jenkins stepped off a plane at the Alameda Naval Air Station, one of the first flights of returning former prisoners of war to the United States. Captain Jenkins had been a POW for more than seven years, and as the senior man on the trip he moved to a microphone to address the crowd of about 500 cheering well-wishers. A teen-ager broke through the lines carrying his 2-year-old brother. The child, looking a bit confused, handed Captain Jenkins a box of Valentine's Day candy. Then the naval officer spoke: "As we boarded the aircraft at Clark Air Force Base, a young girl gave me a huge sign which read, 'Waiting sure takes a lot of patience.' Out there, our patience sometimes faltered but our faith never did—in our God, our families, and our country."

Just a few days earlier, Michael Heck, then an air force captain, had landed at Travis Air Force Base, another California field not more than an hour from Alameda. No brass came out to greet him, no crowds, no cheers, no Valentine's Day candy. In December, Heck had been the pilot of a B-52 that was bombing North Vietnam. On the day after Christmas he had refused to fly any more missions. His faith in his country had been shaken. He had decided, as he said later, "that a man has to answer to himself first." Now he was home to face an "other-than-honorable" discharge.

Harry Jenkins and Michael Heck are just two of the millions of Americans who fought in Vietnam. But their experiences raise some difficult questions about the war, about all wars, and about all men. What does the technology and impersonality of modern warfare do to one's moral sensibility? Where does a soldier owe his loyalty—to his commander or to his conscience? When are the death and destruction of war justified? Does the United States still have a role in protecting small countries, or should we fight only when our own vital interests are threatened?

These men offer different answers and thus symbolize, in a way, divisions that still rend the nation. One reason for their differences, perhaps, is that they were shaped by two different eras. Now 45, Harry Jenkins grew to manhood during World War II and enlisted in the navy right after high school. His hero was James Cagney, recklessly courageous in *Ceiling Zero*, flying the U.S. mail in the early days of aviation. He still holds the beliefs in American power and wisdom which he got from the textbooks and Saturday matinees of his youth. His whole purpose is to follow orders, to fight when called up, to die if necessary. Like most of his fellow POWs he believes that Vietnam was worth it, that the war ended with "peace with honor." Otherwise, his life would be hollow; the beliefs that sustain him, shattered.

Michael Heck is 30, a product of the late fifties and early sixties, a time when the civil rights movement and the Cuban missile crisis started planting doubts about the all-knowing wisdom of established authority. If he had a hero it was the Reverend Martin Luther King, defying a southern sheriff with his quiet methods of nonviolence. His faith in the American mythology changed slowly. But after seven years as a pilot, he found himself bombing hospitals, and he could not go on. Today, he represents those Americans who despise their own country and distrust their own leaders. To them, "peace with honor" is simply a joke, a sad joke, and there is a bitter edge to their laughter.

The war that these men fought—one much of the time in a prison camp and the other in 262 combat missions—is not over. Thousands of their fellow airmen are still stationed in Thailand and Guam. Bombs are still dropping on Cambodia. Men are still faced with choices, still struggling to know what is right and to do their duty.

I talked to Harry Jenkins at his home in Coronado, a peaceful little community across the Bay from San Diego, where on sunny afternoons retired admirals blossom forth in bermuda shorts to tend their azaleas. It is a comfortable ranch house, a bit on the pastel and fluffy side, which Marj Jenkins bought while her husband was still a prisoner. Jenkins is a lean man, almost 6-foot-5, with a beaklike nose and sideburns that barely reach the top of his ears. He reminds you of a huge, quick bird, resting tensely on a tree limb. His words come rapidly and strongly. Five rows of ribbons were strung across his tan, short-sleeved uniform. It was hard to realize that he had spent almost four years in solitary confinement.

Harry Tarleton Jenkins, Jr. was born in Suitland, Maryland, a suburb of Washington, D.C., the son of a wholesale florist. From the time he was 8, he wanted to be a navy flier: "I don't know what really prompted me. It might have been the Robert Taylor movies; it might have been enthusiasm over model airplanes. I was quite a model-airplane builder. Maybe it was just the excitement, the speed, the newness of it. . . . But I can recall, if I ever went downtown into Washington with my folks, or went for any reason, if I saw a naval aviator on the street my week was complete. I would rather have seen that than the president, it was that big a deal."

On Sundays his parents would take him and his two brothers—both joined the air force and one was killed in action—to the Washington airport to watch the planes. In high school, Harry saved his money to take flying lessons and joined a military program called the Cadets. "I guess the best thing you could say is that I enjoyed the regimentation of it. I think it was in 1939, the fleet made a visit into Norfolk, and I got to go aboard an aircraft carrier for the first time. This was just magnificent. It was the most beautiful thing I had ever seen."

In 1945, at 17, Jenkins entered the navy. From the beginning, he was a "hot jock," a fighter pilot, one of a special breed. As one naval officer put it, "Aviators are different. I don't know whether they're trying to prove their manhood or what, but they're the most egocentric people I know." Reviewing *Ceiling Zero* in *The New York Times* in 1936, Frank S. Nugent said Cagney's friend Tex had been killed because Cagney "still was playing with aviation, considering it merely an exciting way of expressing his own reckless courage and disregard for the fears of others." There remains in the "hot jock" a brawling machismo, the sort of spirit that 100 years before sent explorers across the plains to subdue the wilderness. With the frontier gone, they sought other challenges. Jenkins talks enthusiastically about his first airplane, the old Corsair: "You had to fly it. You could get in trouble easy and when you were in trouble it came fast and you were in deep trouble. I don't know, I guess all these things intrigued me. I'm not a daredevil, but my wife is always riding me for having no fear. It's the challenge of being able to walk to the thin edge and come back."

One of Jenkins's great regrets was missing World War II. In a time when veterans had been tossing away their medals and draft resisters fleeing to Canada, his words seemed a bit strange and nostalgic: "I don't know that I felt any real surge of patriotism, other than that attached to the war. And you know all young men, when there's a war going on, particularly as World War II was, they're kind of anxious to be part of it. There's an excitement about war; there is about every war, I guess. That war was of course so much different than this war. I wasn't home during this one, but from what I've read there has been a lot of controversy about this war, and in World

War II there wasn't any. We were going to get in there; we were going to show them and get it over with. We were invincible! We felt it; the whole nation felt it."

That pride in country, that sense of invincibility, became a part of Harry Jenkins. "I used to walk down the street, and wearing those wings, I just felt like I owned the world. . . . I still like to wear the uniform. To me, it commands respect. I don't see why anyone would not be proud to wear a uniform."

During most of the Korean war Jenkins was assigned to train pilots at Pensacola, Florida, and that was even more frustrating. He felt bereft, cut off, like the professional athlete who never got into the game. "It was the excitement that I was after, and the fact that my friends were out there and I wasn't. I joined the military and the military job is to fight a war when it comes along. I had pictured myself as a fighting man, and I wasn't fighting. That's our sole purpose—if we're called to fight, then we're ready to fight." Jenkins made several cruises to the Far East in the early sixties, and finally shipped out to the war zone in 1965 as a squadron commander flying off the U.S.S. *Oriskany*. "I was kind of anxious to get into it. I'd spent twenty years being paid and trained and lined up for that and I just didn't want another one to slip by. I just felt that I would feel a lot better looking at my face in the mirror every morning to be able to say, 'Yeah, I had a part in it.' "

There was also that enormous competitive urge, the desire to prove himself, and to share the masculine camaraderie of those who have passed the trial by fire. "I think probably if you talk to ten aviators, every one of them will tell you that he's the best there is. They're always up there looking for something to jump on, have a little dogfight with, to prove that he's better than the other guy."

As he started flying combat, Jenkins gave little thought to politics, or even to patriotism. "I had no animosity toward the Vietnamese; they were somebody we had to fight." He flew where he was told, bombing "something that looked like a jungle." The only two times he even stepped foot in the country he was attacking were to attend press conferences in Saigon after particularly successful raids. This sanitized form of warfare turned more personal after the squadron started gunning for truck traffic in North Vietnam. "One day my wingman and I saw what we thought was a truck, parked under a tree, hiding on the road. Before we attacked we went down to see what it was. We went right down over the rice paddy beside that field, maybe at 20 feet, and it was a busload of people. I remember a woman standing in the door of the bus as we went by, and we didn't attack it, because we weren't to strike buses. That was a much more personal thing, to look at the people that you might have been killing, instead of dumping bombs in the jungle."

But he says, "It didn't sicken me at all—that some of those people would be killed and hurt. It's a fact of war. When the enemy comes on the air and says we're bombing women and children and old men—we're not doing it purposely but we know it's happening. People who act like this is something utterly horrible and detestable are romantics. . . . If I would go out and drop a bridge it made me feel really good. First of all, it was a test of the preciseness with which I could maneuver that machine. Second, it slowed down the enemy's effort to oppose our friends—and that was what we were there for."

Like most pilots, Harry Jenkins never thought the enemy would drop *him.* Only the other guy would get hit. But on November 28, 1965, after he had been flying about six months, he was on a road reconnaissance mission near the demilitarized zone. As he flew to look at what seemed to be a parked truck, he took a direct hit from an antiaircraft gun. "I lost control of the aircraft and had to eject. It wasn't anything spectacular. It was the first thing I had fired at me that day."

Jenkins was the 55th American taken prisoner in North Vietnam, and the ninth-ranking officer in the camps. From the beginning, he prided himself on being "unmanageable," a "tough nut." Often, he refused to follow orders, particularly the camp rule that prohibited communication between prisoners; often, he was caught and punished. But even under torture, he does not think he ever made a statement or radio tape that was damaging enough for his captors to release publicly. In 1967, he was one of eleven senior men placed in "Alcatraz," a special, high-security prison where all inmates lived in solitary confinement and wore leg irons fifteen hours a day. One time, he was caught tapping a coded message to the next cell and spent eighty-six straight days in irons. In all, he spent more time "solo" than almost any other prisoner, and as he puts it, the key to sanity was "pacing, praying, and planning." Many of his comrades have praised him for the emotional stability he provided for others.

During his time in prison, Jenkins thought a lot. This sort of thing did not happen to "invincible" Americans, to James Cagney and Robert Taylor, and it angered him: "I got to thinking that some country the size of Vietnam would make the noise they had about dragging the American giant down.

They didn't do it, they can't do it, and if they speak honestly they'll admit they can't do it. But they make a big noise about it. It's like a little yappy dog nipping at the heels of a big horse going down the street. It just made me mad and I was kind of glad to see that we were continuing to pound them. The longer I was there, the less I liked them."

Like many returning prisoners, Jenkins admits to a "spiteful" feeling toward his captors. "They cry about their women and children getting killed. Hell, they should have thought of that before they started the war. Let's just say that if anyone comes around collecting for North Vietnamese relief, they could get a black eye." His feelings against the antiwar movement are almost as strong. Activists who visited Hanoi during the war "shamed our nation in the eyes of the enemy," he told a press conference. And he says, "Everybody has his right to speak his opinions in this country. But also, our country is dedicated to the principle that the will of the majority rules. And when this will has been established, then I think it is the country's job to support it, not to create all the opposition we can and undermine it."

It just never occurred to Harry Jenkins to question his orders, to question the reason he was fighting in Vietnam. "I guess some people say I have blind faith. . . . When our government commits us to something, I feel no reservation at all to support that commitment right down the line."

These feelings were only reinforced by his experiences in North Vietnam. Like many prisoners, Jenkins went through a process one has called "reverse brainwashing," in which the men constantly encouraged each other to believe that the war was just and that the president would gain "peace with honor." How else do you survive for seven years? Yet Harry Jenkins is not very happy with the navy he has come home to. "The military" he complains, "is no longer a strictly disciplined, hard-hitting bunch of guys." He criticizes servicemen's unions and the AWOL rates; he feels that beards and long hair are sloppy, and lead to "nonuniformity." Why is uniformity so important? "I think in a military sense, the ability to function as a unit is important. . . . You have a commonality in everything that you can, and I think that a parade of troops going by looks much more impressive if everyone is smartly dressed the same way."

To a man whose whole life has been based on discipline and uniformity, the idea of doing your own thing could hardly be more alien. He finds the country self-indulgent: "We're not as tough as we used to be." He is offended that X-rated movies are so popular; it bothers him when his three children—ages 13 through 21—ask for another bicycle or a new car; he is pleased that they are not doing anything "illicit," like smoking marijuana, but looking at society at large, he would agree with the former POW who exclaimed in dismay, "The hippies have won!"

He would like to see a return to the days when a kid could go to the movies and see Robert Taylor in a dress-white uniform, "squiring some good-looking thing on his arm, with a good-looking automobile and all. . . . That's not patriotism, but it paints a picture for a guy when he's very susceptible to influence of that sort. And he might decide, 'Boy, look at that, that's the way to go!' " On the other hand, Jenkins has been delighted with the public response to his press-conference comments condemning the antiwar movement and amnesty for draft resisters. Hundreds of letters have poured into the house, and as Marj puts it, "They're thrilled that there are still people with old-fashioned American values. A lot said they're glad someone made a stand for America and not against it."

Although Jenkins has some regrets about time lost from his family, essentially, he is a professional military man whose career comes first; he had been home only a few days when he was on the phone with Washington, asking if he could get command of a carrier. Marj was furious, but she is a "good navy wife"; she shares her husband's belief in his country and his job, and she goes along. Even after seven years in a prison camp, he would go to war again. "Now, I have a limited number of years left, and I hope that we don't have another war in that period, but it could happen. The world is certainly not stable in any way right now. But if it comes, that's why I have the job that I have. If that possibility were not there, then there would be no sense in the government paying me."

If Harry Jenkins looks like a pilot, Michael Heck looks like anything but. Rather short, a bit pudgy, he could easily be mistaken for a prosperous young real estate broker, mod enough to sport a small moustache. He has been divorced twice, and the day we talked he was staying with old friends in the suburban San Fernando Valley. His dress was strictly California casual—jeans, T-shirt, no shoes. The only decorations on his chest were two small feet, the emblem of the shirt company.

His family followed the classic pattern of migration to California: seeking a better climate and better jobs. One grandfather ran a clothing store in Council Bluffs, Iowa, the other a small farm in Oklahoma. Michael was born in San Diego in 1942 and raised in Chula Vista, a suburb south of the city, while his father worked on an assembly line in a defense plant. Later, the elder Heck shifted to real estate. San Diego is a company town for the military, and to young Mike, the armed forces seemed to be an economic and political necessity. "Back then," he recalled, "we really believed about the great threat of monolithic communism. We'd all been sold pretty well on that."

In high school Heck had few friends, but he liked being a "mover behind the scenes" and wound up as commissioner of student activities his senior year. Through the Methodist church he met several conscientious objectors, including a counselor at a summer camp. "I remember being impressed with the depth of his feeling and yet being a little puzzled because I couldn't understand the necessity for it," he said. There was no war on, and Heck did not think he would have to join the military at all. Politically, Mike inherited a strong liberal bent from his parents. He got interested during the fifties in the civil rights movement; he was "disturbed with things like Little Rock," and staunchly supported John F. Kennedy in 1960.

Wanting a small college in Southern California, he chose Whittier, President Nixon's alma mater, which retains a certain Quaker tradition. His aim was to study political science and then go to law school, but he soon became intrigued with the theater and wound up performing in everything from rock musicals to *Macbeth*. The Vietnam war was expanded then, as were antiwar demonstrations, which he thought were alienating people, doing "more harm than good." Recalling the year he graduated from Whittier, 1964, Heck said, "Even though I didn't like American involvement over there, I basically still felt that the South Vietnamese government was probably a legitimate government and they were being harassed by the North Vietnamese. I remember when the Gulf of Tonkin came along, like a lot of Americans, I thought it was really great when Johnson ordered the bombing of North Vietnamese ports or whatever. I thought, 'That will get this thing over with and get us out of there.' "

Michael Heck had more complicated, ambiguous views than Harry Jenkins: "The Communists seemed to have such success in converting people to their way of thinking. If our way of life is so much better, I wondered, why aren't we successful? At the time I thought, 'It must be our approach; we must be going about it wrong.' " Several professors taught him the necessity for rationality in foreign affairs, and one stressed the "absurdity" of American involvement in Laos. The Cuban missile crisis further eroded his good-guy, bad-guy attitude, and he remembers thinking, "Wait a minute. How come we can put our missiles in Turkey and then we can tell them they can't put missiles in Cuba? That seemed a little hypocritical to me."

In 1966, Heck was taking graduate work in theater. When his supervising professor left, he dropped several courses and soon he was facing the draft. Going in as an officer, he reasoned, would be a "worthwhile experience," so he shopped around for an opening. The air force had one—for pilots—and in a burst of indifference Michael Heck enlisted. He had no plans to fly in combat. He was assured that he could pick his job, and he intended to choose a cargo carrier. But soon, he found, there was "no truth at all" to the promises. After pilot training he received one of his last preferences, a light cargo plane called the C-123, and by 1968 he was sent to Thailand.

Already the questions were mounting in his mind. He had thought that the swift application of American power would end the fighting. "But somewhere along the line, it became obvious this wasn't working. We had been bombing for three years over there in North Vietnam and it didn't seem to be having any effect."

The C-123s were flying forward air-control missions. It was Heck's job to fly along the Ho Chi Minh Trail, spot enemy trucks as they came down that intricate network of jungle paths, and drop a flare to tell the bombers where to hit. But it was a frustrating assignment: "It became very apparent to me very fast that we were not doing what we were supposed to be doing. We were supposed to be stopping truck traffic, but we couldn't do it, because they moved at night. They were not dumb, and the system we were using to try to hit the trucks at night on the trail was absurd."

Heck felt no guilt then about his participation: "I didn't have to agree with everything I was required to do, and I had a duty to perform. . . . So I could accept things; I could say, 'Certainly, we can't have a military where everybody is making his own decision about every issue,' and I still believe that."

Finally he rotated home, and then got trapped by Catch-22. If an air force pilot has not formally given notice that he intends to leave the service when his hitch is up, he can be reassigned to a new aircraft, and have his tour automatically extended by four years. Heck had not filed a separation date. "I didn't have any direction. I wanted to give the air force a fair chance; I wasn't sure I was going to get out." So without any choice, he was assigned to B-52s—and locked in for another four years. "A lot of guys get nailed like that; they don't really understand the rules."

He returned in 1970 to the war zone, now to fly B-52s. An awesome weapon, the B-52 is also so mechanistic that, as Heck tells it, airmen would sink into lethargy: "We flew missions and it was so routine, such an impersonal thing. In B-52s you are at 30,000 feet. You fly along dropping bombs; it's just another point in the mission. Like you say, 'Well, at point A, I take off, at point B, I climb, at point C, I turn right, at point D, I level off, point E, I drop my bombs, point F, I turn right, point G, I descend and land.' There wasn't any sense of involvement for people."

This lack of involvement, Heck feels, led to a kind of moral insensitivity: "If somebody like me, or a lot of people, had to get out there actively and point a gun at somebody and shoot it, I'm sure I would have reached my decision a long time before I did. But at that altitude it was just routine." He attributes other factors as well to this insensitivity: "The whole way of life over there has to do with it. You're living on a base, you're around nothing but military people. You're not exposed to any other attitudes. There's safety in numbers, I guess. Everybody goes on and keeps doing it."

After his second tour, Heck did not return to Indochina until last spring, when the President renewed the bombing of North Vietnam. His attitudes had continued to change. One reason was the Calley case, which made him "think considerably about the question of conscience versus military orders." Another was former General Telford Taylor, and his comments on that question of conscience. "His position and that established by Nuremberg is that no man has the moral right to completely surrender his conscience to any authority, military or civilian. A man has not only a right, but an obligation to disobey an order that is conscientiously objectionable," Heck has written. A third influence was Lt. Col. Anthony Herbert, who accused superiors of covering up evidence of war crimes. "He was a professional military man, who was trying to do his duty over there within a certain scope. He saw things going on that were being hushed up by other people and he wasn't going to let that happen any longer. Too many professional soldiers will not make a ripple for fear of not getting promoted or getting in trouble," Heck said.

Once back in the war zone, his disillusionment accelerated. By then he had come to believe that the "democracies" America had been fighting for in Southeast Asia were really military dictatorships. He was horrified at the numbness he saw in himself, and in others. Now he shudders at the memory of the airman who admitted, "It makes me feel good to hurt them." As Heck recalls, "People would say, 'I don't care one way or another about the people in Vietnam, but I think we ought to go out and nuke them all [nuclear bomb them] just to get out of here.' I mean, I heard people say that! And this terrible dehumanizing effect tied into the numbness that everybody felt. There's no morality involved with this; it's just a matter of their own personal comfort."

But he continued to fly, partly because he feared the consequence of quitting. "I had visions of being thrown in jail, plus being stoned or being spat upon when I walked down the street." In addition, almost in spite of himself, he had developed a certain pride in his work. It was virtually the first physical challenge this rather bookish fellow had ever mastered, and even today he is quick to point out that he was appointed a "cell leader," commanding a group of three planes and more than twenty men. Moreover, he adds, "I had given my word, and that's very important to me." In October, he hoped that peace really was at hand, and that he could avoid making the decision. Michael Heck did not yearn for martyrdom.

Then on December 18, the bombing of Hanoi began. He describes his state as one of "moral shock." The losses were severe. "All of a sudden, when you walk by a trailer next to yours, and you see them putting the personal effects of people who lived there into little wooden boxes and storing them someplace—that brings it all home to you. . . . After the first or second raid, we saw the pictures in the paper of the hospital that had been hit, of the civilian areas that had been hit, and the embassies that had been hit, and we weren't surprised. A half-mile of error is not unusual, in fact it's an *acceptable* error. It was terror bombing, plain and simple. They called it military objectives but it was psychological objectives and anybody should be able to see that. It was bludgeoning somebody into doing something you wanted them to do."

Heck had flown three missions over the North. There was a pause for Christmas, and then on the next day, a bombing schedule was posted. When the planes returned, Heck found out that they had gone north again. That night he sat up and thought, "They really intend to bomb these people back into the Stone Age. . . . My God, they're going to do it, they're going to totally wipe out the country. . . . How can I be a part of this? How could I have been? What's going to happen to me if I don't fly again?" After much agonizing, his answers came to him. "It doesn't make any difference if I don't fly. . . . What are they going to do, put me in jail? I can live with that a lot easier than what I'm doing now. It doesn't make any difference what anybody else thinks."

The next morning, having made his decision, Heck told his navigator, who said, "That's great, I hope a hundred guys do it with you." Heck remarks now, "Of course they didn't—including him." Then the pilot reported to his commanding officer of his base in Thailand. It was no longer "a matter of choice," he told him, he just could not continue to be part of the war. A military lawyer was of little help and kept advising him not to "cause trouble." A chaplain helped him prepare a conscientious objector application, but that was withdrawn when the American Civil Liberties Union called from New York and volunteered to represent him. He applied for a straight discharge, but when it finally came through, it was under "other than honorable conditions," the worst discharge an officer can receive without a court-martial. Heck is now planning to appeal that decision on two grounds: that he never violated a direct order, because his name was removed from the flight roster, and that his spotless record of 262 missions warranted better treatment under any circumstances.

One inevitable question is whether Heck was just scared, and he admits that seeing his buddies get shot down did shake him up. But he believes that his record speaks for itself. "I'd gone through an entire tour previous to that one where we were under fire every night; it was not particularly new for me. It's very hard to answer someone who believes I did it out of cowardice. But the people I flew with never made any allusion to that at all—that's the best argument I can give to that."

Like Jenkins, Heck received a flood of supportive mail—a reflection of the divisions created by Vietnam. One letter that touched him deeply came from a woman in Massachusetts who called him a "man among men" for his courage and explained, "Four and a half years ago my three children and I lost what was dearest in the world to us—their father. My husband and I both felt his going to Vietnam was the right thing to do but now I see how blinded and misled we were."

Looking back, Heck feels that his experience helped him sharpen and define his own values. "Life itself is the first priority, and I totally reject national honor, pride, religion, or anything else that makes people go fight and die. I think there's only one thing that's gotten more people killed than national honor, and that's misguided religious zealotry. Honor implies looking good. Really, that's all it does."

That is the story of two pilots who flew in the war in Indochina, but some hard questions remain. Was the war worth it? Harry Jenkins criticized the way it was fought: "I think the job could have been done cheaper, if we had decided to fight to start with, but we tried to fool around." Basically, however, he believes in the mission he performed: "I think we were supporting the principle this nation was founded on. I think we fought to prevent the forceful subjugation of a people to a foreign government and I think we prevented that."

To Michael Heck, the war was a disaster: "Regardless of how someone feels about the government of South Vietnam, and the outcome of the war, it was not worth the sacrifice in lives lost. Our motive was to insure a government leaning in our direction, and even if that was an admirable objective—and I'm not sure it is—a war that kills 50,000 Americans and close to 1 million Vietnamese is just not justified." In particular, Heck feels that the "terror bombing" of populated areas during Christmas cannot be justified.

But Harry Jenkins believes that it was the Christmas bombing which brought him home: "I really think that showed them. As early as 1965, those people told us that if they waited long enough, the American people would make this war end. But when President Nixon won by that unbelievable margin, and when the B-52s came in, they finally realized they were messing with something that could grind them right back to the Stone Age in every sense of the word." To Captain Jenkins, such bombing also reinforces the credibility of American military power. He does not think we can assume the role of "world policeman." But there are still times, he feels, when fighting is necessary. "At times when someone's freedom is threatened, and they sincerely need help, we should be willing to give it to them. The basic concept of friendship is that when someone needs you, you'll be there."

Michael Heck feels the world is much more complicated than that. "Showing everybody how tough we are is a 1950s concept: It's John Foster Dulles brinkmanship. Just the fact that Richard Nixon is making peaceful overtures to China and Russia shows that type of diplomacy is not necessary. The whole idea of them and us, the good guys and the bad guys, is outmoded." Often, he says, critics accuse him of wanting to "give away" Thailand and other Asian allies, and the suggestion infuriates him. For one thing, Heck feels we are more frequently defending tyranny than the "freedom" Jenkins talks about. More importantly, he believes that the obligations of "friendship" have been largely discredited, that most foreign conflicts are none of our business, and he cannot accept the idea that "Vietnam or Thailand or any country is ours to give away or not to give away."

Harry Jenkins is ready to fight again. Michael Heck is returning to college, as a graduate student in theater at the University of South Carolina. His ambition is to teach, "to get people to think about things." Perhaps he might get to direct his favorite play, Joseph Heller's *We Bombed in New Haven*. Its hero is a pilot who refuses to fly a bombing mission—over Minnesota.

1973

THE PLIGHT OF THE CHICANOS

After years of struggle, Cesar Chavez and the United
Farm Workers Union won contracts in 1970 with most
California grape growers. It seemed that unionization
would finally come to the fields. But the organizing drive
stalled, partly because the union was inexperienced and
inefficient in administering the contracts it already had.
The growers continued to believe that Chavez was a
"radical" who would expropriate their lands, and they
could not shed the endemic racism of whites who had
always dominated their Chicano field hands.

Thus when those contracts expired in 1973, most of
the growers dropped the Farm Workers and signed up
with the Teamsters. Violence flared again. The American
Federation of Labor-Congress of Industrial Organizations
stepped in and won a promise from the Teamsters to
withdraw from farm labor and let the Farm Workers Union
take back the contracts. That truce fell through, and by
mid-1974, Chavez was in trouble. He appealed for public
support, but his cause no longer held the same romance
and power, so attempts to revive the boycott of grapes
and lettuce sputtered. But as Chavez told me many times,
he would never give up. There was nowhere else to go.

Most people tend to think of Chicanos in terms of
Chavez and the Farm Workers, but more than three-
quarters of the state's Mexican-Americans live in urban
areas like San Jose and suffer from a different set of
problems: gerrymandering to limit their political power,
schools that fail to understand the problems of Spanish-

speaking children, and discrimination in jobs and housing. But the traditional image of the sleepy Mexican is fading fast. Slowly but surely, Chicano power is becoming a reality in California.

Cesar Chavez,
The New American Hero

Sal si puedes, Spanish for "escape if you can," is the self-mocking name that Mexican-Americans give to the barrio in San Jose where Cesar Chavez spent part of his childhood. The rest of those years were spent tramping the back roads and fields of California's verdant San Joaquin Valley, a member of the faceless, nomadic army who pick the fruits and vegetables most Americans seem to think appear by magic in their supermarkets. What made Cesar Chavez different was that he accepted the challenge of *sal si puedes*. He has tried to escape, and take his people with him

Chavez is the head of the United Farm Workers Organizing Committee, the most recent in a long series of unions that have tried, with little success, to organize the poverty-ridden farm workers. For more than four years the United Farm Workers Organizing Committee has been striking the growers of California table grapes, and for almost two years it has been promoting a nationwide boycott against the fruit.

In the process, the union has attracted support ranging from the labor establishment to the Black Panthers. Housewives have traded bridge clubs for picket lines; Charlotte Ford and George Plimpton have raised money at chic cocktail parties; clergymen of all faiths have preached that not eating a grape is a holy act. Since the death of Martin Luther King, Cesar Chavez has become the nation's favorite radical.

What is the source of the union's strength? What lies behind the mystique of Cesar Chavez? In his excellent new account of Chavez and his movement, *Sal Si Puedes*, Peter Matthiessen offers this perceptive explanation: "Chavez is the only leader in the nation who has gained the fierce allegiance of the New Left without appeasing it. The students and the black militants are not drawn to Chavez the Revolutionary or Iconoclast or Political Innovator or even Radical Intellectual—he is none of these. In an ever more polluted and dehumanized world, they are drawn to him, apparently, because he is a true leader, not a politician: because his speech is free of the flatulent rhetoric and cant on which younger voters have gagged: because in a time starved for simplicity he is, simply, a man."

Matthiessen is not a political writer but a novelist (his last novel was *At Play in the Fields of the Lord*) and a naturalist. (Some of the book's most eloquent sections describe the despoliation of California by irrigation and pesticides.) He focuses on Chavez as a personality, and that is an important part of the story. For Chavez is a truly humble man, a man of the land and of the people who are close to it. When he refuses to wear a tie, when he accepts only $5 a week in expense money, when his tastes for luxury extend to Diet-Rite soda and matzos, it is not merely for the effect. That is the way he is.

He has been accused in recent years of a nascent messiah complex, and he does wear a Jewish mezuzah because he thinks Christ wore one. ("He certainly didn't wear a cross," Chavez explains.) But when he looks at his family and says, "Beautiful! Three generations of poverty!" there is more pride than bitterness in his words. (He is also a man of great gaiety. Matthiessen remembers leaving Chavez at the headquarters of the San Francisco archdiocese. Moments later the author heard a rapping sound and there was Chavez, silhouetted in a window high above the street, dancing and clowning for his friend below.)

Chavez is more than a humble man. He is an exceptionally shrewd organizer. He opposes Chicanos who glorify *la raza*, the Mexican race, when he sniffs even a hint of racism. At a time when white liberals have been ousted from the civil rights movement, he has not only recognized their good intentions but given them something concrete to do. And at a time when violence seems to have become a fact of public life, Chavez has maintained the principles of nonviolence. A deep admirer of Gandhi, he rejects the current notion that a group's militancy should be equated with the number of guns it has stashed away. "We are as militant as anybody," he once told me, and he is right.

For the real importance of Chavez lies in what is happening to the membership of the union. While others talked about participatory democracy, the farm workers were practicing it. "He wanted the people who did the work to make the decision," said Dolores Huerta, Chavez's able chief lieutenant. "He wanted the workers to participate, and he still does, because without that the union has no real strength. This is why he would never accept outside money until the strike began: He wanted the workers to see that they could pay for their own union."

Chavez is not averse to asserting leadership, and even ruling by fiat—as he did the night he prohibited Mexican-Americans from discriminating against the union's Filipino minority—but by and large the decisions flow from the bottom up. "Whether he wins *La Huelga* (the strike) or not," Matthiessen quotes one observer, "Cesar Chavez . . . has taught his people to do for themselves."

Learning to do things for themselves has changed the farm workers. People with little formal schooling are organizing successful boycotts across the country. Moreover, they are losing the sense of shame society hammered into them for so long. Today they are proud to be Chicanos, though five years ago, as Chavez remarked, "They wanted to be anything *but* Chicanos."

They are demanding equality and dignity in communities where the growers have ruled them like feudal lords, and they are gaining a new sense of their own potential. "It's so great when people participate," enthused Chavez when he saw the artwork in the union's new headquarters. "It's only a very small revolution, but we see this art beginning to come forth. When people begin to discover themselves like this, they begin to appreciate some of the other things in life."

One of the criticisms of Chavez, however, is that he has not thought enough about the "other things in life." While working to improve the life of the farm worker, he has not done much to help some of the young people leave the farms and get the education they are clearly capable of absorbing.

At times, success seems very far away. The boycott has made an impact, but the growers have shown little sign of giving in, and the Nixon Administration offers no prospect of outside help. The defense department even dramatically increased its quota of grapes for the troops in Vietnam. Many workers, moreover, are still too poor and insecure to join a union. Yet the struggle goes on. "We can't go back," Chavez's cousin once said: "We got nothing to go back to."

1970

Huelga!

Salinas

Red Lewis flicked his cigarette butt toward a field laden with ripe green cauliflower. "I'm harvesting my crops," he said grimly, "that's what I planted them for." His partner, Joe Violini, spat into the dust and said, "You're goddamn right, that's what we're doing."

Across the field, a group of Mexican-Americans formed a ragged picket line and waved the red banners of the United Farm Workers Organizing Committee. *"Huelga! Huelga!"* they shouted. Strike! Strike! "The growers thought we were kidding," said Tanis Reyna, a 21-year-old Mexican-American wearing sunglasses and a brown beret. "They think that because we're losing work time that we won't last, but we've got nothing to lose. We'll wait till we get what we want."

Red Lewis and Tanis Reyna symbolize two sides of a struggle that has engulfed the Salinas Valley in tension and terror. One is a white farmer, determined to run his land and his life the way he always has without outside interference. The other is a Mexican-American field hand, feeling the first rush of anger and militancy, demanding more security and better working conditions in his backbreaking job.

Several weeks ago, the International Brotherhood of Teamsters announced that it had signed contracts with 200 California growers covering field workers. Cesar Chavez, leader of the Farm Workers Organizing Committee, called the agreement a "stab in the back." Field workers, he said, were the province of his union, which recently won a five-year battle to organize workers in the California grape industry. The teamsters at first agreed to transfer the contracts to the Chavez union, but then backed down. The growers also resisted the transfer, saying they preferred to deal with the teamsters.

The farm workers struck on August 24—a week before a riot erupted 300 miles away in the Mexican-American barrio of East Los Angeles in another indication of Chicano militancy. Most of the Salinas Valley's 6,000 field hands stayed out and farmers were forced to use schoolboys and families to harvest their crops. Shipments of lettuce, the area's chief crop, dropped to one-third normal. Other crops were virtually shut down.

Last week, Interharvest and Freshpict, two of the area's biggest growers, signed contracts with the farm workers, but the others were holding out. And as the strike lengthened, tempers rose. Reports of beatings were rampant. Threats and accusations filled the valley like a fog rolling in from Monterey Bay.

This lush, narrow valley stretches for nearly 100 miles through central California. It was the birthplace of John Steinbeck and the scene of some of his most famous novels, including *East of Eden* and *The Long Valley*. In some ways the valley has not changed much since the 1930s, when Steinbeck was writing about it. The fields are still a marvelous mosaic of leafy tesserae: yellowish green beans, emerald-green lettuce, blue-green broccoli. The aroma of ripening strawberries and celery and garlic conveys the land's great richness.

Men still believe in simple virtues here—thrift, hard work, patriotism. The town band turned out to send the Salinas sons off to fight World War I, and today the newspaper carries letters urging Washington to "win" the war in Vietnam. But in other ways Salinas has changed a great deal. It has grown from a town of 4,000 in Steinbeck's youth to 60,000, "spreading like crab grass toward the foothills," as he wrote in *Travels with Charley*. When prosperous farmers in *The Long Valley* came to town, they ate at the Hotel Cominos on Main Street. Today the hotel has a seedy look and a sign that says, "No Credit, No Checks Cashed." The well-to-do now eat at the Towne House or the Tee 'n Turf, all neon and plastic and red leather.

Steinbeck was born in 1902, the son of a miller. His old house is a confection of turrets and wrought-iron railings and scalloped siding. Now the gentry live out from town in sleek ranch houses without a curved line in them. Steinbeck's farmers were usually small, independent operators, rooted in their land like the huge eucalyptus trees they planted to break the fierce valley wind. But in recent years huge corporations—United Fruit, Purex, S. S. Pierce—have moved in.

In the thirties, the natives feared and loathed the thousands of Okies who fled the Dust Bowl for the Promised Land of California. Now the Okies own businesses and property, and loathe the current wave of newcomers, the Mexican-Americans.

This is not a new story. When white Americans moved in they "were an outrage to the Spanish-Mexicans and they in their turn on the Indians," Steinbeck wrote in *Travels*. "Could that be why the Sequoias make folks nervous? Those natives were grown trees when a political execution took place on Golgotha. To the Sequoias everyone is a stranger, a barbarian."

Red Lewis was one of those Okies. He came West in 1935 with a new bride and large ambitions. "I was one of the better class of Okies," he quipped the other day, "I had two mattresses." He found work in the packing sheds and was made idle for sixty-one days during the bitter lettuce strike of 1936. But he saved some money and made friends with the right people. Today he is the packer and shipper for 1,600 acres of cauliflower.

Mr. Lewis is a tall, square man but these days he drives around with a German shepherd in his station wagon, which has an American flag tied to the aerial. "I have nothing against unions," he said. "I still have my union book from the strike of '36. But my workers don't want to belong to Chavez's union; this is being forced on them."

Why then were they all on strike? "Many families refused to picket, but they've been threatened and intimidated so much they went out," he said. "Agitators from outside are getting the people out on strike."

Joe Violini was born in this valley 58 years ago, the son of a Swiss immigrant dairy farmer, and has lived in the same house, on the same land, since 1922. "For a fella who was born and raised here," he said, "it's damn hard to eat this stuff. People who aren't even citizens are telling you what to do. That's what it amounts to." The farm workers' union is only the latest thing that is troubling Joe Violini. He complains about taxes and welfare. And a few years ago the state put a new road right through his property, cutting off his view of the Salinas River.

"You don't have any control anymore," he said, his blue eyes burning under the felt brim of his cowboy hat. "You act like you own the land, but you don't. Goddamn," he went on, "years ago if you worked and paid your bills you were all right. Now you have problems other people create for you. I can't quite put my finger on them but they're there."

Several hundred yards away, the striking field hands could put their fingers on their problem—Red Lewis and Joe Violini. "Those growers still think they're living in the thirties," said Ray Huerta, the leader of the pickets. "They think they can just ship us back to Mexico." Were they being intimidated to join the farm workers' union? "We've been waiting for Chavez for some time now," said Mr. Huerta, who wore a black, Zapata-style moustache. "We don't want the teamsters shoved down our throat."

"The union would give us security in our jobs," added Carmen Reyna, one of six brothers and sisters marching on the line. "The way it is now we have no one to defend us if something goes wrong. There's nobody to back us up." "The foreman is always on top of you when you're working," said Miss Reyna's brother Tanis. "We don't have any guaranteed hours, no travel time, no health plan, no paid vacations, no holidays. And they make us use the short-handed hoe. Now that they have to work in the fields they'll find out it's no picnic."

Like the growers, the farm workers feel that the current dispute is only a manifestation of a deeper problem. Carmen and Tanis Reyna are both high school graduates, but they were unable to find work in Salinas and were forced back to the fields. "The only place there's no discrimination," said Mr. Huerta, "is when they take you into the army."

The picket lines here are mainly manned by the young, those who will not accept the conditions under which their parents have lived for so long. They drive around town with red flags waving, honking their horns to one another and flashing "V" signs out the window. The strike has almost a festive air.

"This picket line really means something to us," Mr. Reyna said. "We've got to win. We've got to. It means we're taking pride in our race. We want to be called something. Chicanos. We just don't want to be nothing."

1970

Escape If You Can

San Jose

Helen Garcia worked at the Salvation Army sorting old clothes. She had to leave every morning at six because it took three buses and three hours to reach the job from her home here on the East Side of San Jose. With five children, Mrs. Garcia had to work, but she did not like the travel time, and a friend got her a job as a grocery clerk. She had been working only a few days when a young man, apparently crazed by drugs, entered the store last week waving a gun. Everyone thought he was kidding until he fired a shot into an ice machine. Then he shot Mrs. Garcia. She died 15 minutes later.

Helen Garcia was one more victim of the barrio, the Mexican-American section of San Jose. The area has been called Sal Si Puedes, which means "escape if you can."

Cesar Chavez, the leader of the Farm Workers' Union, who lived here for many years, once explained the name: "That's what that barrio was called, because it was every man for himself, and not too many could get out of it, except to prison."

Mainly because Mr. Chavez's efforts on behalf of field workers have received so much attention, there is a popular impression that most Mexican-Americans are rural harvest hands. In fact, at least 80 percent of the more than one million Chicanos in California live in urban barrios like this one, and here is where their problems—and potential power—are most significant. Nationally, the percentage of Chicanos living in urban areas is almost as high.

At first glance, Sal Si Puedes looks like a rather pleasant working-class suburb, with small frame and stucco houses, cars in the driveways, well-kept yards, and sprays of flowers.

But it is like the impression made by a middle-aged woman with heavy make-up in a dim light. When you look harder you see the cracks and wrinkles—the broken windows, the sagging roofs, the overcrowding, the shacks hidden in tiny alleys that would be unfit for chickens, let alone human beings.

Still, many residents have a certain affection for their community. "I didn't know I lived in a ghetto. I thought I lived in a pretty nice place," said Mrs. Armida Rivera, an active member of Our Lady of Guadalupe Church.

"Remember when Robert Kennedy came to San Jose?" she went on. "That's the church he went to, our little church. I have a paper to prove it."

The tides of community life flow through the tiny grocery store where Mrs. Garcia died. One evening recently a steady procession of people came in to buy milk and bread (mainly with the food stamps the federal government issues to poor families) or beer, cigarettes, and candy.

A Chicano man and an Anglo woman, carrying a black baby, picked out some bread and soda and paid with pennies.

"You know how it is when you run out of money," the girl said sheepishly.

When the pennies were counted she had a few extra—enough to buy the boy a yellow lollipop.

The black population on the East Side is growing steadily, and while there is some tension and competition between the two groups, it was not evident in the store.

A young black man came in and Lydia Torres, the clerk, knowing his craving for them, automatically brought him a jar of green olives. "It's just something I'm stuck with," the man laughed. "I picked it up in the service. This jar will be gone in an hour."

The store is owned by Ernie Abeytia, a local political leader, who performs little services for his customers. He cashes checks for people with no identification and gives customers a break when they're a few cents short on the bill. The store is filled with the intoxicating aroma of fresh tamales, shells of ground corn stuffed with meat and sold hot from a big blue pot on the counter. The store sells at least a dozen kinds of chili and chili powder, and Mr. Abeytia has learned to stock black-eyed peas during the New Year holiday for the recent arrivals from the South.

On Sunday morning the store features hot homemade menudo, a Mexican soup made with beef tripe and hominy and flavored with cows' feet.

"Menudo is very traditional throughout the Southwest on Sunday morning," Mr. Abeytia said. "It's great for hangovers—it's a real belly liner."

Although Chicano traditions like menudo endure, the old image among Anglos of the lazy, feckless Mexican is changing rapidly in San Jose. Mr. Abeytia ran for the State Legislature this year and lost by only 145 votes, even though many Chicanos are prevented from voting by complicated citizenship and language requirements.

After years of complaints about police brutality, the Chicanos recently decided to organize a unit called the Community Alert Patrol to monitor police actions. A radio operator listens to police radio communications and dispatches an observer car to the scene of any trouble. The observers, usually responsible older men with no arrest records, do not interfere with the police. They just take photographs and make tape recordings. Reports of brutality have dropped sharply in the two months the patrol has been operating. "But the cops," said one member of the group, "never know when they're being watched."

The Peace Officers Association of San Jose charged that the patrol was getting aid from the Mexican-American Community Service Association, a group that in turn receives money from San Jose's United Fund campaign. The peace officers threatened to boycott the United Fund if the Community Service Association got any more money. Within days the fund suspended the association.

The incident made Chicano leaders more aware than ever of how little real power they have in the political system. Yet, despite the rhetoric of some young militants, most Chicanos remain committed to that system.

"A lot of people like me don't go along with this militant deal. They get so wound up they want to force issues," said one community leader who refused to be identified. "There's all this talk about revolution, but that's not what the majority of Chicanos want. They're fighting the system just to get ahead, to get some breaks, to get a job. We just want our equal rights like everyone else."

1970

THE FAMILY BESIEGED

Of all the things people are looking for in California—and anywhere else—what they want most is a satisfying relationship with another person. The Holy Grail is not status, money, or security, although that is part of it. It is, simply, love. But the other magic word these days is "freedom," and what struck me so often was that people did not see the potential conflicts between those goals. They did not see that love, at its best, requires tolerance, patience, even compromise.

I remember having a discussion with my mother about "kids today" and at one point she blurted out, "What do they want, to be happy?" To her, growing up in the Depression, struggling for security, happiness was a distant goal. People now insist that they deserve more than comfort, that they deserve to be happy, and they are right. But if they are going to get more, it seems to me they are going to have to give more. As it is now, marrieds want the freedom of being single and singles want the intimacy of being married, but relatively few people are willing to do the demanding work of reconciling the two.

Divorce—People Aren't Willing to Make Do Anymore

Los Angeles

In 1957, Diane and Winslow Smith got married. Diane had to quit college, but Win was finishing law school, and although she was not in love, he was. Besides, her parents approved. "We didn't think," Diane remembered, "we just did it."

Last year, the Smiths—not their real name—became one of almost 900,000 American couples to get a divorce. Diane, now 36, mother of two and a college student again, explained why: "In considering the divorce, I thought of my survival, rather than: What am I doing? How could I do this to Win? When I went to a shrink, I began to break out of the old things. He was one of the old things I broke out of. I started dating and felt young again. I got a divorce because I felt it was the only way I could expand and grow as a human being."

Divorce in America has become an "epidemic," as one lawyer put it. In the twelve months ending last July, there were 9 percent more divorces nationwide than in the previous year. Marriages also increased, but by only 1.4 percent. In the single month of July, divorces jumped 17 percent over July, 1972, while marriages dropped 7 percent. Here in California last year, there was 1 divorce for every 1.6 marriages.

Experts in the field generally estimate that one out of every three couples getting married this year will ultimately break up. But some think that projection is too low. *The New York Times* has interviewed dozens of these experts, including lawyers, judges, counselors and therapists, as well as numerous individuals who have recently gotten divorced. If there is any consensus explanation for the divorce statistics, it is this: Marriage has been caught up in a revolution of rising expectations. People want more out of their marriages than their parents ever did, and in the words of one counselor, "They're not willing to make do, or slide by anymore." They also have the time, and the money, to worry about their personal needs in a way that was seldom possible a generation ago. Divorce, in one sense, has become a great leisure-time activity.

Traditionally, marriage was devoted to certain purposes: economic survival, emotional security, the procreation and raising of children. In the play *Fiddler on the Roof*, when Tevye the milkman asks his wife, "Do you love me?", her answer is an incredulous shriek: "Do I what?" As Stuart Walzer, a Los Angeles divorce lawyer, said, "That was the strangest question he could have asked her."

As Tevye tells his aghast spouse, "It's a new world, a new world, love." And while Tevye's children might have married for love, in the new world of his grandchildren, love is only a part of what many couples are demanding from each other. As Richard E. Farson, a prominent psychologist and the new head of the Esalen Institute, has written, "Marriage is now burdened with the expectations that husbands and wives should enjoy intellectual companionship, warm intimate moments, shared values, deep romantic love, great sexual pleasures. Couples expect to assist and enhance each other in ways never thought of as being part of the marriage contract."

These new expectations are much harder to meet than traditional ones, particularly when they are hammered into the public consciousness by the mass media, broadcasting the message expressed by one beer commercial this way: "You only go around once in life, so grab all the gusto you can."

The result, according to the experts, is that people feel they are somehow "missing out," that their gusto quotient is below par. They want, in Diane Smith's words, to "expand and grow as a human being" and feel "young again." And when they do not, they blame the person closest to them—their spouse.

Some observers see the divorce statistics as a sign of health, a sign that people are finally striving to reach their "human potential." Others see them as a mark of moral decay. Most experts welcome the ideals of personal growth and fulfillment, but they worry that other ideals are in danger of being lost—commitment, responsibility, even sacrifice.

Whether it is praised or condemned, divorce has become a major fact of American life. It is an age when the governor of Maryland can, with impunity, move out of the executive mansion and announce he is leaving his wife. A woman like Diane Smith can decide that her own "survival" is more important than the well-being of her husband or children. This amounts to a basic change in values. People might still promise to remain married "until death do us part." But many of them really mean, "until it does not feel good anymore."

In his book *Future Shock*, Alvin Toffler says that in a time of such rapid change, it will be almost impossible for a couple to grow and adapt together over a lifetime. The norm, he predicts, will be "temporary marriages," different relationships for different stages of life.

If marriage is changing, if people are playing new roles and trying to meet new expectations, the social context in which marriage takes place is also changing. Once a relationship goes sour, it is much easier to get a divorce, for a wide variety of reasons:

L A W S. The laws in many states have loosened up considerably in recent years. In California, for instance, there is now "no fault" divorce, with no need to prove that one partner was to blame for the break-up. In addition, the spread of legal services programs has enabled many poor people to get divorces that they could not previously afford.

A T T I T U D E S. The stigma once associated with divorce has virtually disappeared in many places, and as it becomes more common, it becomes more acceptable. This is particularly true in a place like Los Angeles or Manhattan, where you sometimes feel odd if you are not divorced, but a judge in Charlottesville, Virginia, said, "There's been a tremendous change in attitude toward divorce in Virginia. It used to be a stigma, a disgraceful thing to happen to one's family. But morality has changed. People don't look upon it as a disgrace any more, even in the rural-conservative areas. They just think, 'Well, they couldn't make it.' "

R E L I G I O N. Many religions are less able to enforce their tenets against divorce. The divorce rate among Roman Catholics, for example, is approaching that for the rest of society, and the church is under enormous pressure to modernize its procedures for granting annulments and welcoming divorced persons back into the fold.

M O B I L I T Y. In his book *A Nation of Strangers*, Vance Packard reported a "striking similarity" between regions with high mobility and those with high divorce rates. Just the act of moving causes immense strains on a relationship, he noted, but the problem runs much deeper. At a time when people are seeking greater emotional gratification, they are separated from people who could give it to them: extended family, old friends, teachers, clergymen. As a result, said Mary Jane Hungerford, a California marriage counselor, "Two people are thrown in on themselves almost completely." One example of the problem: Who takes care of the new baby, and the new mother, when all of her relatives are thousands of miles away?

The problem of two people trying to grow and adapt together is aggravated when the husband travels a lot on business, or works in an urban setting far removed from his suburban household and suburban wife. They can wind up living in one house—and in two different worlds.

Above all, mobility shields a couple from traditional community and family pressures. Mr. Packard quotes a salesman in Sunnyvale, California, as saying, "There's no morality here and I guess it is because nobody knows anybody so that you can get away with stuff you couldn't in the old days when everybody knew everybody and what they were doing."

THE STATUS OF WOMEN. Divorce is almost always a trauma, but the impact can be lessened by the ability of a woman to make her own way in the world. "Women are no longer afraid," said Lillian Paradise, a Manhattan lawyer. "They're beginning to develop themselves, to take courses in school." Tilla Vahanian, a New York psychotherapist, added, "Women are seeking their own thing with more courage, and they're passing up alimony because they know they can earn their own living." In some cases, this also allows a man to walk out of a marriage with less guilt. As Judge Harlow Lenon of Portland, Oregon, said of young couples, "They're not really terrified by divorce anymore. Each is confident that each can get along without the other. There is a new sense of independence."

CHILDREN. Most experts agree that children are less of a deterrent to divorce, since parents are less willing to defer pursuit of their own happiness for the sake of their offspring. Moreover, as Dr. Irving Fosberg, a New Orleans psychologist, put it, "Once children were almost a total bar to getting a divorce. Now with day nurseries and day care centers and a change in attitudes, that is changing. Now parents feel 'It isn't fair to the child to grow up in a household where the parents don't love each other'; previously they would have felt divorce was an immoral thing to do."

THE SINGLES SOCIETY. People getting divorced today are not alone. They can move into a singles apartment complex, go to a singles bar, take a singles trip, and find dozens of ready-made companions who are in the same boat. They can go to a church group or a consciousness raising group and receive advice and support. They can lead an active sex life without acquiring an unwanted mate, or child, or reputation.

Divorced persons also have it easier in the business world. For example, banks that once closed down a man's line of credit when he faced divorce are now willing to keep it open. "Society," explained Stuart Walzer, "is developing institutional norms that take divorce into account." If divorce is easier, however, the more important question remains: Why is it happening? What is tearing the American family apart?

In some places, and among some groups, the reasons for divorce are much the same as they always have been. Ronald R. Tweel, a Legal Aid attorney in Virginia, said that 90 percent of his divorce cases center on alcohol. "It's a pattern," said Mr. Tweel. "They drink, then they lose their jobs, they get abusive and start beating up their wives."

Another traditional reason for divorce is money. The daily struggle for economic survival can implant considerable bitterness, particularly among the poor. But the revolution of rising expectations makes money a problem, even when survival is not in question.

"I hear the damnedest arguments about who will get the hi-fi and the cars," explained John M. Bischoff, chief deputy clerk of the Domestic Relations Court in Washington, D.C. "So you know money was what was wrong in the first place. The wife says, 'You slob, why don't you make more money so we can live like the Joneses?' That's what lower- to middle-income people worry about most."

Sex is another classic reason for divorce. But this area, more than almost any other, has also been affected by rising expectations and temptations. Marriage was once considered an opportunity, sometimes the only opportunity, to have sex; now it is often considered a limitation on one's sex life. Magazines that once preached "togetherness" are telling women that they deserve to have orgasms. Men are urged to live by a "playboy philosophy" that seems to be based on an endless supply of soft leather, smooth liquor, and sensuous lovelies. Topless bars, X-rated movies, and adult bookstores are now fixtures in many neighborhoods.

"It's almost impossible in this culture to be monogamous," asserted Ralph Keyes, the youthful author of a new book entitled *We, The Lonely People.* "Just walk on a beach on a Saturday and watch the bikinis—it's absurd! Go to a party and you have some talk about vaginal lubrication. It's like being at an endless and fantastical smorgasbord."

Women are as subject to this stimulation as men, and are increasingly able to act out their impulses. "There is more freedom for women now; many of them are working outside the home," said William Parker, a referee in the Domestic Relations Court of Dayton, Ohio. "Perhaps there is more opportunity for misdeeds for women than there used to be." Or as one lawyer put it, "Familiarity breeds attempt."

One sign of this new freedom among women is that more men are filing for divorce than in the past, and more are asking for custody of the children. "The ex-husband is often horrified at the wife's conduct," said Judge Lenon.

Inside marriage, women are also pursuing sexual fulfillment. Susan Fuentes, a sex counselor at the American Institute of Family Relations in Los Angeles, said, "I have women come in all the time who feel cheated by their sex lives. They have demanded therapy, and I mean demanded it!" But one result of this female aggressiveness, she said, is a sharp increase in male impotence.

Sexual satisfaction is only one of the new demands placed on marriage. As Dr. Farson noted, people expect that a whole range of needs will be met—companionship, intimacy, love, "peak experiences" of all kinds. In a recent study conducted by the Family Service Association of America, 87 percent of the married couples interviewed said that "communication" was a major area of conflict in their marriage. Children (46 percent), sex (44 percent) and money (37 percent) trailed far behind.

As Gary Brainerd of the American Institute put it, "It's a whole cultural tone; people are more aware of their emotional needs." Added Susan Fuentes, "They want it to be good all the time." This awareness, this "cultural tone," flows from a number of sources. One is the mass media, according to Meyer Elkin, director of family counseling services for Los Angeles County: "Every medium of communication is exploding the message at you—you've got to be happy! And unless you have this, this, and this product, you won't be happy!"

Dr. Farson thinks movies and television have perpetuated a "syrupy sweet," over-romanticized view of family life, and adds, "The implication that a constant state of affection and unity in family life is actually achievable gives cause to rising dissatisfaction in one's own marriage."

A second source of awareness of emotional need is the youth movement of the late sixties, the era of "flower power" and "doing your own thing," mind-bending drugs and mind-blowing music, long hair and colorful clothes. As Dr. Melvyn Kinder, a psychologist in Beverly Hills, put it, "The hippie movement, the drug revolution, fed into the divorce rate in many ways, particularly in terms of the rejection of old values. It didn't last; we didn't have a Woodstock Nation, but a lot of the values did get transmitted—they were quickly absorbed into the adult culture." "I see a lot of 45-year-old couples who kind of wish they could be like their children," added another therapist.

A third reason for the "cultural tone" is the movement for human rights that started among blacks in the early sixties and is currently flowering among women. Like the hippies, the feminists have influenced many people who never joined their movement; their ideas have been absorbed by the mass culture, almost by osmosis.

Dorothy Davis, a Los Angeles lawyer, remembers that when the first excerpt from Betty Friedan's seminal book, *The Feminine Mystique*, was published in a magazine, "it caused so many divorces you wouldn't believe." The reaction of women to that, and subsequent feminist writings, is that "they sort of fear they have lost out on life," said Ms. Davis. "And they're angry at their husbands for allowing them to get to this terrible spot."

In a recent letter to *The New York Times*, Dr. Paul E. Kaunitz, a Connecticut psychiatrist, said he has witnessed a "disturbing" increase in recent years of women seeking divorces "in the absence of customary reasons." Dr. Kaunitz explained, "The plaint of the wives has been consistent: 'I must find my identity; I must no longer be a slave and a prostitute; I must find my independence.' A large proportion of these women have attended consciousness-raising groups."

The "cultural tone" that raises new expectations for marriage flows from a fourth source: what has been called the new or "humanistic" psychology. The "gestalt" theories of the late Fritz Perls are probably the most influential in the field, but these ideas have blossomed in a hundred variations of sensitivity training, encounter groups, "bioenergetics," transactional analysis, psychotherapy, and many more. One local joke has it that young lawyers trying to start a practice line up outside weekend-long encounter groups, or "marathons," to get the divorce business as the couples leave.

The basic message transmitted by the "new psychology" was summarized this way by Dr. Farson, one of the early leaders of the movement: "You are a beautiful, unique human being, fully worthy, with potential beyond your wildest imagination. Moreover, you've got to get yourself into the driver's seat. You are responsible for yourself. If you are hurting, fix it! Take action! No one will do it for you."

"But what action can a person take in life?" Dr. Farson adds. "Many of the important things—race, IQ, health, even your job—you don't have control over. The one thing you do have control over is your marriage. You can pick up the phone, get a lawyer, and get a divorce."

This adds up to a very powerful message. At a time when traditional sources of moral authority, from the church to the state, have lost much of their power, the psychologist can become a priest, preaching a gospel of salvation through personal gratification, and sanctioning almost any action needed to reach that state of grace, including divorce. For many, the concept of sin has been reversed. Once you were prohibited from indulging yourself; now you are scorned for not doing so.

These ideas leave many experts on marriage torn and confused. They generally applaud the concept that people can, and should, strive for better relationships, deeper communication, more intimacy. But many feel that this "new consciousness" can cause enormous frustration. They worry that people have been "sold a bill of goods," that they have been tantalized with an impossible ideal that can never be met in real life. "People are expecting themselves and their spouses to be superhuman," warns Dean Smith, a marriage counselor in Orange County, California. "A marriage can only be as good as about 60-40—60 percent is okay and 40 percent could be better. That's as good as a marriage can be, because that's as good as people can be."

"You can't have love without pain, and without hate, the two are inseparable," added Mr. Smith. "But people have developed the idea that when you're in love that doesn't happen—love is all nice and pleasant, no angry feelings. They seem to be saying, 'I'm so good, I don't deserve any pain in my life; I'll never forgive my mate if he or she hurts my feelings. I'd better find somebody else.' But painless love is the most frustrating goal in the world."

"There's more of an attitude that if it doesn't work now, let's forget it," said Dr. Jerold Kuhn, executive director of the American Institute of Family Relations. "Everyone wants instant gratification. Tenacity is not a virtue, particularly."

"Any commitment or restriction is seen as an enemy of growth," explained Dr. Carlfred Broderick, a practicing therapist and professor of psychology at the University of Southern California. "But marriage, and many other institutions, require a social covenant: You have to give up a certain amount of freedom because of social responsibility. But in marriage, more and more people are saying, 'I'll be damned if I'll give up anything.' "

Many experts feel that this refusal to make commitments, to "give up" one's total freedom, to "work" at a marriage through a process of compromise and toleration, is a major cause of the rising divorce rate. "Making a commitment to your marriage is like making a deposit in a bank account against a withdrawal," said Dean Smith. "If you haven't made any deposit, and a problem comes along, the relationship goes bankrupt."

Meanwhile, the frantic search for happiness, for fulfillment, for gusto, goes on. And the divorce rate goes up. The mood was probably best expressed by the 45-year-old business executive who explained why he had left his wife of twenty-three years and moved in with his secretary: "I wanted more than I had. I didn't know what it was I wanted, but I knew I didn't have it."

1974

Five Marriages

After Jim left her, Barbara Burton went back home, back to the Middle West, looking for comfort and support. What she found was an aunt who told her, "We just don't do things like that in this family." But today, they do things like that in most families.

The Burtons met in college and were married soon after. Jim was a writer, a good one; within a year or two he accepted an attractive offer to come to California, and life slowly started to change. Jim wrote stories about rock music, the drug scene, young political hotshots who whisked around the country on someone else's credit card and romanced a bright-eyed envelope stuffer in every campaign headquarters. "It was the kind of culture that said, 'All right, if you're not happy, split,'" Barbara related. "Follow your inclinations! Flower! Have experiences!"

The talk and the dope and the music had their effects. As Barbara remembers it, her husband started saying things like, "What am I doing? I'm almost 30 years old and this life is not fulfilling. I want to be free, I want to be able to feel. I'm tired of this deadness around the house, I want to be around someone who excites me."

Their sex life epitomized the problem, and Barbara tried to liven it up. But it is not so easy for the granddaughter of a Lutheran minister to feel "free" and "exciting" in bed, even if everybody is telling her she should. "When somebody says sex isn't important, I find that ridiculous," said Barbara, a pretty woman who smokes rapidly to ease her edginess. "It's the distillation of everything else, a mirror of how you are as a person. I didn't see myself as a sexual person, and I never thought I had a sex drive. It was something to be gotten through to please a man. I grew up in a very religious house, and while I never really accepted it, I went along with it. I felt that certain things were right or wrong, without knowing why."

The Burtons had a baby, and it only made things worse. Jim felt more trapped and refused to deal with their growing financial problems; Barbara felt more uptight and fantasied that a brain tumor was preventing her from having an orgasm. Then one day Jim told her that he was having an affair with another woman, that he was leaving to go live with her.

Looking back, Barbara compared the expectations of her friends and family in the Middle West to the ones she encountered in California: "I don't think they expect to be thrilled all the time. I didn't; I was content to be happy with the parts of my life that were happy, and not question the other parts, but Jim wasn't. I really did assume that people loved each other and stayed married and worked things out. But divorce just seems more possible out here. It seems like the thing one ought to do if you're unhappy."

After the divorce, Barbara took a "terrifying tumble" into loneliness and fear, but with the help of psychotherapy, she is pulling herself together. Now she wants what she feels she has missed, to be "thrilled," to "go completely berserk in bed." She is living with a youth of 23, an unemployed playwright, and trying to stamp out the ghost of her minister grandfather.

"I don't feel guilty from a moral standpoint," she said, and then paused. Finally she admitted, "Yes, I do. It comes up mainly when I have problems with my daughter. I come apart; I think God is punishing me. I'm 30 years old, and it doesn't go away. I'm like a child."

Cynthia Jackson is 21 and black. She was pregnant when she got married at age 18, and was divorced sixteen months later. For her, two of the most traditional reasons—money and in-laws—helped cause the break-up.

"I was the only one in the house who worked," recalled Cynthia, a secretary. "We were living in his parents' house with his parents, five brothers and sisters, and grandmother. He would be lazy about going to find a job, so when it came time to pay the bills it came out of my paycheck, which left me nothing."

Another prime reason for divorce is that people get married for the wrong reasons, and the Jacksons were no exception. "We really didn't get along anyway," Cynthia said. "I really didn't want to be there. I knew I wasn't in love with him, and I really got married because I thought my mother wanted me to, because I was pregnant. He had no initiative in getting anywhere and I certainly didn't want to live with his folks forever."

Cynthia does not consider herself a women's liberationist, but she is an assertive young woman who knows what she wants, including a good sex life. "He didn't satisfy me," she said of her ex-husband. "I think he was just interested in satisfying himself."

She has also absorbed, from somewhere, another idea of growing importance—that children should not be a bar to their parents' happiness. As she put it: "I thought about my daughter when I was deciding on the divorce, but I don't believe in saving marriages for the sake of the kids. When my daughter grows up she'll try to make it for herself, not for me. So I'm going to live for myself and her right now by doing what I want to do and getting what I can to make things better for us. I don't think staying married for her benefit would have done it."

"You know," concluded Cynthia, "I might get married again, but if I do I will have checked out all sides of the person, including money, sex, and how well we get along as two people being together. When I was younger I dreamed I would get married but not divorced. I thought I would only be married once. But all those storybook dreams about marriage we have as kids are just a lot of crap when it comes to reality."

They were a good Catholic couple, the Donovans. Paul went to Georgetown and Fordham Law; Denise went to nursing school and would never dream of sleeping with him before they were married. But the heat was on them both, so they did get married, in 1963. He was 25, she was 21, and as Paul put it, "We took it for granted that marriage was permanent."

They also took for granted what Denise would do. "We didn't think she'd be anything but a wife and mother," said Paul. "That was her role; that was the profession she had chosen."

Paul worked in a Wall Street law firm, but found it stifling, and moved his family to Los Angeles after about five years. The move was stimulating to both Donovans. As Paul recalls, "It's a much freer life in every respect out here. You can do your own thing, you can dress the way you want, wear your hair the way you want, and no one gives a damn. And my wife became more mobile. She had a car, and it let her explore the city. In New York she had depended on me to get around."

After their third child was born three years ago, Denise went back to work part-time. Both her mother and Paul's, girlhood friends in the Bronx, felt a wife should not work, but family ties loosen up when they are stretched across a continent. "When you see your family a lot they influence you, and you do what's expected of you," Paul explained. "But you find it a lot easier to live your own life when you don't have to answer to them."

At the hospital where she worked Denise got involved with a

"dynamic, free-thinking crowd," many of them unmarried. She decided to go back to school to get a degree in psychology, and when her father's death left her deeply depressed, she entered psychotherapy herself. According to Paul, the therapy transmitted this message: "You have to be selfish. Only if you're good to yourself will you be good to other people. Consequently you should go out and perfect your talents. Otherwise you'll feel that your growth has been stunted, and you'll resent your family for preventing you from doing that."

Paul went along with her plans—she also tried some acting—even when it meant that she was out three or four nights a week and sometimes all weekend. But he mourned the loss of his creature comforts, and his place as undisputed ruler of the household. Neither of them could just jettison the old ways without feeling it.

"A certain amount of resentment builds up," recalled Paul. "Almost unconsciously you find yourself getting teed off, and a sort of iciness starts to develop or some damn thing. The whole situation built up resentment in me, and guilt in her, and we fed on each other."

Lonely at night, Paul started going out, too, leaving the kids with a maid. Hungry for attention, the youngsters turned wild when their parents were around, and the parents blamed each other for the problem. Then about a year and a half ago, Denise got involved with the women's movement, and as Paul remembers the result, "The movement articulated the fact that women have been put down, and that men were selfish bastards. Denise felt trapped because she had married so young and had always been tied to a husband and children. She felt that she had had no chance to do exactly what she wanted, with no responsibility to answer to anyone else. But she felt tremendously guilty about her husband and children, and the logical way to eliminate the guilt was to eliminate the husband."

Meanwhile Paul was having doubts of his own. "As you get older you begin to wonder," said this 35-year-old husband of ten years. "Is this all there is? Am I going to live this way for the next twenty years, or would I be happier with someone else? I started feeling that there's got to be something better."

When Denise decided they should split, Paul was ready. But you do not tear up the past so easily, not when you are a good Catholic girl from the Bronx who thought marriage was forever. The guilt weighed so heavily that Denise committed herself to an institution for three weeks to make the decision. To this day Denise has not told her mother about the break-up. But then her mother is 3000 miles away. She does not have to know.

Elaine met Alex Goldstein on her seventeenth birthday, at her home on Long Island, and despite her parents' objections, she dropped out of college to get married. Alex was in business, and they lived and traveled abroad for a number of years. Skiing in Austria, sailing on the Nile, two "delightful" daughters; "We really had a good life, a normal married life," Elaine remembers.

After settling in Arizona for a while the Goldsteins moved to Southern California, and while the surface of their 27-year marriage remained unruffled, whirlpools swirled beneath. As Elaine recalls one painful moment: "I told him, 'I know I'm getting older, I know I haven't been so great for you, but hang on.' I remember him turning his back and walking out; he didn't want to hear what I was saying."

There was a boss in New York that Alex greatly admired. The man kept a mistress stashed away there for his "business" trips, and Alex's own eyes began to wander. Then Elaine had to go East for six weeks, to take care of her aged mother, and when she returned, her husband "seemed very different."

"He had grown his sideburns, he was wearing mod clothes, he walked differently," Elaine remembers. "Even his driving changed. He used to be very conservative and safe; now he was taking mountain turns on two wheels."

Several weeks later, Alex sat her down and said, "I have fallen in love with Iris, and I want a divorce." Elaine's reaction was "total shock—he was a part of me." Then the doorbell rang. It was a process server with the divorce papers.

Iris was their next-door neighbor, restless in her third marriage, nineteen years younger than Alex, who was now 51. Elaine tried to explain what happened: "Alex was impotent at times; it worried him and it worried me. Here's this gorgeous gal who apparently wanted him, and it does a lot for a man's ego. It was all right for everyone he knew—why not for him? As they all say, 'Live for now, catch it while you can,' and he was looking for someone who would give him a new life, a chance at youth again. I can't say he did the wrong thing, but it's been absolute hell for me. I went in playing by one set of rules," she said sadly, "and now I've been chucked out under another set of rules."

At age 48, Elaine went out and found a job as a librarian. She is coping, but she does not hide her bitterness. "You know what bothers me as much as anything?" she raged. "My memories are ruined. Was he a decent guy all those years, or was he a louse all along?"

An intelligent, well-tailored woman, Elaine Goldstein always considered herself a liberal. In one way, she welcomes many of the changes she sees around her; but in another, she finds them frightening. "Morals are what society says they are," she said. "We're in a state of flux, and that's good, I'm all for the self-examined life. But I don't really think that out-and-out hedonism is right. There's got to be something more than someone trying to satisfy himself. There's got to be a value beyond yourself somewhere, doesn't there? Or is it all just a giant joke?"

"I'm sure when we first married we loved each other," said Lois Gilmore, a 30-year-old newspaper editor. "But I changed a whole lot, and Andrew didn't change all that much. He wanted all those old things, like me to stay home and have children. But the longer I kept working, and the more I liked working, then I realized I didn't want to stay home."

At first, Lois wanted a lot of the "old things," too, like security. She had met Andrew while she was still a student in Missouri and looked him up in New York several years later. They began dating—she was a cub reporter, he an investment analyst—and she hoped he would "save" her from the "miserable" life of singlehood.

Besides, marriage was the only model she had ever known. "I was really dumb, I really was," Lois confessed. "I grew up in a small town where I never knew such a thing as an older unmarried person; everybody got married or there was something wrong with you. I'd never met anybody who was a career woman."

Andrew's pursuit of better jobs took them hopscotching across the country, and the small-town girl from Iowa began to rebel. For one thing, Lois felt that Andrew was "infringing" on her life, forcing her to leave good jobs and good friends. For another, she felt that as a substantial wage earner, she should have more say over the family finances. The traditional wifely role, the "old things," weighed heavily on Lois Gilmore.

"Andrew was a very strong person, and if anything, I was a weak person when we got married," Lois recalled. "And for whatever reason, I got stronger and ended up a very strong person, too. I finally decided, screw trying to please him. I think for two or three years into the marriage I was willing to please him and I thought that was the way you were supposed to do things—that's what wives did. And here I was being crazy and liking my job and enjoying going to work instead of staying home and cooking pot roasts. So in effect, he was married to a stranger, and he didn't like me as well as the person he'd married."

The final break came after Lois joined the Los Angeles chapter of the National Organization for Women and started attending consciousness-raising sessions. She had gotten married in 1968, a "long time ago in terms of women," as she put it. And the group gave support to her new feelings. As she recalls, "You find—at least I found—that all those crazy feelings that you have, that you sort of feel guilty about, are really nothing to feel guilty about. Like the feeling of wanting to be your own person and make decisions about your life yourself. So in the Women's Liberation movement I got support from other people who felt that way, and to that degree, I didn't feel like such a weird person."

Many of the women she met were single and they convinced her that it was "not so bad" to be unmarried these days. They gave her courage, and she remembers thinking, "If they can do that, then why am I living in a situation I'm not happy with?"

Things were not "miserable" with Andrew, Lois said. But toward the end "it was just blah. We were like roommates, living together." Blah was not good enough. One day she said to her husband, "Well, somebody's got to do it." And she moved out.

1974

Swinging Singles—
Lonely Is the Word

Los Angeles

Steven Rabin is 26 but he looks older. His dark hair is thinning, his face is thickening, his heavy glasses keep slipping down the bridge of his nose. He wears brown suits and white shirts appropriate to his job as an assistant cashier for a large life insurance company.

Steven Rabin does not exactly fit the image of the "swinging single." But one evening recently he somewhat hesitantly sipped a glass of complimentary champagne and signed the lease for an apartment in a South Bay Club, where, he was assured by a colorful brochure, "the fun is."

The South Bay Clubs are a string of nine garden-apartment complexes in California limited to single people between the ages of 21 and 40, but they sometimes seem more like cruise ships. Each attractive, if unimaginative, complex contains a staggering array of facilities, from pools to tennis courts to men's and women's gyms, and a full-time social director.

The clubs represent a new way of life for young singles on the West Coast, and the trend is likely to spread. Ten more South Bay Clubs are under construction, including one in Phoenix, Arizona, and dozens more are planned for such cities as Houston, Dallas, and Washington.

When a resident gets married he is required to leave. But two clubs exclusively for young marrieds—without children, which is almost an obscene word around South Bay—are going up right across the street from existing singles clubs. Long-range plans include special resorts, at a ski area or a famous beach, just for the use of South Bay residents from around the country.

Land costs would make it impossible to provide such luxurious facilities in the middle of a city like New York. But in Manhattan, singles already congregate in many of the new apartment buildings on the East Side, using local bars as their party rooms and Central Park for athletics. Why these clubs have flourished tells something about the attitudes and life-styles of the young people they serve.

Steven grew up in Cincinnati and attended college there. He started working in Chicago and was transferred to Denver and then to Los Angeles in less than two years. A few distant relatives were his only contacts when he moved here. "This seems like a friendly place," he said, as the social director poured another glass of champagne. "In Chicago I lived in the kind of building where you never knew who lived next door. Here you can come downstairs and find someone to talk to or spend the evening with. With my personality I need that. Unless I'm forced into something I could sit home forever." Asked how he met people in Chicago, Steven said softly, "You didn't."

Life in Los Angeles can be even more difficult, especially for the shy newcomer. There are no central business districts, and no built-up apartment areas where young people gravitate. Practically everyone is from someplace else—often someplace quite far—and few have relatives or school friends to fall back on. "They're all strangers in some way," said Ludmilla Anderson, the bubbly manager of the Mid-Wilshire South Bay Club, a new addition to the chain near what passes for downtown in Los Angeles.

It is not surprising that the Sunday newspapers here regularly advertise more than a dozen matchmaking services, based on the assumption that "the art of loving is in all of us . . . but a lasting love often eludes us, for it must have the right person."

Even for the socially adept young person, the bars and beach resorts where singles usually meet can prove frustrating, and even a bit dangerous.

Doran Christie, a pixieish, dark-eyed girl from Bernardsville, New Jersey, drove to California with a girl friend last fall after graduating from Kent State University in Ohio (and was surprised when her mother did not object). She described one local meeting place this way: "Manhattan Beach is a big place to meet guys, but you're going to be picked up—that's why you're there. I don't go for that. I have nothing against meeting people in bars, but they're usually so packed you can't carry on a conversation.

"You have no idea what it's like. All you do is shout at each other over the noise, and if you leave together, you know nothing about each other. Everyone is always putting on airs, trying to impress each other. You never get down to the essentials of the kind of people you are."

Doran and her roommate, Maryann Leonhardt, were playing pool together one evening. Unattached residents casually wandered in and out of the brightly lit room. Several men stopped by and chatted; a few gave advice on how to hold a pool cue. "This is a more relaxed atmosphere," said Doran. "You can be friends with people here. Also you know they're not married," she added with a grin. "They might be divorced with seven kids but they're not married."

Friendships have a way of ripening. Most clubs average several marriages a month, and the party room is usually booked far in advance for Saturday afternoon wedding receptions.

The people at South Bay Clubs represent a definite type. Most are neither clods nor swingers, and certainly not eccentrics. They make an average of more than $8,000 a year as computer programmers and schoolteachers, stockbrokers and secretaries. (The rents start at $150 and run up to $310 for two bedrooms.) Few have long hair or black skin.

The cultural high point of one week recently was a movie, *King Solomon's Mines,* sandwiched in between various bowling, bridge, and billiard tournaments. Most residents think grass is what grows next to the tennis courts, and political radicalism is about as popular as Zen Buddhism.

South Bay Clubs basically are pretty straight places. As Howard Ruby, one of the youthful owners of the enterprise put it, "This is the other America you don't hear about. It's clean-cut people who don't wear sandals and beards—guys and girls living very normal lives. It's almost blasphemous how American it is."

South Bay Clubs reflect desires of a mobile, affluent, independent generation—as well as the annoyances of urban living. "To get to the beach you have to get in a car and drive two hours on the freeways," said Maryann Leonhardt. "Here you have everything in your backyard."

It's a life-style that grows on you. Mrs. Anderson recently received a call from a former resident who was splitting up with his wife and wanted an apartment. Several days later she received another call. "Could you hold the apartment a few days?" he pleaded. "I'm going back to my wife, but I want the apartment if it doesn't work out."

To those who cherish the variety and vitality of urban life, who like to live near children and old people, who will trade inconveniences for charm, the South Bay Clubs seem sterile. "It reminds me of my dorm back at school," said one disgruntled resident, as she sipped a beer and sat near the pool in a flowered bikini. "Or some fancy motel."

But South Bay Clubs answer a need, and they know it. As Bill Lee, a

28-year-old computer programmer from Alabama put it, "Lonely is the word to describe a lot of people here."

1969

THE CHARLES MANSON PHENOMENON

Charles Manson and his followers were ultimately convicted for the Tate-La Bianca murders and are now in jail. Manson himself was on Death Row for a while but was moved back into the general prison population after the Supreme Court ruled against the death penalty. Several of his acolytes who escaped the law, including Sandra Good, spent months sitting outside the Los Angeles County Hall of Justice, waiting for the release of the messiah, but I have lost track of them recently.

Of all the stories I did in California, the one that I remember most vividly is "One Man's Family." It is important to understand why that pathetic little band called itself "the family," what they had missed, and what they were looking for. For all of his hideous perversions, Charlie Manson made his girls believe in themselves, and that is something their parents seldom did. I kept thinking about those girls as I read about Patricia Hearst and the Symbionese Liberation Army. Patty and Sandy, Charlie and Cinque. They represent the same horrors, and ask the same questions.

One Man's Family

"Neither repented they of their murders, nor of their sorceries, nor of their fornication, nor of their thefts."

—Revelation, ix, 21.

"Why don't we do it in the road?"

—The Beatles.

Los Angeles

The day had been soft and bright, the sort of glistening Saturday that fills the beaches and the tennis courts and the gardens of Southern California with ruthlessly robust, pleasure-pursuing multitudes. In midmorning, police were called to an isolated, expensive home on Cielo Drive, back in the wooded hills above Hollywood. What they found was a scene of unimaginable horror: Five people had been brutally murdered, including Sharon Tate, a stunning blond film actress who was eight-and-a-half months pregnant. The word "pig" had been scrawled in blood on the front door.

Terror streaked through the beaches and the tennis courts, clawing at the August sun. Angelenos feverishly bought guns and watchdogs, private police and burglar alarms, and behind their padlocked doors they traded theories and rumors about the murders with morbid fascination.

Meanwhile, Hollywood carried on. The victims were buried with the obligatory number of weeping movie stars and harassed press agents in attendance. Screen director Roman Polanski, Miss Tate's husband, called a press conference to defend his wife's reputation and say that her unborn baby "had been her greatest picture." Before leaving, he found time to pose for magazine photographs in their blood-stained living room.

But even Polanski's performance could not still the rumors: The murderer was a drug pusher, a victim of past sexual abuses, "rough trade" picked up on Sunset Strip for fun and games, a friend who had freaked out on speed and turned violent. All the stories had a common thread—that somehow the victims had brought the murder on themselves, that they were responsible for the violence. The attitude was summed up in the epigram, "Live freaky, die freaky."

For months, police made little headway. They announced the discovery of a "major" clue—a pair of eyeglasses that limited the suspects to several million myopic men with bullet-shaped heads. Then they started hearing rumors about a roving "family" of young people—mostly of middle- or upper-middle-class background, slavishly devoted to a bearded guru—who had been arrested in the desert near Death Valley for stealing cars. A member of a motorcycle gang gave the police some leads, and then one of the girls who had been arrested in the desert, Susan Denise Atkins, told a cellmate about the band's lethal activities.

On December 1, police announced they had issued warrants for the arrest of three young people: Linda Kasabian, 20, Patricia Krenwinkel, 21, and Charles (Tex) Watson, 24. A week later, a grand jury, after deliberating for twenty minutes, indicted the three, plus Miss Atkins and Charles Manson, the 35-year-old leader of the nomads, for the Tate murders. They also indicted the five, plus Leslie Van Houten, 19, for the murder of Leno and Rosemary La Bianca, wealthy grocery-store owners, who had been killed the day after Miss Tate and her friends.

The arrests evoked a new surge of public panic. Suddenly, all the rumors appeared to be wrong. A national magazine had to scrap a feature detailing twenty theories about the Tate murders: According to Miss Atkins, the killers did not even know who their victims were; the deaths were arbitrary, random. Dying "freaky" could happen to anyone.

The police are convinced that Miss Atkins is telling the truth, since she is supposed to know details only the murderers could have known. Her explanation of the motive behind the crimes, however, remains murky. Manson ordered his followers to commit the murders, she said in a copyrighted newspaper article, "to instill fear in man himself, man, the Establishment." The Tate house was chosen because a previous occupant, Terry Melcher, a record producer and the son of Doris Day, had not kept a promise to help Manson get a recording contract. At another point, Miss Atkins said the group hoped to foment a race war between blacks and whites.

Whether Miss Atkins is telling the truth, and whether Charlie Manson and his "family" did commit murder, is a question that can be answered only after what is likely to be a lengthy and highly publicized trial. (The pretrial publicity has been so extensive that the judge has ordered all principals not to make any public comments that might prejudice a jury.) But what cannot be denied is the existence of Manson and his strange family of wandering young people. Living on the fringes of a hostile society, they posed just by their presence a basic challenge to the values and institutions of their parents. Where did they come from? What were they like? What road did they travel to that crowded courtroom in which a nervous assistant district attorney formally told them that they were charged with murder?

The most compelling, but in some ways the most understandable, member of the family is Manson himself, a man whose life stands as a monument to parental neglect and the failure of the public correctional system. Charles Milles Manson was born in Cincinnati on November 11, 1934, the son of a teen-age prostitute named Kathleen Maddox and one of her boyfriends, a man remembered only as "Colonel Scott." In order to give her child a name, the pregnant girl had married William Manson, an older man who quickly left the scene. In 1939, Mrs. Manson was arrested for robbery, and the boy was sent to live with his grandmother and an aunt near Wheeling, West Virginia. Charles later remembered his aunt as a "harsh disciplinarian," but his uncle secretly gave him money for the movies and took him on hunting and fishing trips. When the uncle became ill with tuberculosis, Mrs. Manson, then out of jail, reclaimed her son and moved to Indianapolis.

Mrs. Manson recalled in later years that people fell in love with her personable little boy. She promised herself to provide him with a good home, but every vow was soon broken by liquor and men. She would put him to bed, say she was only going out for an hour, and then leave him all night by himself. When the remorse flooded in, she gave the child 50 cents and yet another promise. At other times, she abused him.

Mrs. Manson tried to place Charlie in a foster home, but the arrangements fell through. Then she sent him to the Gibault School in Terre Haute, a boys' school run by Catholic priests. She could not keep up the payments, however, and Charlie came home, but not for long. "I didn't want to stay where mother lived in sin," he told juvenile authorities. Only 14, he rented his own room, and supported himself with odd jobs and petty thievery. His mother turned him in to the city's juvenile center, where he met the Reverend George Powers, a Catholic priest. "This particular boy seemed very lonesome, just craving attention and affection," recalled Father Powers, who arranged for Charlie to go to Boys Town, near Omaha, Nebraska.

Even then, the youth displayed one of his marked adult traits, a charismatic personality. "He was a beautiful kid for his age, a warm and friendly boy; he won everybody over," the priest remembered. ("Charlie had to be persuasive," a friend said recently; "it was the only way he could survive. Otherwise, he would have been dead long ago.")

Charlie stayed a total of three days in Boys Town before running away with an accomplice named Blackie Nielson. The pair were arrested for robbing a grocery store in Peoria, Illinois, and when he was returned to Indianapolis, Charlie was sent to the Indiana Boys School in Plainfield. He ran away eighteen times before he was arrested in Beaver City, Utah, for stealing a car. He wound up in the National Training School for Boys in Washington, D.C.

After his release in 1954, Charlie went back to West Virginia and within months married a local girl, Rosalie Jean Willis. She became pregnant, and he started stealing cars. By the time the baby was born, Manson was in jail in Los Angeles.

Rosalie moved to California to be near her husband. Kathleen Manson displayed an uncommon streak of maternal sympathy and came to help care for her grandchild. But by the time Charlie was released in August, 1958, his wife and mother had gone, leaving him alone again. Several arrests for car theft and pimping followed; in 1960, he was convicted of forging government checks and was given a ten-year sentence. During his stay in McNeil Island Penitentiary in the state of Washington, Manson dabbled in philosophy, took up the guitar, and taught himself to sing and compose songs. As a habitual probation violator, he was not eligible for parole, and served seven years until his release in March, 1967.

The long stretch had left its mark. "If Charlie has any roots, it is in the penal system," said one acquaintance. "Inside, you have to be aware of everything, and when he came out, Charlie was like a cat. Nothing got by Charlie. If something happened within 100 miles of him, he made sure he knew about it. Every time he came into a room, he cased it, like an animal.

Where were the windows? What was the quickest way out? He never sat with his back to the door." A man who served ten years himself said, "I knew lots of guys like Charlie in jail—little magicians with eyes that really psych you out. Doing time strengthens you, you know. You learn how much you can take and how much you can give."

Soon after his release, Manson made his way to Haight-Ashbury, the district in San Francisco where the hippie movement was in brief, bright flower. The true hippies, the gentle folk who believed in peace and love and sharing with others, who had some sense of themselves and their direction, were like a primitive African tribe suddenly exposed to civilization. As the news media spread their story, the hippies were quickly overwhelmed by runaway teeny-boppers, motorcycle gangs, and a wide variety of mentally deranged types who found their openness all too inviting.

Manson's probation officer remembers he was "shaken" by the friendliness of the natives—but, before long, he learned how to exploit it. A slight man, about 5-foot-7, with chestnut hair and burning eyes, Manson started to collect a harem of young, impressionable girls who had fled to the Haight in search of the community of love advertised by the press and TV. A guitar, a pleasant voice, a boyish smile, sinuous mannerisms, a smooth line of talk—these were the ingredients of Manson's appeal.

"He was magnetic. His motions were like magic, it seemed like," said one of his girls. Susan Atkins recalled, "One day, a little man came in with a guitar and started singing for a group of us. . . . Even before I saw him, while I was still in the kitchen, his voice just hypnotized me—mesmerized me. Then when I saw him, I fell absolutely in love with him." One observer of Manson's courtships said, "You either hated Charlie or had a strong attraction to him. He cut right to it; he cut through the pitter-patter. It was sex, and the women knew it; there was no foreplay involved."

To his girls, Charlie Manson was a "beautiful man" who "loved us all totally." To many outsiders, he was a relentless recruiter who came on very strong with every girl he met, a cynic who treated his harem like possessions and seldom showed any real affection. "In a way, he was very frank and truthful," a close friend explained, "but in a way he was very treacherous with his words—there was no meaning behind them."

To Dr. David Smith, the founder and director of the Haight-Ashbury Free Clinic, these two sides of Charlie Manson were not really contradictory: "To take one example, if you get to know any paranoid schizophrenics it won't puzzle you at all. The schizophrenic usually believes in a mystical system in which he is right, and he can plan in the most calculating and cunning way possible. He himself does not really know whether he is a con man, or whether he really does love the girls. He vacillates between one emotion and the other; one of the characteristics of a schizoid personality is the inability to sustain one emotion. It doesn't confuse me that he would be able to convey sincere emotion and carry on in a very plotting way. Of course, he would hide the cunning side as much as possible from those he wanted to involve in his system."

As the Haight was increasingly taken over by the hard-dope pushers, the psychotics, and the rapists, Charlie packed his crew into a converted school bus and headed south in the spring of 1968. The group of fourteen—nine girls and five boys—were arrested near Oxnard for sleeping nude in a field; one of the girls, the mother of a newborn infant, was also charged with endangering the health of a child. But the charges were dropped when the group agreed to leave Ventura County.

Once in Los Angeles, they "crashed" in Topanga Canyon, originally a haven for many stable hippies, which, like the Haight, has been overrun with itinerant panhandlers. For a while, the group lived with Gary Hinman, a musician, in his Topanga home (Hinman was found dead last July, and Susan Atkins and another family member, Robert Beausoleil, have been charged with the murder). Then one of the girls met Dennis Wilson, a member of the Beach Boys singing group, who invited the family to stay in his luxurious home in Pacific Palisades. But Wilson never quite gave in to Manson's demands for total loyalty and the family left after several months.

They finally settled at Spahn's Ranch, an old movie set in the craggy, desolate Santa Susana Mountains, just north of the San Fernando Valley. The ranch's owner, 83-year-old George Spahn, was blind and feeble and desperately afraid of Manson. But he also liked the attention of the girls, who cooked and cleaned for him, and the group was allowed to stay. The family lived at the ranch for about a year, leaving this fall after deputy sheriffs staged several raids, looking for stolen cars and motorcycles. It was then that they decamped for the desert, where they made their last home before the arrests in October.

Once Manson succeeded in making recruits, he tried to eradicate their "hang-ups" about conventional society. By "hang-ups," he essentially meant anything he did not like, and their removal was not a very difficult process. He was dealing with lonely, insecure people in need of a father figure, people who did not have much ego to begin with. What he did, in effect, was to tear down that ego and substitute himself, thus achieving enormous control over his followers. They became empty vessels for whatever he poured in. As Susan Atkins said bleakly, "I never questioned what Charlie said. I just did it."

Probably the major hang-up most girls brought to the group was sex. But Charlie was so persuasive, and so brutal when necessary, that any girl who stayed quickly accepted the idea of having sex with him, or any other member of the group, on demand. He preached that women should be totally submissive to men, an idea he put into a song that was recorded by the Beach Boys. Charlie's title for the song was "Cease to Resist," and although the Beach Boys changed it to "Never Learn Not to Love," they kept this lyric: "Submission is a gift, give it to your lover." Recurring throughout the song is a pleading, wailing voice singing, "I'm your kind, I'm your kind, I'm your kind."

Once he controlled the girls, Manson was able to use them in his ceaseless pursuit of new acolytes. "The women around the place were always his property," recalled one boy who lived at Spahn's Ranch. "You were always welcome to share them, but then you became his property, too." Charlie's technique, another acquaintance said, was "to put you under some obligation and then milk it dry." Four or five boys became somewhat permanent members of the family, but those with some measure of self-confidence resented Charlie's desire for total mastery and drifted away.

The girls were offered to visitors who were in a position to help Manson, as well as ranch hands at Spahn's (at least one cowboy who accepted the gift ended up with venereal disease). Sometimes, one of the girls recalled, "Charlie had to chase guys away and remind them we weren't running a whore house." But Sandra Good, one of the few family members not in jail, found nothing wrong with the arrangements. "If a guy wanted to use women, or play power games, the girls said, 'Uh, uh,'" she said. "Charlie treated us right; he loved us totally. And the fellows in the family were supergentle and right with the girls. They loved us; they didn't use us. And there aren't too many men like that."

Manson's ability to "psych people out" and discern their hang-ups was so acute that some of his disciples believed he could read minds. "He could play any role you wanted him to—a father, a lover, a little boy, anything," said Sandy Good. A man who was close to Manson for several months added, "Charlie was a man of a thousand faces; he had a different one for everybody. That's why he didn't grow a beard for so long: He felt it would reduce his ability to communicate with people."

Manson knew what to say to make people feel good, to bring them out of themselves. Sharon Rayfield, a girl who lived near the Spahn Ranch and rode horses there, said, "I always thought I was ugly, but Charlie made me feel beautiful." Another girl recalled the time when the family was having one of its frequent songfests. The girl was "playing inhibited" and refusing to join in, convinced she could not sing. Charlie sat down next to her and yelled at her to sing. "I started to cry," she recalled, "but after he yelled a few more times I finally started to sing. It was a tremendous relief. It was what I had always wanted to do, but I didn't have the nerve. I was just making myself miserable by not singing."

Then there is the story about Dean Morehouse, a former Methodist minister who met Manson in San Jose several years ago. Manson gave Morehouse his first LSD and the two became friends—until Manson ran off with Morehouse's beautiful 15-year-old daughter (who remained a member of the family to the end). Morehouse and another man, who had given Manson a Volkswagen bus, took off after the family. After three days, they found them near Los Angeles; Morehouse approached Manson, burning with fury. "You're just angry because you want to do to your daughter what I'm doing," Manson told the irate father.

"Then he told me he loved me, and all the girls said, 'We love you, Dean,' and I realized I was angry only because of my own hang-ups," recalled Morehouse, who is now in state prison for giving LSD to minors. Several months later, Morehouse returned to Los Angeles and found the family living at Dennis Wilson's house. "Charlie said I would be a prophet," said Morehouse, who wants to start his own sect, The Universal Order of Metaphysics, when he gets out of jail. "Then he said to Dennis, 'Isn't Dean beautiful?' and he got down and kissed my feet."

Manson was adept at picking up and playing on the dissatisfactions of his followers. One of his favorite lines was, "People spend too much time worrying about the moon and not enough making love." He gloried in nature and denounced the evils of urban life. A man who lived with the family for a while said, "Charlie's ability to speak was really something. He could point to a black wall and say it was white and you would almost believe it. Anyone with some intelligence can point out the wrongs in society, and if he can talk convincingly, he can attract a following. I remember he used to say that giving acid to kids was no worse than sending them to military school, and that made sense, even to me.

"He once took me out to a new housing tract in Chatsworth, near the ranch. It was all finished, but no people had moved in. We got out and walked around. He asked me what the place reminded me of, and I knew right away—a graveyard. That is what he was against—stone-cold, ugly houses. It was just horrible. I'm sure he took other people there; it was all very effective."

Fantasy always played a large role in the life of the family. They were frequent users of LSD, when they could get it, but often their fantasies took the form of childish games. "When we were at the ranch, we would play cowboy and cowgirl, and talk Okie talk to each other," said Sandy Good. "Out there in the mountains, we became mountain folk and the city people were the flatland foreigners. Sometimes, we'd put on long dresses and play like it was a long time ago, back in the pioneer days."

To get to the Spahn Ranch from Los Angeles, you drive through the western end of the San Fernando Valley, a farming area before World War II that now harbors more gasoline pumps than orange trees. Huge signs proclaim the virtues of new housing tracts with names like Vista Del Norte and Hidden Lake. But when you climb off the valley floor and into the hills, you cross into a different world.

The Spahn Ranch, a cluster of dilapidated buildings arranged like a Western street, complete with board sidewalk, is still used occasionally for B-minus movies, but most of its meager income comes from renting horses to day-riders or movie companies. The family squatted where it could—in the jail and the saloon on the movie set, in an old bunkhouse back in the woods, or outside during the warm months.

They foraged for food in garbage cans—they once startled a grocery-store owner by collecting refuse in Dennis Wilson's Rolls-Royce—and ate huge communal meals cooked by the girls. They shared the few clothes they had, when they bothered with them at all. Manson hated the hang-up of material possessions and his attitude permeated the group.

But he also used possessions, as he used the girls, to win over recruits. A master of the dramatic gesture, he once gave a new boy his favorite shirt and told him to defecate on it. "It took away the ego thing the kid had," Morehouse recalled. When Sandy Good joined the family, another girl gave her a beautiful ring that had once belonged to the girl's grandmother. "Isn't that expensive?" Sandy asked. "What does expensive mean?" the girl replied.

People often gave the family presents, and the family was not above asking for them. One day, several of the girls were hitchhiking to the beach. They started talking to the man who picked them up, and one of the girls said, "Can we have your car?" The man, somewhat flustered, said he had an old Studebaker with a busted transmission that did not run. The girls asked him for the keys, and one of the boys, an expert mechanic, put the car back in working order. One girl gave Manson $5,000 she had in stocks, and another donated $10,000; a third girl is said to have stolen $5,000 from friends on Manson's orders.

But Charlie was also generous with what he had. He gave Dean Morehouse money to meet some overdue car payments, and George Spahn enough to cover taxes and a horse-feed bill. Manson also donated $2,000 to the Fountain of the World, a religious retreat near the Spahn Ranch where the family occasionally went for meals and Saturday evening musical shows. "Charlie didn't want any physical possessions," Morehouse insisted. "The only thing Charlie wanted was people—and their souls. He wanted to deliver their souls."

As time went on, Charlie seemed to consider himself something of a prophet and even a savior. He preached an eclectic and confused doctrine that all people are one person and part of God. "I am Charlie and Charlie is me," is a line used by many of his followers. In this sense, Manson maintained, there can be no death, since the oneness of God endures. Indeed, he considered all things part of an inseparable whole. One day, walking through the woods, he picked up a stick and started stroking it. "That is making love," he said. Another time, one of his girls was collecting brightly colored stones in the desert and he handed her a plain gray one. "Take this one, too," he said. "This is just as beautiful as the others."

Doctors familiar with paranoid schizophrenics and habitual users of LSD—who often share similar symptoms—find many of Manson's attitudes quite understandable. Such people, they point out, find it difficult to distinguish between fantasy and reality and have delusions about their own grandeur. Moreover, an LSD trip makes a person aware of a consciousness apart from his physical body, and imparts a feeling of oneness with the universe. This experience, the doctors believe, could lead a person to believe there really is no death.

In the past eight months or so, people detected a change in Charlie Manson. While he could be loving and warm with his followers, he could explode with anger at those who crossed him. George Spahn recalls having a fierce argument with Charlie because the family's motorcycles were scaring the horses. When Spahn finally called the police, Charlie hid outside. After they left, he came back screaming. "He said, 'Open your eyes, you goddamn son of a bitch. You're a liar: You really can see,' " Spahn recalled, sitting in a fly-covered ranch house littered with dogs and Western saddles. "He called me every foul name you could think of and made me say over and over, 'I can see, I can see.' He held me hostage the better part of an hour. Every once in a while, he'd throw a fist past my eyes, thinking I would blink. Then he threatened to cut my throat. Finally, he sat down and got real quiet. There were two girls with him, I think, and he never said a word. That got me even more scared than before. I don't know much about dope, but they had to be full of it; they were shaking and shaking, like a horse does before he dies. Then, before they left, Charlie said, 'George, I love you.' "

Charlie's control over the group grew more rigid and intolerant. "You were either for him or against him," recalled one friend, and Susan Atkins has said, "We belonged to Charlie, not to ourselves." Friends of the family noticed a vacant passivity in some of the most avid followers. Clem Tufts, one of the boys, once took Dennis Wilson's Ferrari for a joy ride and smashed it up. When he returned, unhurt, and was asked why he had taken the car, Tufts just shrugged and said: "I wanted to see how fast it could take a curve."

Manson was not satisfied with preaching to his small circle of disciples He wanted to carry his message to the world and he deeply admired the Beatles for their influence on young people. He even had a fantasy that he would some day meet the Beatles and they would greet him as a comrade. The main reason he wanted to get a recording contract was not for the money, but for the chance to make new converts. (Manson apparently has some musical talent and some tapes he made of his own songs may now be put into an album.)

Susan Atkins has testified that Manson was angry with Terry Melcher for not helping him get such a contract, but Charlie's hatred of the Establishment went much deeper than that. Juan Flynn, a ranch hand at Spahn's, put it this way: "He got stepped on quite a few times, and when he cried out, no one paid any attention. You have to live at the bottom in order to know who's stepping on you. Charlie often said he wasn't successful to the Establishment, but he felt he was successful to himself in love."

Manson's feelings about society showed in his attitude toward children. He often preached that the power structure corrupted young minds, and he urged his girls to have babies they could raise in their own way. At least four of the girls did have babies, including Sandy Good, who was feeding her three-month-old son, Ivan, as she talked: "In the city, where I was before I met the family, everyone was having abortions. The first girl I met in the family was pregnant and she wasn't married, but she was happy about it. Babies are perfect, if you don't let them grow up with all that garbage in their heads. They're total love. If you don't teach them that certain things are wrong or dirty, they'll have a pure mind."

Recently, Manson's resentment against the Establishment began to blend with a growing phobia about Negroes, particularly the Black Panthers. He claimed that he had been beaten up by a group of Panthers and that they were coming to the ranch to kill him. He believed in the law of karma, the Eastern religious idea that all events come in cycles and have previous causes—and he was convinced that the black man would revolt and oppress the white man in the way that whites had previously oppressed the blacks. And he saw the signs of the coming revolt in a rather unlikely place—an album recorded by the Beatles.

A song called "Blackbird," he believed, was really referring to black militants as it described a crippled creature whose time had come. He theorized that in "Helter-Skelter" the Beatles were actually describing the coming race war when they sang of an undefined upheaval about to occur. And to Charlie, the song "Revolution 9," a lengthy cacophony of odd sounds and snippets, was pointing to the ninth chapter of the Book of Revelation. That chapter describes an angel who unleashed "locusts upon the earth: and unto them was given power, as the scorpions of the earth have power." The locusts were commanded to harm "only those men which have not the seal of God in their foreheads."

Manson's fear of the blacks drove him to start collecting cars—the family has been charged with stealing some of them—and converting them into dune buggies. He believed that his group could survive the revolution in the desert if properly prepared, and might become the last link to white civilization. The girls sewed clothes designed for rugged desert life. Guns started appearing at the ranch and the men frequently took target practice. Guards were posted. A girl remembers dropping someone off at the ranch at 2 A.M., and being greeted by a menacing machine gun.

Escape routes to the desert were plotted. Caches of gasoline and other necessities were buried all over the Death Valley area. Charlie tried to recruit some motorcycle types to act as guards but was unsuccessful.

Shortly after the Tate murders, police raided the Spahn Ranch looking for stolen vehicles, and a week later Charlie decided to get out. He led his followers to the deserted Barker Ranch near Death Valley, the place where he wanted to make his last stand and where he was ultimately arrested, despite an elaborate look-out system complete with walkie-talkies.

The inevitable question remains, however: Why? What caused the void, the terrible emptiness that drove so many young people to Haight-Ashbury, the East Village, and dozens of other places, seeking refuge from the culture of their parents? What is still sending them out into the world, so lost and confused? And what makes these troubled adolescents so vulnerable to spiritual gurus like Charlie Manson?

Manson's family was only part of a much broader phenomenon, but the reasons behind it are neither clear nor easy. Even the sketchy hints that are discernible remain unsatisfactory; many youngsters from backgrounds similar to Charlie's girls' never run away and still think LSD is a college football team. But one factor seems to be the breakdown of the family and the community as structured units in which children can find security, affection, and ideals. This is particularly true in California, where one out of every two marriages ends in divorce, and where the past ends at the eastern slopes of the Sierra Nevada. Here there is only the restless present—new communities sunk no deeper into the earth than a tumbleweed, a personal freedom that is as corrosive as it is liberating, a flailing-about for meaning and identity.

Almost every girl in Charlie Manson's family came from a disrupted home. Susan Atkins was 15 when her mother died and her father left home in San Jose to look for work. When she got into trouble with the police, her father complained that the courts were "too lenient" because they let her out of jail. "She once did some beautiful things," he told a home-town reporter recently, "but that was a long time ago. I don't know what went wrong."

Linda Kasabian's parents were married only briefly, if ever. She grew up in Milford, New Hampshire, and saw her father, a bartender in Miami, only twice in fifteen years. She was married at 16, divorced within months. She had a child by her second husband, who brought her to California and then abandoned her. Now she is pregnant again. "She was ensnared," her lawyer said, "by what she thought was a loving group of hippies." Her mother said when she was arrested, "There is no hate in her, at all. She was searching, searching for love."

Sandra Good is the daughter of a wealthy stockbroker in San Diego who divorced her mother when the girl was 2. Sandra and her brother and sister were sent away to school most of the time. "All my mother cared about was her social climbing," recalled Sandra, a soft, pretty girl with reddish brown hair. "She'd do anything to get in the social column. I was scared of her; I was terrified." After Sandra was arrested in the Death Valley raid, her baby was placed in a foster home, and she asked her father to post bail so she could recover the child. He did so, reluctantly, and she went to live with him when she got out of jail. She stayed a week. "My stepmother had this expensive tea in the house and I kept drinking it, so she hid it," Miss Good said. "My father gave me $200 when I left, and said that was it: He wouldn't give me anymore."

A girl who has lived in the hippie world for years tried to explain the situation this way: "Sure, the girls were obviously weak, but it's not that hard to be fooled, especially if a woman expects to be led by a man. He was offering not just a physical living situation, but sex, a family, everything a woman is looking for. Love is blind, you know." Another girl added, "Women have been falling for the wrong men for years."

But the girls' backgrounds are only part of the story. "We can't be dismissed as uneducated or deprived kids, or the products of tormented childhoods. We're pretty typical. A lot of parents can identify with us as their kids," insisted Sandy Good, who has been cleared of all criminal charges. She is now living with her baby on welfare in a shabby motel room in Independence, California, the little mountain community where some of the girls are still in jail. She hopes, against all odds, that the family can be reunited and will help her raise her baby. She has nowhere else to go.

To support her point, Sandy ticked off the occupations of the girls' fathers: stockbroker, scientist, psychologist, real estate man, insurance salesman, auctioneer, minister. Many of the parents had some college education; so did some of the older girls. One girl with a master's degree had been a librarian. Sandra had been studying marine biology. Leslie Van Houten, a legal secretary, had been a high school homecoming princess. "You can't categorize us," said Sandra, with a look of triumph. "We're going to blow people's minds."

Dr. David Smith believes part of the explanation for the girls' rebellion lies in the state of the society that raised them. "If you're going to believe in the institutions and conventions of a society, then you have to believe in that society, and that is very difficult," said the doctor, who also teaches toxicology at the University of California and recently finished an academic paper on the Manson family. "Things like the Vietnam war and environmental pollution are just as important in adolescent alienation as family background.

"The thing that is different now, as opposed to the thirties, is the instant information environment. There were pollution and graft and unpopular wars years ago, but people didn't find out about them right away. Today, youth gets an instant feedback about what's happening. It makes them question the quality of American life and institutions, and this questioning comes at a very vulnerable period."

There is also a third possible explanation. Simply put, Charlie Manson gave the girls a chance to do something, even if it was only the most rudimentary of tasks. Neither their family lives, nor school, nor their jobs had enabled them to say, "I have accomplished something; I am worth something."

Marx predicted the alienation of the assembly line, but that same sense of incompleteness has permeated many areas of modern life. Perhaps the society needs to provide new rites of passage for the young, new tests and opportunities in which they can earn their adulthood and a higher sense of themselves and their possibilities. As Sandra Good explained her experience, "When I joined the family, I just didn't think I could do anything. But after a while, I made a dress from an old piece of cloth. Then I started cooking without recipes. I got pretty damn creative. I could cook, sew, sing, play the guitar. You don't have to learn; it's in you. You have to believe you can do it, and not be afraid to let it out."

A fourth factor is the yearning to "be simple," to "get back to nature," to escape the "hassle" of city life, of stultifying schoolwork, of the "instant feedback"—news pollution—of crisis and disaster. "I used to think I had to read a million books a day," Sandy said with a smile. "Now, what I want to do is watch the sun come up. When I came into the family, it was like I had walked into a dream. Maybe you get the same feeling on an isolated Greek island. There were no clocks, no radios, no papers, no books."

Whatever the causes, there are thousands of young people just like Charlie's girls who have broken with their families and are looking for a new home and new values. Dr. Smith understands the positive side of their protest, but he also senses a danger. "The second leading cause of death among adolescents is suicide," he declared angrily. "There is an incredible increase in drug use. There is a great rise in things like the hippie subculture and youthful activism. And through it all there is a common thread—the alienation of young people from the central core of American society. Yet the leaders say nothing is different, we don't have to change, we don't have to resolve the alienation of these kids."

Did Charlie Manson and his family commit murder? Only a jury can decide that. Whether or not such a group is *capable* of violence is another matter. Dr. Smith believes the possibility for violence exists in any group in which individuals are totally committed to the righteousness of their leader, and thus give up their own ability to think independently—in other words, the "I was only following orders" syndrome.

"If you set up infant consciousness as an objective [Manson preached that a child's mind, unsullied by society, is perfect], you have to strip away all the social controls you've learned from your parents and society," the doctor said. "You can thus see where the mechanism for violence might come from. If the delusional system turns hostile, and you're committed to whatever your spiritual leader says is right, and he says, 'Kill,' you can kill. I think the mechanism of violence that can operate in these groups is the same as what is indicated by the recent stories from Vietnam. What you do with soldiers is strip away all normal social controls, and you substitute a form of nationalism. Then you get involved in an emotional situation, and if the leader says to shoot women and children, they shoot women and children."

1970

The Tate-Polanski Circle

Los Angeles

A beautiful actress. A hair stylist who was a Hollywood socialite. A Polish emigré. A wealthy young Radcliffe graduate. Four lives whose twisted paths crossed on the night of August 8. They—along with an 18-year-old youth—were murdered in an isolated hilltop home.

The murders remain unsolved, and in the absence of facts, amateur detectives are having a field day. But the savage killings did more than provide local cocktail party chatter. They brought into focus several life-styles—disparate yet connected—that displayed some of the glamour and intrigue that have long fed the Hollywood script mill.

Sharon Tate was 26 when she was murdered, a stunning actress who literally "stopped traffic" the first time she visited New York. At the time of her death, she was eight months pregnant with the child of her husband Roman Polanski, the noted film director, who was in London.

The Polanskis met several years ago while working together on a film. Since then, they had been near the center of a loose group of filmmakers who were described with all the current cliches: mod, hip, swinging, trendy.

This group was not only more youthful but also more international than the Hollywood Establishment. Its members were "rootless vagabonds" as one studio executive put it, at home in a dozen places, and yet belonging nowhere. Their names never appeared on the maps tourists buy on Hollywood Boulevard to find the homes of the stars; they had no homes.

The Polanskis were unusual: they rented a house. Most of their friends lived in apartments and hotels, restaurants and shooting locations, airplanes and steamships. As one successful actor put it, "It's a peculiar thing about movie people. The film industry is not in any one place. It rotates among London and Los Angeles and New York and Paris and Rome. Wherever you are, you always run into the same people."

Yet if the Polanskis and their friends represented a new breed in Hollywood, much remained the same. As one writer said, "There is a lot of talk about the new Hollywood, but it is the same old Hollywood, only it's 1969. It's still the American dream, still the race for money and fame."

Charles Champlin, movie critic of the *Los Angeles Times*, described that Hollywood this way: "The impermanence makes for an edginess, an urgency, an unreality—or, more precisely, for an almost involuntary detachment from the ongoing concerns which move and occupy most mortals. It can make for a particular kind of hedonism: eat, drink and be merry, for tomorrow your agent may not return your calls."

The Polanskis' friends were a diverse group that included such actors as Peter Sellers, Yul Brynner, and Warren Beatty; Michael Sarne, a British director, who made *Joanna*; Simone Hesera, another young director; Dick Sylbert, the art director for *Catch-22*; John Phillips, formerly of the Mamas and the Papas, a singing group; Brian Morris, who once ran a discotheque in London and is opening a new club here; Hatami, a photographer, and Victor Lownes, head of Playboy International.

For the most part they were talented and successful. They made pictures people talked about—*Bonnie and Clyde, Rosemary's Baby, Blow-up*. They were self-indulgent but not very self-centered. They did not especially seek publicity nor care who they were seen with. They were loyal to one another and invested in one another's enterprises. They were handsome and young and free.

"One of the most moving things at Sharon's funeral," said Ruth Gordon, the veteran actress who worked with Mr. Polanski on *Rosemary's Baby*, "were all those adorable girls, all those girls with their long hair and miniskirts."

"We were always out enjoying ourselves, it was always great fun," said Peter Sellers. "If Roman had a premiere in Paris, why we'd all fly over there for it. Or we would have lunch in London and dinner in Copenhagen."

It was revealing that the Polanskis, who also rented a house in London, had decided to raise their baby in California. Like many of their friends, they enjoyed the casual dress, the informal social life, the closeness of the mountains and the deserts and the ocean.

The Polanskis and their friends had money, and they spent it. Their clothes were expensive and stylish—bell-bottom pants, open-necked shirts, wide belts. They liked fast cars (Mr. Polanski drove a red Ferrari) and motorcycles. Skiing vacations in the Alps were almost a ritual. They talked about three-star restaurants in Paris and discotheques in New York with equal facility.

Many of them preferred marijuana to Scotch, but as one of them put it, "So does everybody else these days, this is speakeasy time for pot." Some of them might have dabbled in harder drugs, such as cocaine, but there is a limit when you have to be on a movie set at 7 A.M.

They were more European than American in many ways, especially in regard to sex, which was always plentiful and, actually, rather unimportant.

Mr. Polanski became close friends with his wife's former escort, Jay Sebring, the hair stylist who was murdered with her. The director was devastated by his wife's death, and yet he had made no attempt to hide his friendships with other women.

"We are living in the midst of a sexual revolution, and we are certainly a part of it," said one young actor. "But read *Couples*. They're doing it in Massachusetts, too."

The Polanskis "exuded a warmth and a magnetism people just wanted to be near," said one friend, and their rustic, comfortable house was always open. "There was a constant party," Mr. Polanski recalled at a news conference last week. "There was never a night without friends."

Scattered among the friends were hangers-on, people who thought knowing Mr. Polanski could be useful, and he did not always discourage them. "Roman sometimes seemed to need an entourage," said one acquaintance. "It was rather sad, actually." A Hollywood press agent added, "They never seemed to want to be alone."

There was a constant desire for company and action. When Gene Gutowski, Mr. Polanski's partner in a producing company, rented a villa in Cortina, Italy, last winter, he wound up with seventeen house guests. And Brian Morris designed his new club, Bumbles, to be mainly a gathering place for his friends. "My dream," he said, "is to have Bumbles clubs all over the world and connect them with closed-circuit TV. Then no matter where you were, you could see all your friends any night you wanted."

One outsider who became an accepted member of this Hollywood scene was Jay Sebring. Many top stars were considered his close friends, and he flattered both their hairlines and their egos. When a particularly important man called, Mr. Sebring dropped everything to give him a trim, according to John Madden, his business partner.

A short and slender man, Mr. Sebring drove motorcycles, bought a Porsche, learned karate, and went to auto racing school (his last name he took from a race track in Florida). Beautiful girls were almost a trademark. When he opened his San Francisco shop, Paul Newman went to the party, and when he died, Henry Fonda and Steve McQueen went to the funeral.

There was another life-style illuminated by the violence of August 8, a style that contains another kind of unreality and hedonism. The style is that of the emigré, the Polish emigré in particular, who fled the repression of his homeland and was looking for a new start in iife.

Voyteck Frokowski and his girl friend, Abigail Folger, were killed outside the house where Miss Tate and Mr. Sebring were found. Mr. Frokowski, who knew Mr. Polanski in their student days, left Poland about two years ago and came to America after a brief interlude in Paris.

Bright young Polish intellectuals have left their country and settled here in recent years to form almost an underground railway. "When someone needs something, we all help out," said one writer, "and when someone new comes over we gather the troops for him. Sometimes we have parties on Polish holidays."

When Mr. Frokowski landed in New York he stayed with Jerzy Kosinski, the novelist, whose book, *Steps,* won the National Book Award last year. When he went west, he looked up his old friend, Mr. Polanski, who was probably the best-known of the emigrés.

"Everyone who comes out of Poland tries to latch onto Roman," said Gene Gutowski, another refugee. "They phone up," he said, "and say, 'Do you remember me? Can you help me? Can you write a letter to this person or that person?' It bothers him sometimes, but he is very loyal, and he always helps if he can."

While some of the emigrés were very industrious and successful, others, like Mr. Frokowski, had more of a flair for living than for work. "People here always ask you what you do and how much you make," explained one Pole. "In Europe they never ask you that. Here Frokowski had to make stories up, but he was never routinely employed. He moved in strange ways. He didn't want to do anything but read and see friends and observe."

At the same time there was something "brooding and disturbed" about Mr. Frokowski, and many of his Polish friends, one colleague said. "We belong to a generation which survived the war in a peculiar way and shouldn't have," he said. "We were put on a crooked orbit at the age of 6 or 7 and we have never known what will happen to us and we don't want to know. We mistrust the future, we've seen what happened to people who did trust the future."

Gibby Folger represented yet another way of life. Heiress to a fortune made in the wholesale coffee trade, she attended Catalina School for Girls, had a sumptuous debut and emerged from Radcliffe as a bright, well-educated, and aimless young woman.

She traveled in Europe. She worked in a museum in San Francisco and a bookstore in New York. She campaigned for Robert Kennedy, and she cared for children in Watts. Her relationship with Mr. Frokowski told something about both of them and their friends.

"Gibby was very much alive with Voyteck," said one friend. "He changed her outlook. She realized she didn't have to conform to that damn Protestant ethic. I remember once asking her how she was and she laughed, 'Well, I'm not my old constipated self anymore.'"

1969

PERSONALITIES, LARGE AND SMALL

Mae West was generally panned in *Myra Breckinridge* and has not made another movie since. Her agent told me she hated my piece because I quoted a neighbor saying that she "shuffled" along the beach like an "old lady."

About six months after I interviewed him, Joe Wambaugh quit the police force. One of the main reasons, he said, was that he could no longer do his job effectively. At the time we talked, he was still trying to convince himself that nothing had changed since he had become a celebrity, but finally the fantasy collapsed. *The Onion Field* hit the best-seller lists and received top reviews, as did the TV dramatization of *The Blue Knight* and his *Police Story* series.

Nothing ever went right for Rodger McAfee. His dream of a rock festival to raise money for a socialist cooperative never materialized. Angela Davis even denounced him as a white liberal. I don't know where he is now.

76—And Still Diamond Lil (Mae West)

Hollywood

"I hold records all over the world. That's my ego, breaking records. So don't say they put me in someone else's room." Mae West was not happy. Her soft voice took on a tense shrillness as she continued. "I'd like to see someone break records like that and I'll respect them as a star. 'Till someone can do that, I feel I'm in a class by myself. The only other person I know who could write his own movies and star in them was Chaplin. When I had my act with the muscle men in Las Vegas they gave me a diamond bracelet after a two-week run. When they do that you know you're making money for them. All the notables and big-money people came to see me. Someone else had the Coca-Cola crowd."

The tirade had been triggered by a casual remark that Miss West was getting Barbra Streisand's old dressing room at 20th Century-Fox during the production of *Myra Breckinridge*, Gore Vidal's garden of sexual hybrids. (Miss West is also receiving $350,000, a limousine, and top billing over Raquel Welch.) Mae West is 76. She hasn't made a picture in twenty-six years. But in her own mind she is still a movie star, a reigning sex queen. And she does not like to be compared with another woman, even the fellow Brooklynite who did for the nose what Mae West did for the bust. In some ways Miss West is right. She is still there on *The Late Show*, captured forever in her swirls of feathers and diamonds, purring at a practically pubescent Cary Grant, "Come up and see me sometime." There is no other Mae West. She is an institution, a living legend, as much a part of American folklore as Paul Bunyan or Tom Sawyer or Babe Ruth.

Visiting such an imposing personage can be a bit unnerving; it's a little like having a chat with Cleopatra. My first interview with Mae West was at her apartment, a small place in a slightly shabby Hollywood building, which she rented when she arrived here in 1932 and has kept ever since. The living

room has been described often, but it is still rather startling, all off-white
and gilt, fluffy chairs and sofas, ornate pottery lamps with bare-breasted
maidens playing lutes, bouquets of dusty flowers, a white piano on which
stands a spectacular nude statue of the young Mae West. There are photos
of her swathed in furs and feathers, an oil painting of her swathed in nothing
but light. This is the stage for her performances, and she keeps you waiting,
building up the suspense. When she appears it is in a swirl of pink and green
chiffon, bright yellow hair, false eyelashes blackened with mascara. Only
slight wrinkles at the corners of her mouth and a puffiness in her throat gave
away the secret. She is surprisingly small (about 5 feet 2 inches tall, 124
pounds), despite the famous $43\frac{1}{4}$-inch bust, and soft and feminine. There is
nothing she would rather talk about than her own incredible career.

It started back in Bushwick, a family neighborhood of horse-drawn
carriages and ragtime music, where Mae West was born on August 17, 1893.
From her father, "Battling Jack" West, a man celebrated for his pugilistic
abilities inside and outside the ring, she derived a toughness bordering on
belligerency. From her mother, Matilda Delker Doelger, an occasional
corset and fashion model, she inherited an anatomy rivaling the structural
wonders of the Brooklyn Bridge. She was 7 when she persuaded her dancing
teacher to enter her in an amateur-night contest sponsored by the local Elks.
She was billed as "Baby Mae—Song and Dance," and she got furious when
the spotlight was slow in picking her up. Needless to say, she won the
contest. Soon she found a permanent job in Hal Clarendon's stock company
at the Gotham Theater in East New York. After a dramatic career studded
with such deathless roles as a moonshiner's daughter in the Kentucky hills
and a poor white slave in Chinatown, she turned to vaudeville at the age of
14.

She worked up a song-and-dance routine with a young jazz singer,
Frank Wallace, who, like a good many men, started proposing matrimony.
An older woman on the bill advi. .d Mae that her magnetic properties would
soon cause her trouble and that marriage would make her "respectable." In
1911, at the age of 17, before a judge in Milwaukee, she took marriage vows
for the only time in her life. The vows were hardly compelling—she left
Wallace within months—but they proved resilient; she did not get a divorce
until 1943.

After leaving Wallace she won a featured part in Ned Wayburn's review, *A La Broadway and Hello, Paris.* On opening night she took seven encores and *The New York Times* reported the next morning that "a girl named Mae West, hitherto unknown, pleased by her grotesquerie and a snappy way of singing and dancing." A string of reviews, vaudeville acts, and fleeting romances followed swiftly. In 1918 she was playing opposite Ed Wynn in Rudolf Friml's musical *Sometime,* and one night after a performance in Chicago went slumming to a jazz spot on the South Side. She saw black dancers shake with "a naked, aching, sensual agony" in a dance they called the "shimmy shawobble." The next night, when it came time for an encore she introduced the "shimmy"—eight months before Gilda Grey, who made the dance famous, opened in New York. "She was a good vaudevillian, but she wasn't good enough to play the Palace," recalled Don Prince, the theater's former press agent. "Some genius took her out of second-class vaudeville to first-class Broadway." That genius was her mother. Here is how Mae remembers the story:

"It was 1926, and the Shuberts were looking for a play for me to do. They couldn't find one and my mother said, 'You rewrite all your vaudeville parts, why don't you write your own play?' I had often thought of things, but I was usually too lazy to write them down. This time I didn't want to make a mistake and do something that wasn't right for me, so I sat down and wrote my own play.

"I sent the play over to the Shubert office under the pen name Jane Mast—I didn't want too much Mae West involved. They sent it back—I learned later some girl in the office hadn't even shown it to J. J. Shubert—so my mother said, 'Why don't we produce it ourselves and make all the money?' We gave it to a director, who read it and said, 'My God, this is what Broadway has been waiting for!' We came back from lunch and I said, 'When do we start?' We cast the whole play in a day.

"When we went into rehearsal the director was very excited. He kept saying to me, 'You've got something I've never seen in anyone.' I finally asked him what it was I had. 'You've got a sex quality,' he said in this deep voice, 'a *low* sex quality.' The way he said it, it sounded like the best kind to have. He kept saying the play reeked with sex, sex—he said it so often I began to like the sound of the word. One day I told him I wanted to change the name of the play to *Sex.* Up to that time they only used the word in medical textbooks. He said, 'Oh, my God, if we only dare,' and I said, 'I'll dare.' "

Sex, with Mae West in the role of a waterfront prostitute, opened at

Daly's Theater on April 27. *The Times* review was not exactly ecstatic: "A crude, inept play, cheaply produced and poorly acted." That critic's influence was so great, however, that the play ran for eleven months. In the meantime, its frank sexuality spawned several imitators, and the blue-noses massed their forces. The police raided *Sex* and two other plays and charged the principals with "indecent performances."

Mae West could not have planned things better if she had the most able press agent in New York. She was convicted and spent eight days in the Welfare Island jail. The papers were filled with the cataclysmic news that Miss West's tender skin, so used to silken underwear, was being irritated by the prison's rough cotton garments. She emerged from her incarceration somewhat chafed, perhaps, but a national figure.

Her next play was a study of homosexuality called *The Drag*. She produced it in such theatrical meccas as Paterson, New Jersey, but it was so controversial that it never made New York. Miss West has always been particularly popular with homosexuals, perhaps because in her perpetual opulence she looks a bit like a flashy drag queen. "They're crazy about me because I'm so flamboyant," she said recently. "They love to imitate the things I say and the way I act, and they like the way I move my body."

As her notoriety grew, she wrote and starred in several more plays, including *Diamond Lil*, a musical about a well-kept dance-hall girl on the Bowery of the Gay Nineties. No one accused her of composing great literature, but her performances had a rather stimulating effect on at least one reviewer, who gushed, "So regal is Miss West's manner, so assured is her artistry, so devastating are her charms in the eyes of all red-blooded men, so blonde, so beautiful, so buxom is she that she makes Miss Ethel Barrymore look like the late lamented Mr. Bert Savoy." The play was later rewritten as a novel and became the basis for *She Done Him Wrong*, the biggest hit among Miss West's ten films. It was no accident. *Diamond Lil*, she said in later years, "I'm her and she's me and we're each other."

Broadway was hit hard by the Depression, and in 1932 the talkies lured Mae West to Hollywood. With the typical modesty of the loyal New Yorker, she announced on her arrival, "I'm not a little girl from a little town making good in a big town. I'm a big girl from a big town making good in a little town."

The first Mae West picture was *Night After Night*, a gangster epic starring George Raft. Mae insisted that she write her own dialogue, and her very first scene set the pattern for her film career: As she walked into a saloon festooned with glittering gems the hatcheck girl blurted, "Goodness, what beautiful diamonds." Mae turned and cracked, "Goodness had nothing to do with it." The line became the title of her autobiography. Raft, in his own autobiography, recalled with some displeasure that Miss West "stole everything but the cameras."

The movies displayed a new facet of Mae West; she became a comedienne, almost by accident. "There were a lot of things censors wouldn't let me do in the movies that I had done on the stage," she recalled. "They wouldn't even let me sit on a guy's lap—and I'd been on more laps than a napkin. I had to do something different, so I put in some humor. That way I could get away with more things. I never meant 'Come up and see me sometime' to be so sexy, but I guess I was thinking about sex all the time. I wasn't conscious of being sexy until the censors got after me. It was always natural for me, it was never a strain. I guess that's why it goes over so well."

In her next picture, *She Done Him Wrong*, Mae recreated the role of Diamond Lil, though the name was changed to Lady Lou for the benefit of the ubiquitous, if not very perceptive, censors, who refused to allow a movie based directly on the play. Production was delayed because Paramount Studios didn't have a leading man. Miss West and some executives were walking on the lot one day and spied a handsome young actor. "Who's that?" asked Mae. "His name is Cary Grant," came the answer. "He's never made a picture; we just use him for screen tests." She replied, "If he can talk, I'll take him." Grant met the test and won the lead as an undercover agent posing as a Salvation Army captain.

As the sharp-tongued, mushy-hearted girl friend of a saloon-owning political boss, Mae was in top form. "When women go wrong," she philosophized, "men go right after them." With Grant, the lines whizzed by. "I'm sorry to be taking your time," he said. She looked up with a leer: "What do you think my time is for?" He resisted for the moment, but she sensed a weakness. "You can be had," she snapped; then, in a delightful scene, issued her famous invitation to second-story sensuality. Grant seemed shaken by the proposal, and Mae could only laugh. "Come on up," she repeated, "I'll tell your fortune."

She Done Him Wrong was followed quickly by *I'm No Angel.* In one scene, Mae, upbraided by a wronged wife, ushered the lady out the door and, burdened by boredom and disdain, turned back to the cameras. "Beulah," she called as she sashayed across the screen, "peel me a grape."

The two movies made Mae West very famous and very rich. In 1934 she earned $340,000 and the next year $480,833—it was the second highest salary in the country, exceeded only by that of William Randolph Hearst, who once editorialized, "Isn't it time Congress did something about Mae West?" Her self-assured swagger, her adenoidal and ungrammatical Brooklynese (one of her best lines was "Diamonds is my ca-re-a," and she still says "pernt"), her joyous celebration of sexual delights became known around the world. A grande dame threw a "Mae West party" at the Eiffel Tower that was the social event of the year. The couturiers quickly picked up her style and ladies of fashion were soon dressing in figure-hugging froufrous of the Gay Nineties. Someone called her "the figure that launched a thousand hips." After an appearance on the Edgar Bergen and Charlie McCarthy radio show drew a howl of outrage, NBC paid her the singular compliment of banning her name from their air. Crowds stormed theaters in Vienna protesting her pictures. When she returned to New York for personal appearances, thousands of hysterical fans mobbed her at Penn Station. She entered the dictionary when British airmen used her name for an inflatable life jacket that somewhat resembled her awesome chest. Princeton scientists designed a new magnet in the shape of her torso. Everyone from college boys to women newspaper reporters voted her the most popular actress. A New York newspaper ran a six-part series proclaiming "This Mae Westian Age."

Why was it a Mae Westian Age? "There had been sex sirens before, like Theda Bara, but she was so sexy she was sinister," said Stanley Musgrove, a producer and close friend of Miss West. "They all portrayed sex as a heavy, evil thing. Mae was breezy and humorous. It was the first instance of blatant camp. I don't think she knew what she was doing; it was just there." Miss West described her impact this way in her autobiography: "Women became more sex-conscious, and this, for some men, was a big break; for others, a bother. Sex was out in the open and amusing." The censors and other guardians of public morals did not share in the gaiety, but from Mae West's viewpoint, she had always been something of a put-on. "I make fun of vulgarity," she said. "I kid sex."

In her career, as in her comedy, Mae West showed good timing. "You feel good when you're around her, and that imparts itself on the screen," said Robert Fryer, the producer of *Myra Breckinridge*. "That's why she was such a success in the Depression. She really made people forget their troubles." Douglas Gilbert, writing in the *New York World-Telegram* in 1933, thought Mae West symbolized a revolt against the "modern" woman of emancipated ideas and emaciated shape who had dominated the twenties: "No argument can dislodge her present position. She has given the gate to those proud beauties who once ruled our screen. The great Garbo today is a trifle passé. 'Legs' Dietrich, as she is dubbed in the studios, shakes her slender limbs to apathetic houses. . . . Against Mae's ample bosom figuratively rest the modish aspirations of our girls. Her well-rounded arms encircle a nation's desire for escape from a synthetic life to one of substance and color."

In all of her pictures Mae West played essentially the same character—herself. But sometimes she was like the mirrors in a barbershop: an almost infinite number of images, each reflecting the other, Mae West playing Mae West playing Mae West. The character usually had a big build-up, fancy clothes (often diamonds) and considerable power. She was always the center of attention. She was never a mother or an aunt, seldom a wife, usually an illicit girl friend. "My fans," said Miss West, "expect certain things of me." She wrote virtually all of her own dialogue, and to her it did not matter that the characters were so similar. "It is not what you do," she said many times, in many contexts, "but how you do it."

"Too much of a good thing," she once remarked, "can be wonderful." But gradually the critics and the public began to disagree. As the thirties waned, so did Mae West. Even *My Little Chickadee*, her famous encounter with W. C. Fields (whom she detested for his drunkenness), was panned when it appeared in 1939. One critic saw her final picture, *The Heat's On*, in 1943 and wrote, "The heat is definitely off." After that Mae turned back to the stage. She toured the country in several mediocre plays of her own composition and revived *Diamond Lil* in London and New York; while the crowds were enthusiastic, they seemed interested in her mainly as a historical curiosity. "Like Chinatown and Grant's Tomb," one critic wrote, "Mae West should be seen at least once."

In the mid-fifties she put together a nightclub act that spoofed the girlie shows: eight muscle men in loincloths and Mae, resplendent in her "Diamond Lil" finery, adored by them all. Recently there have been a few television guest shots and several rock 'n' roll record albums, but little else. She received a few movie offers but turned them down. Occasionally the papers announced that she would appear in a new TV series or play, but the projects never seemed to come off.

While her career declined, however, her old films enjoyed a revival among youngsters who were not even born when she made her last picture. When *She Done Him Wrong* and *I'm No Angel* shared a double bill recently in Hollywood, they out-grossed any new picture issued by Universal Studios, which owns her old prints. Part of the reason is the campiness, the outrageous exaggeration—Mae West as a pop poster. Moreover, like Fields and Bogart, she had a flip insolence and self-assurance that appeals to an iconoclastic generation. She is, after all, the woman who said such things as "Good women are no fun. . . . The only good woman I can recall in history was Betsy Ross, and all she ever made was a flag." Arthur Knight, the film critic and historian, feels there is also an element of escapism in her resurgence: "She's part of a whole enthusiasm for the thirties, along with Fields and the Marx Brothers and Bogart. The kids are looking back at a time that seemed freer and easier—no wars or race problems, just nice gangsters. And I think they feel a little guilty about being part of an affluent society. Look at all the jeans and raggedy shirts they wear—it's kind of a do-it-yourself Depression."

Mae West says she is coming back to movies "because my fans have been pleading and demanding for me to come back." Maybe that's true, but there is an element of sadness in it all. Many of her fans seem to be demanding what she was, not what she is. Our idea of glamour has changed radically—indeed, even the word is outmoded. Raquel Welch poses for publicity photos in torn shirts, the grubbier the better; Mae was never photographed in anything but a full-length gown. Movie stars are less important and more realistic today; Mae West was always outsized, larger than life. She is fine as a period piece, rather out of place as a contemporary.

But Mae West feels no pity for herself. She owns considerable real estate (a Hollywood apartment, a beach house in Santa Monica and a ranch in the San Fernando Valley) and a large collection of diamonds (when she wears some of her better stuff the insurance company sends along a guard).

She lives alone, but has the constant attention of Paul Novak, a former muscle man in her nightclub act, who serves as chauffeur, butler, and general handyman. Her private life remains, as always, very private. She has spun a cocoon for herself and nestled inside, largely unaware of and unconcerned about the world.

Her day is very orderly. She gets up late, goes over fan mail, tends to business and personal calls, often rides to her beach house or to the ranch, where her sister, Beverly, now lives. (Most of her fan letters—she gets 200 a week—come from younger people who see her movies on television; a sizable number contain the flowery rhetoric of a rather obvious homosexual. However, one recent letter from a professor at Brown University said he used a collection of her "wit and wisdom" in his English course.) Occasionally, Miss West does some writing, and she has several screen plays finished. She left school at 13 and seldom reads. The architect who designed her beach house once returned for a visit and noticed that she had ripped out a set of bookcases. "They look pretty silly without books," she explained.

In the evening she occasionally goes to a movie or has dinner with such friends as George Cukor, the director, or Robert Wise, who is producing a TV special for her. (Though many of her pictures were set in saloons, Miss West has always disliked liquor. As a young girl she sampled some strong spirits and had a bad fight with her mother, whom she adored; the morning after she swore off booze.) Several years ago, Cukor arranged a dinner party at which he introduced Garbo and West to each other. Mae, who is often nervous around other women, was apprehensive as the time approached. "What will Garbo want to talk about?" she asked Cukor. Then she brightened: "If she's anything like me, she'll talk about herself."

According to reports, Garbo arrived late and was somewhat startled when Mae kissed her on the cheek. "I wanted her to feel at ease," Mae explained. Said a friend, "Garbo, of course, was more interested in Mae than Mae was in Garbo, so Mae spent most of the evening talking about her career. Garbo wanted to know especially about her muscle men."

Mae West's overriding interest is the care and feeding of Mae West. "My secret is positive thinking and no drinking," she once said, but it involves more than that. She exercises continually—with small barbells, a walking machine, a stationary bicycle. She has been called "a Mount Rushmore of the cosmetician's art," and the pampering of her face, hair, nails, and teeth take up a good part of her day. She eats lean meat and salads; she does not smoke and dislikes others to smoke around her. When she is at the beach or the ranch, she takes long walks. "I sometimes see her in the evening, after the crowds have gone," said a neighbor in Santa Monica. "She walks along the beach on the arm of a man and is usually wearing his coat to keep warm. When I see her on the street she is all porcelain and perfect, but on the beach she shuffles a little, like an old woman."

Miss West is used to being worshiped, and when I paid my first visit she was a little nervous in the presence of a stranger who was not yet a card-carrying idolator. "I am the greatest screen personality since Valentino," she said, striving to establish her eminence. "I didn't say that, though; the studio did." What had she been doing recently? "I've lived the same way ever since I can remember. I concentrate on myself most of the time. Everything I do pertains to myself. Everything I wrote, like *Catherine Was Great*, was for me." Did she star in that? She laughed "I star in everything."

The mention of the Catherine play, which she opened in 1944, started her reminiscing about the years after World War II. "When I wrote that, Lee Shubert called up and said, 'I'm sending out a guy to produce it. He's not too smart, but he'll run his legs off for you.' It was Mike Todd. That ran for a few years and then I wrote a new play, *Come On Up*. They wanted me to bring it to New York but I didn't want to work that hard and I closed it down. I also wrote a screen version of *The Drag*. They're ready for that now. I was always ahead of my time. I wrote *The Constant Sinner* in the late twenties—the story of a black man and a white woman. I'm always thinking of what I'm going to do next. At 17 I was the youngest headliner in vaudeville and I wrote all my own plays and movies and my autobiography. I've always been two people. Most stars are just told what to think, but I told the director what to think."

We were interrupted by costume people from the studio. Miss West's role in *Myra* is Letitia Van Allen, an actor's agent who holds many of her auditions in a huge bed in her office. The clothes were all black and white—tunics and pajamas and flowing coats. We were called into the bedroom for a showing. There was the famous bed with the mirror on the ceiling ("I always like to see how I'm doing," she once explained) and a set of white barbells in the corner. "What, no pockets?" she said, striking a jaunty pose in a pants suit. A studio aide hustled to make a note. Another change, and Mae was in a kidding mood. Her voice dropped to that nasal whine, her hand went to her hip and she drawled the first line of her part: "Awright, boys, get your résumés ready." But the clothes weren't right. "I look like a house," she kept muttering. Someone objected, "You aren't wearing a corset now, are you?" She snapped back, "Of course I'm wearing a girdle."

After the fitting, she had appointments with a manicurist and a hairdresser. We arranged to meet a week later at Perino's, her favorite restaurant, a richly appointed and richly priced place that, in typical Los Angeles fashion, offers an odd mixture of French, Italian, and American dishes.

Mae arrived in a floor-length white gown with semiprecious stones at the neck and wrists. Two huge diamonds glittered on a ring and smaller stones shone forth from a bracelet. As she entered slowly on Paul Novak's arm, she looked, in her own word, "regal."

We talked about her childhood in Brooklyn ("Sunday school always gave me a headache") and her parents, an indulgent mother and an irascible father. "I had a mother who thought I was the greatest thing on earth," she recalled. "By the time I was 12 I had a lot of boyfriends and she would always let them come in the house. One of my boyfriends was Joe Schenck, of the vaudeville team of Schenck and Van—his mother was a nurse in our house for a while. I've always had multiple men in my life; that's been the pattern ever since I was a child. That's how I can write parts in pictures for five or six men; I had that in real life. Once my cousin told my father that I was staying out late with the boys and he was furious. He came home and I picked up an iron rod he kept near his bed. I thought he was going to hit me and I was going to hit him first, but he never touched me."

During most of her career, Miss West managed to keep her private life so secluded that newspaper stories of the day said she had never been "romantically linked" with anyone. In her autobiography she frankly recounted a long series of often brief affairs. "If Kinsey is right," she wrote, "I have only done what comes naturally, what the average American does secretly, drenching himself in guilt fixations and phobias because of his sense of sinning. I have never felt myself a sinner or committed what I would call a sin."

Did she regret never having settled down and had children? "I never wanted children. I thought it would change me—mentally, physically, and psychologically. I was always too absorbed in myself and I didn't have time for anybody else. I was talked into marriage once and maybe it was a good thing—I might have gotten married ten times if I had been free all those years. But you know, a woman becomes a different person when she gets married. She lives for her husband and her family. I wanted to live for myself." ("She says she never wanted to be a mother," observes her friend Stanley Musgrove, "but you should see her with her pet monkeys. She calls them 'baby' and calls herself 'mama' and cuddles them like kids. It's a tip-off on how she really feels." She is so devoted to her monkeys that when one was sent to a kennel she visited regularly and sent fruit. She also financed an eye operation for one of the monkey's kennel playmates.)

The subject drifted to current movies. "They haven't got the glamour any more," she said between forkfuls of crab legs in mustard sauce. "Even in clothes and cars they don't have glamour. Take a Ford, it looks the same as a Cadillac; there's no distinction left. It's even true of diamonds. There are so many good phony ones on the market anyone can wear them and be happy.

"I don't think nudity is sexy. Now they're doing it because they have to change. There were so many great pictures in the thirties and forties and fifties, so many great stars and directors. They don't have that today—to be a star you have to be a little better than anyone else. All the great plots have been done, so they have to slap something together and throw in a naked body. I saw a picture recently, I think it was called *Childish Things*. They have a nude woman riding a carousel and a rape scene. It didn't do anything for me. Take *The Sound of Music*. That was great. It didn't have all the noise and confusion and crazy lights they have now, but it made a lot of money; people will come to see that sort of thing."

I asked her how she had liked the book *Myra Breckinridge*, whose main character changes sex several times in the course of the story. "It didn't grab me," she replied; but later she confessed, "I didn't even read the damn script all the way through—it was too much work. I've just been working on my part. I lie down every day and scribble lines on little pieces of paper, and when I have enough I put them together for a scene. I can tell you that I have affairs with all the leading men and I finish up owning everything. My fans would be disappointed otherwise." Among the other stars of the movie are Miss Welch, who plays Myra, a rapacious young woman on the make in Hollywood, and Rex Reed, the celebrated interviewer (*Do You Sleep In the Nude*), who makes his screen debut as Myron—Myra before her sex-change operation.

Miss West is writing all of her own dialogue for *Myra*, and Fryer, the producer, is still a little surprised that he approved the arrangement. "I would never do it for anyone else," he explained, "but no one can write Mae West's dialogue better than Mae West."

We talked about her health secrets. "You have to be healthy on the inside or else it shows on the outside," she said as raspberries and cream showed up for dessert. "You have to eat good and not go to extremes. You know, I was born with a double thyroid—they stimulate your sex glands and everything. I guess that's why I have so much energy. And I don't do anything that's bad for me. I don't like to be made nervous or angry. Any time you get upset it tears down your nervous system. That's why I have only 'yes' men around me. Who needs 'no' men?"

Mae urged Paul Novak to order a piece of chocolate cake, and he reluctantly agreed. When she finished her berries, she coquettishly stole a bite from him. The whole idea of a 76-year-old woman flirting left me rather stunned, but I asked one last question—what she wanted to be remembered for. She didn't hesitate. "Everything."

1969

Cop of the Year
(Sergeant Joe Wambaugh)

The Other Ball is just another bar jammed between a gas station and a fast-food joint on one of those broad, bleak avenues that stretch across the Los Angeles basin for miles, but never seem to begin or end anywhere. I walked in late one afternoon out of a bright sun and could hardly see in the sudden darkness. As I approached a girl in a blond wig and a black leotard who looked official, she turned around. The front of her little suit had been cut out, and staring up at me were two sensational boobs that clearly would have offended the accepted community standards of McCook, Nebraska. My eyes began to focus a bit better.

I asked her for Bill Coleman, the owner, and was led toward the back of a narrow room. To my left, on a small stage surrounded by ringside seats, another well-developed young lady clad only in an orange G-string sort of strolled around—you could hardly call it dancing—while snapping her fingers. The spectators tried to look as if they weren't looking—and yet tried not to miss anything—which is rather hard to do. Coleman is an ex-cop, and The Other Ball is a cop's bar. It's actually in San Gabriel, about ten minutes from East Los Angeles, a place where the boys can come when they are off duty—or on—to have a drink, swap "war stories," and occasionally make a discreet date.

One of Coleman's good friends and, when he is off duty, regular customers is Joseph Wambaugh, a burglary detective at the Hollenbeck division of the Los Angeles Police Department. Sergeant Wambaugh also happens to be a novelist, the author of two highly praised and eminently successful books about cops—*The New Centurions* and *The Blue Knight*. This fall Wambaugh published his third book, *The Onion Field*, a nonfiction account of the murder of a Los Angeles policeman and the psychological deterioration of his surviving partner. Predictions are that it will be his biggest book yet, and the film rights sold for more than $350,000 even before publication.

I started talking to Coleman about his friend Joe, and soon we were joined by several others. Critics have frequently described Wambaugh's work as "realistic" and "authentic," and the cops at the table agreed. "Any policeman," said a young captain, "can pick up a Wambaugh book and point to any character and say, 'Yes, I knew a guy like that.' " The officers enjoy TV shows like *Dragnet* because policemen are portrayed sympathetically, but they find them unrecognizable. "If someone offered Joe Friday a free cup of coffee he'd say, 'No, ma'am, just the facts, ma'am,' " snorted Coleman, whose chunky, chiseled face reminded me of Johnny Cash. "The fact is, policemen put on their pants the same way you and I do. They drink a little, they gamble a little, they even get laid once in a while." The captain whooped at that: "Joe Friday never got laid!"

Joe Wambaugh, a very conservative, very Catholic family man, apparently resists most temptations, but many of his friends, and characters, do not. They are not "supercops," able to leap tall buildings and crack cases in a single bound. They are human beings, sometimes rather weak human beings, who happen to wear police uniforms. *The French Connection* helped publicize the image of the cop as semitough, a bit nasty and uncouth, but still able to nail the bad guys in the final reel. Wambaugh's cops don't have any answers. For them frustration is an occupational disease; justice is sometimes done, and sometimes not. They beat up suspects, harass homosexuals and others they don't like, they lie in court, they cadge free meals, they goof off on the job. Some take bribes, and a few get blow jobs from prostitutes in the back seats of their squad cars. All this does not exactly make for an ideal homelife, and Wambaugh is one of the few writers who looks at the "psychological violence" of a policeman's lot—the tension, the drinking, the playing around, the unhappy marriages, the suicides. Obviously this is not the image conveyed by most books or TV shows—let alone community relations programs—but Joe feels he has to keep faith with his fellow officers and tell their story honestly, warts and all.

But even if Wambaugh's characters are different from most lawmen of legend—and maybe because they are—he is probably the major figure in the current rush to blanket the mass media with cop stories. Serpico, Ironside, Batman and Robin, Hec Ramsey, Eddie Egan, McCloud, McMillan, Madigan, Toma—where are you, Gene Autry, now that we need you? Around Los Angeles, where so many films and TV shows are made, working cops are in great demand as technical advisers and bit players. Dick Kalk, Wambaugh's former partner, got several parts and joined the Screen Actors

Guild. He even had *Daily Variety* sent to him at the station house before the captain told him to stop. Another Hollenbeck dick, and a close associate of Wambaugh's, regaled friends at The Other Ball with stories about advising actors at a TV shooting. In demonstrating how to stop and frisk a suspect, he barked, "Freeze, asshole!" and then threw the actor so hard against a wall that he tore a chunk out of the fellow's hand. The director had a heart attack, but the guys in the bar roared.

The cop craze has made Wambaugh a lot of money. His own empire last season included the movie version of *The New Centurions* with George C. Scott and Stacy Keach, and a two-hour television pilot called *Police Story*, on which he was a consultant. This year *Police Story* is a weekly, hour-long series. In addition, *The Blue Knight* has been made into a four-hour TV "mini-series," with William Holden as the lead.

Wambaugh will not discuss his net worth. Suffice it to say he would never have to work again. But he does work—compulsively—and his unshakable determination to be "real" in everything he does has caused him many problems. He's had constant battles with TV executives he feels have tried to perpetuate the "fantasies" that dominate most cop shows, and he readily admits that many of them think he's "psycho."

The writer's unsettling experiences with Hollywood have also affected his personal life. He took a six-month leave from the police department to finish *The Onion Field*, and nobody thought he would be back, including himself. But when the leave was up last February there he was, ready for work. The job is like a "Linus blanket," he concedes, an anchor in the "real world" he has always known. He is frightened of floating free, of tearing up old roots and not having anything to replace them, of joining that grinning, chatting legion of "personalities" bobbing up and down in front of a TV camera or a photographer's flashbulb.

Joe lives in San Marino, a staid, wealthy community east of Los Angeles, the sort of place, he says, where neighbors have "brand names," rather than screen credits. I went to see him one evening, and his wife, Dee, opened the door of their huge, Spanish-style house; his two sons, both adopted, played in the backyard pool. Tanned and attractive in white shorts and red top, Dee Wambaugh is certainly one of the few wives in San Marino who pours beer for her guests with her own hands. The furniture was all steel and glass and rich leather; the paintings, primitive Caribbean island scenes. The books ranged from old college texts (*Poetry and Criticism of Matthew Arnold*) to a matched set of Fitzgerald to something called *Writing for Television.* I remembered I had heard his friends joking that he keeps a book next to his bar about how to mix drinks.

Sergeant J. A. Wambaugh, L.A.P.D., came into the room carrying his blue cord jacket, his tie loosened. As he sat down he brushed himself off and explained, "I just put some burglars in jail and it was pretty messy." On his belt I could see a service revolver, a pair of handcuffs, and a leather sap that was a bit larger than regulation size. "It's a holdover from my vice days; it gives me a feeling of security, I guess," he explained. "If you hit somebody with the ones we have now, all it does is make them mad and they beat the crap out of you."

A slight man—he likes to say that he loses all fights—with dark, thinning hair, and a plain face that is about as interesting as an egg, Joe Wambaugh is friendly and accommodating but never quite relaxed. When I told him I had read all three books he quickly said "thank you" before I could say whether I liked them or not (I had). Back in East Pittsburgh, Pennsylvania, his father had been a small-town police chief and then a steelworker before the family came to California to bury a relative when Joe was 14 and decided to stay. Out here the elder Wambaugh became a washing-machine repairman and his wife worked as a maid, but things were always tight. There were no college graduates in the family, no professionals. Joe was a "terrible" student in high school in Ontario and right after graduation he joined the Marines. A year later, when he was 18, he married Dee, and perhaps it was the new responsibility that motivated him to work for "something a little better." He started taking night courses at a local college and kept it up after leaving the service and taking a job at a steel mill near Ontario.

As he flitted from college to college, Joe learned something about himself: "All through high school I wasn't good at anything, but I discovered when I was 20 years old, lo and behold, I was really good at something, and that was literature." His dream was to be an English teacher, but as graduation approached he realized he was too "antsy" for classroom life. "I guess like a lot of college seniors I panicked and I wanted to run out and do something. I went out and joined the police department because . . . I don't know why. Because I needed a job. And the pay was pretty good. Also, I strongly suspect there was something in me from the time I was a child, admiring my father's badge and so forth."

After joining the force Joe kept going to school, and earned a master's. Then in the summer of his 30th year, 1967, he started to write. "There's never been an English major who didn't have the urge to write," he laughed. "So there was that, and the urge maybe to write a true-to-life police story. I had never read one before that was really true to life. Maybe, I thought, I could do a short story. That would be my little bit of immortality, if I could write one little short story that was true about policemen and get that published, that would blow my mind forever and I'd be happy." There was something else, too. Joe had heard the story of Ian Campbell, the cop who had been killed in the onion field, and his partner, Karl Hettinger. If he ever got good enough, he thought, he might someday be able to tell their tragedy.

Wambaugh sent several short sketches off to *The Atlantic*, and a young editor sent them back, but she added a little note saying the stories had promise and urging him to try a novel. That's all he needed. With dreams of Fitzgerald dancing in his head, he started writing a novel. The same impulses that sent him to class after long days in the mill or on the beat—and make him run two miles every day—sent him to the typewriter. "Come hell or high water I write a thousand words a day," he said. "I somehow developed a fanatical discipline. I expect a certain amount from myself and I don't let myself rest until I get it. So I have my devils driving me."

The New Centurions was bought by Atlantic-Little, Brown and exploded onto the best-seller lists for eight months; *The Blue Knight* was almost as successful, and Wambaugh thought he was ready for the story of Ian and Karl. His editor told him that it was too difficult, that he was "not capable" of accomplishing what Truman Capote had done with *In Cold Blood*. But the story continued to haunt him, and it was Capote himself who pushed Wambaugh into a decision. As Joe tells it, "I had met him on Johnny Carson and he was interested in us and invited us to his house in Palm Springs. He made two screwdrivers, fresh orange juice and I guess about a half a quart of vodka in them. My wife passed out—conk, like bang! Anyway, we sat there and I said look, I've got this story in my system, but this editor won't let me do it. I told him the whole business with Karl and everything and after I was finished he said, 'My God, that's a story! Would I like to write that story!' When he said that I said, 'My God, I'm going to write that story no matter what!' "

After months of cajoling, Joe got Karl Hettinger and the killers, Jimmy Smith and Gregory Powell, to cooperate. When he took his leave from the force he spent the weeks working and the weekends getting smashed, trying to relieve the agony of the labor pains. Finally *The Onion Field* was done, but the "stretch marks" were still there from the birth, and he could not begin to think about another book. Meanwhile, David Gerber of Screen Gems had talked to him about television, and the idea was appealing, mainly because the cop stories on the tube were even worse than the ones in books.

But the relationship between Joe Wambaugh and network television has not exactly been a fairy-tale romance. As he tells it, "They pay me a lot of money to use my name and be a consultant and all that business, but they're not listening to me. I'm trying to tell them what a police show should be about, what police life is all about. And so far they're giving me cops-and-robbers stories. That's the thing I can't bear about all these shows on television now, the capers and the cops and robbers and all that. What I've gone through with television has been unreal. They brought me in to give them the first true-life television shows about police. Good drama, strong in plot, strong in character, adult shows. And I sit there and I tell them about the way you do it and I look at their scripts and I go over them carefully and then they nod their heads and say, 'Yes, but there's the real world and there's the real world of television. And the folks like lots of shooting and they like sirens and they like chases and they like the caper.' And I keep telling them, that's not what I'm here for. All this bullshit is not what police work is all about. But they can't really free themselves from that preconception yet, and I was terribly naïve to think that they could."

The real problem is the obvious one: How do you reconcile artistic values with commercial ones? How do you translate one man's novelistic vision into a show that will appeal to a mass audience? Can the ugliness and cynicism that make up so much of a policeman's life sell beer and shampoo? A successful writer who has worked for TV cop shows answers this way: "The networks and the advertisers limit everyone to a degree. There's no way TV can provide the authenticity Wambaugh wants. You just can't get grim or offensive. It's been that way for twenty years and it will be that way for another twenty, or as long as sponsors control TV. It's a very collaborative medium, there's a lot of bread riding on each show, and everyone runs a little scared."

Wambaugh realizes the problem and will make some compromises, but not many. He accepted the final gratuitous shoot-out in *The Blue Knight*—with background music by Nelson Riddle—but only after he had screamed so loudly that the producers had revised most of the script. "Joe doesn't need television," explains Irving Feffer, his lawyer. "He has the security to buy his freedom. How many writers can really enjoy the luxury of integrity? Very few, and I don't think NBC likes that." Joe likes the money, he likes the idea of TV trying to do "real" cop stories, he likes his buddies to get work as extras and advisers. But he likes his reputation as a "serious" novelist even more, and he is afraid that a second-rate shoot 'em up with his name on it would tarnish that reputation. Maybe if he had more confidence in himself he would not be so worried, but then, this is the guy who still uses a book to tell him how to mix drinks.

When movie producers started bidding for *The New Centurions*, Wambaugh started meeting Hollywood people; his popularity on the TV talk shows and his own involvement with a series plunged him deeper into the celebrity scene. When he was on leave, Hollenbeck seemed far away. "During that time, of course, all my friends and relatives and acquaintances said I'd never go back," Joe remembers wryly. "How could you go back to an 8 to 4:30 drudgery like that? Now you've lived the good life and you've been away from it and you're doing all these things. You went to Harold Robbins' New Year's Eve party, and after that, I mean, what's left?"

He did go back, but one thing he is sure of. "I'm not there for any reasons of duty," he snapped. "I don't give a damn about public service." Nor is Sergeant Wambaugh merely out to collect material for another book. One possible answer is the pace and flavor of police work, the lure of the "puta," the "whore," as Bumper Morgan calls his beat in *The Blue Knight*. More to the point, the poor rich writer felt bored and guilty. After *The Onion Field* was finished, Joe went through a "terrifying experience." As he describes it, "There was no job, there was nothing. I was just sitting here in this big house. What are you going to do, play one-on-one basketball in your dining room? What kind of life is this? I was going bananas in this place. I can't to this day figure out what a gentleman of leisure does. There must be some duty. I've always had duties and I've always worked many hours. I've always had two jobs, and suddenly I had no job."

Then there was the time Wambaugh ran into Kent McCord, who plays one of the leads in *Adam-12*, a cop show Wambaugh rates along with Walt Disney for authenticity. The actor was upset at Wambaugh's remarks and told him that he, McCord, had been riding around in L.A.P.D. radio cars and knew as much about police work as the Hollenbeck dick. "Where does truth and where does fantasy lie?" moaned Wambaugh. "I could see this fella was serious, and I mumbled a few things like, 'Kid, I was a cop when you were chewing bubble gum.' And as I looked around after this guy left I thought, 'There has to be a real world somewhere.' "

That meeting with McCord, there at a posh NBC party with the top brass sidling up and telling him to put plenty of "scientific detection" into the *Police Story* plots, scared the hell out of Wambaugh. "I began to think, 'What if I became enamored of this kind of life?' " Joe recalled. "You know, there is something about fame, and I guess fame and power are a couple of perverted bedfellows and they go together a lot. And I was really caught up in this world. I really became a personality and did the whole number, you know, the talk shows, the press agent. And I got to thinking, I could get caught up in this, and soon I wouldn't be able to separate fact and fantasy anymore and I wouldn't know where the real world is and where the real people are. That's really scary. I want to know where the real world is and where the real people are, and I want to make sure that I'm one of them if I can. I assure you there's nothing more sobering, really, than going out on the streets every day in East L.A. and investigating a burglary. I assure you that everything down there is very, very real."

A few days before his leave was up, the Wambaughs went to a police party and Joe was given a name tag. "I looked at my wife and I got all misty and I said, 'It says Sergeant Joe Wambaugh.' And she said, 'Big deal.' I said, 'You know, nobody's ever going to call me Sergeant again!' She said, 'Look, Sarge, I'll call you Sarge the rest of your life if that'll make you feel any more comfortable. Now get this nonsense out of your head.' Then we had a long talk. We went to a French restaurant, very un-policeman-like. I had my veau de crème and my expensive bottle of wine and I sat there and she said, 'Now look, Sarge. Do you look like a policeman? Do you feel like a policeman? Isn't it ridiculous for you to even have those childish thoughts about going back?' And I said, 'Well, yeah, of course.' "

Then early Monday morning Sergeant Joseph A. Wambaugh got up, strapped on his gun, and reported for work. Unfortunately it was Lincoln's birthday, and the detectives were off. "He got down there and he was totally crushed," laughed Irving Feffer, who frankly thinks his client is crazy. "Here was his big moment and nobody was there for his great scene!"

Unavoidably, life has changed for the poet laureate of Hollenbeck. After considerable pressure he abandoned his Volkswagen for a Cadillac, but he compromised by getting one in black and white, the L.A.P.D. colors. He eats at fancy restaurants and doesn't look at the prices. Sometimes, a burglary victim will ask for his autograph. Since his mother had been a maid, he resisted getting domestic help for a long time, but her previous occupation did have one benefit. When he moved into his new house he was puzzled by some wiring in the dining room and she told him, "You dummy, that's to step on and call the maid!"

The Wambaughs had lived in a pleasant suburb called Walnut, but with their new wealth they decided to move, and started looking on the west side of town, out near Beverly Hills and Bel-Air, the "beaten track," as he calls it, of the high-living entertainment crowd. "I mean, if you're gonna go you might as well go all the way, right?" he cracked. "But it scared me away. It's a different world over there. Everybody looked different and it was just a little too fast for me."

San Marino is hardly the sticks, but Wambaugh likes it because it is "the old bastion of the old conservatives. I don't like snobbishness and all that nonsense. But on the other hand they still don't have school dances here without parents chaperoning. I mean there's sort of the old tradition still here. It makes me feel comfortable. I was brought up in a strict Irish Catholic traditional sort of way. I had my kids in a Catholic school for a while and I took them out and put them in a public school but I still wanted some of that discipline. Discipline is the word I guess." Joe likes to drop around The Other Ball on Friday after work for a few belts and, who knows, maybe he lets his fantasies romp around the stage with the girls. He has even been known to try his hand at belly dancing at a place called The Seventh Veil, another haunt. But Wambaugh's favorite place is the old Huntington-Sheraton Hotel in Pasadena, a prim old dowager where the music is strictly Guy Lombardo and the dancers "have either blue hair or no hair." Joe Wambaugh will stay a provincial if it kills him.

Tradition or not, when Sergeant Wambaugh parks his Caddie next to those campers at the Hollenbeck station, it is not the same. "Joe is kind of unaffected by everything, but it's affected the feelings of others," said one cop at The Other Ball. "Joe hasn't changed but his friends have. He's a rich guy now. Everybody would like to be rich, and here's one of our guys who made it." For men who scrape along, working two jobs, never quite getting ahead, a guy with real dough is a bit weird, a special type. "You know what the three biggest lies in the world are?" cracked Bill Coleman. "I don't want to be rich; I don't mind being a nigger; and I'm only going to put it in a little way." Dick Kalk likes to joke that he lives only "ten minutes and $150,000 away" from Wambaugh, but there is an edge to the laughter.

"When Joe went to a party, before he was so well known, he could be Joe Regular Guy," said one friend. "He could enjoy himself, watch what was going on. Now he's a celebrity. He's immediately deluged with people who want to know what Bill Holden is really like. He tries to have a normal time like everybody else, but it's not too easy."

"Cops are a strange breed of cat, there's a great deal of jealousy between them," said one drinker at The Ball. "I have a certain amount of jealousy toward Joe. Goddamn it, I wish I had written that book! I had as many experiences as Joe Wambaugh. Why didn't I write it?" One of his partners has been grousing lately that when he works with Joe, "I kind of feel like I'm nothing. When we go somewhere it's always Joe Wambaugh and what's his name."

Behind his back, some cops say Wambaugh "wants to have his cake and eat it too." They say he wants to be considered a martyr for returning to the force. In their frustration they criticize his police work and even call him a "nigger lover" for hanging around with a dark-skinned partner after work. If he buys drinks, they feel patronized; if he doesn't, they feel snubbed. If he had quit, they would have called him a snob. Now, they don't know what to do.

"I think I psyched myself out," concedes Joe. "Probably everybody is acting different toward me, but I refuse to admit that. I just do my job every day that I've always done. But then something happens to jar me back to the feeling that maybe I'm deluding myself. Maybe I'll see someone I haven't seen for a while and they're terribly uncomfortable and they're almost super-apparent in their admiration, treating me like a movie star or a celebrity or something. So I'm troubled over it. I still have a little bit of an identity crisis."

What next? Wambaugh has not written a word since *The Onion Field*, but he muses about trying a comedy, or maybe a novel about The Other Ball, and the girls who stroll to the music, snapping their fingers. As for TV, he quit *Police Story* once in late August and was then wooed back with promises of more realism, but the future looks dim.

He talks about East Pittsburgh, about the steel-mill towns where nothing grows, about the open-hearth furnaces where fathers of his friends met death. He talks, painfully, about his own parents, working-class people who are bewildered by their son's success, pleased and grateful for the help he provides, but a little resentful, too. He jokes that he should write a book and call it, *You Can't Go Home Again.*

Yet he clings to his job, to his badge, to his values, to his past. Fame chases him like a TV cop running down a bank robber. He tries to hide—in the streets of East L.A., in The Other Ball, in his big house with the bell for the maid. But as Joe Wambaugh knows, TV cops always get their man.

1973

A Matter of Conscience
(Rodger McAfee)

Raisin City

Raisin City is just a glorified crossroads 17 miles from Fresno, a handful of stores, a post office, and a Little League field, where mothers in print dresses sit on plastic folding chairs and cheer the players for Rau's Dairy and the Big B Market. Here, the sandy soil grows the sweet, early-maturing grapes prized by raisin producers. As summer approaches, the heavy green vines creep toward the roadside. They seem almost asleep in a sun so fierce that some people buy Cokes frozen solid.

Dairy cows perform their endless pantomime, swishing away flies with their tails. The only sounds are an incessant chorus of birds, feasting on the ripening plums and apricots, and an occasional pickup truck, roaring off to somewhere.

At the Hamburger Spot, a tiny shack at the edge of town, farmers stop for some fresh blackberry pie and fresh gossip. The talk is of eternal things, crops and weather, San Francisco Giants and the perfidy of a management that would trade a pitcher like Gaylord Perry.

The talk is also about Rodger McAfee, the farmer who put up part of his land last February as bail for Angela Davis, the black Communist then accused of participating in an escape plot that left four men dead, including a judge.

At the time, Mr. McAfee proclaimed himself to be a "humanitarian Communist," and this hamlet of about 700 people reacted like a bronco with a burr under his saddle. Today, even with the realization that Miss Davis was found innocent, the waves of anger continue to break over Mr. McAfee. A few days ago, for instance, he tried to lease some dairy cows. "When the man found out who Rodger was," said his wife, Darlene, "he wouldn't have anything to do with him."

The fury of the townspeople is reflected by Sadie Polin, who runs a little grocery store. "This is supposed to be a free country, but if he wants to follow a Communist way of thinking, he should go to a Communist country and try it out. It's not fair to send our boys to get killed fighting communism in Vietnam, and then let it go in our backyard. If this country is so worried about communism, it ought to stop it here, that's what rubs me raw."

"I'm an American 100 percent," added Mac McGuire, as he sat in the grease and the shade of his filling station. "Ever since World War II we've been fighting those devils and I can't learn to like 'em."

Now that an American president has gone to talk to the "devils" in Peking and Moscow, many people here are plain baffled. And some agree with Mr. McGuire that the trips are "a waste of taxpayers' money for nothing."

But while most people want to believe the best about the president, few seem to want to believe the best about Mr. McAfee.

The McAfees and their five sons are living in a house trailer and a wooden cabin on the 1,100-acre farm Mr. McAfee's parents bought them a few years ago. Two goats are tied to the front porch and Mr. McAfee, a beefy 33-year-old, with sweat-stained workclothes and freshly cut hair, seems like a typical dirt farmer.

He is not. The grandson of a Presbyterian minister, and the son of a teacher, he has spent twenty years searching for a cause to believe in. The trek took him from a Communist rebellion in Guatemala to a kibbutz in Israel to a jail in Cuba. Nothing quite worked out until the Angela Davis case. "We've wanted all our lives to contribute to the revolution," said Mr. McAfee, his earnestness showing like the red sunburn on his thick neck. "This was an excellent opportunity to do so."

The McAfee incident here has gone beyond the issue of communism. The incident also seems to have stirred up feeling about race and crime. H. B. Fries, a prosperous farmer, gazed at the rosebushes in the front of his ranch-styled house and said, "All of us know what Angela Davis stands for, and people were sure she was guilty of everything. They're still sure of it, that's the amazing thing."

Art Klepper left the field after a heart attack and now runs a farm supply store in the neighboring town of Caruthers, "Why bow to the minorities when they're just as guilty as guilty can be?" he stormed.

If she was guilty, he was asked, why did the jury find her innocent? "It beats hell out of me," he said. "A lot of 'em get off—these goddamn laws we have now. It's a real shame the Ku Klux Klan isn't as strong as it was when I was a kid in town. It would take care of a lot of these damn deals."

Nobody around here seems to like Mr. McAfee, who has always had an ability to antagonize people, but a few residents respect him. "It's his own business," said Thomas Brown, who owns a hardware store across the street from Art Klepper. "It's a free country as far as I'm concerned, and I hope it remains so. Why shouldn't I be nice to Rodger? He done nothing against me."

But now even people like Mr. Brown are under pressure. Mr. McAfee's latest plan is to hold a music festival on his farm in September for 25,000 people; the profits would be used to enable a farm workers' cooperative to buy some land of their own. Mr. McAfee says the festival will feature classical music, not rock, but the specter of dope-crazed hippies looting the local stores and trampling the tomato crop has Raisin City in turmoil.

To Mr. McAfee, their upset comes not just from ideology, but from their own frustration. More small farmers are going under every year. Unless a man does his own work, and gets a break from the weather, he cannot survive.

The huge corporate farm, with its big capital and buying power, is only slightly less threatening than Angela Davis, or a devotee of the Rolling Stones.

"Many of these farmers are poor people who were pushed out of Arkansas and Oklahoma during the Depression," Mr. McAfee said. "They lost out once and they're about to lose out again, and they want to find an excuse for it all."

1972

TARNISH ON THE GOLDEN STATE

If anything, disillusionment with California has accelerated in recent years. So many people are leaving that Oregon is threatening, only half in jest, to put guards on the border. Yet there are signs that Californians are finally understanding the limits of the land, and trying to plan for the future. A number of cities have placed ceilings on their own growth and even the chambers of commerce have abandoned the notion that bigger is always better. The Bureau of Land Management has come up with a plan for use of the desert, and while off-road vehicle enthusiasts are protesting mightily, some controls have been imposed.

My whole family loved living in California. In Manhattan, where we had lived before, all that could be seen from our living room window was a brick wall. If you strained your neck and risked hurtling to the pavement five stories below you could see a tree. In Malibu we could see 50 miles of blue Pacific; we could go to the beach or have breakfast outside in any season; flowers were constant companions. But the clearest and brightest days sometimes depressed me. They made me realize what this lovely place was like B.S.—Before Smog—and something has been lost that will probably never be regained.

Giving Up on California

Los Angeles

Thirteen years ago, Ardis Evans came to California when her father was transferred here from Minneapolis. In time she got married and had three children. Her husband's dental laboratory thrived and they bought a four-bedroom house in the suburbs.

But they did not live happily ever after. Now, Donald and Ardis Evans are moving to Yakima, Washington. They have had it with California. Mrs. Evans explained why: "There are several things—smog, 6 million people, and the fact that when we wanted to go out for recreation we either had to drive two or three hours to get there, or go twenty minutes to Disneyland and spend a fortune. We're more of the outdoor type; we like hunting and fishing and camping, and that's what the Yakima area will be able to give us."

The Evanses are not alone. Last year, for the first time in this century, about as many people moved out of California as moved in. Estimates differ—some economists say there was actually a net loss from migration—but the situation is clear.

The Golden State, which drew 1000 net migrants a day in the mid-sixties, has grown tarnished. Like an aging movie star, the Promised-Land-on-the-Pacific has lost its allure.

"California always had some great attraction, something glamorous about it," said James Lewis, director of research for the Los Angeles Chamber of Commerce. "You can start with the Gold Rush and go on from there. But we've gotten so much bad publicity about smog and stuff that the glamour is off now."

Even many who stay are unhappy. The California Poll reported recently that only 64 percent of its residents think California is "one of the best places" to live, a drop from 73 percent in 1967, 29 percent of the population said they would like to move; of the people who have been here fewer than eight years, almost half want to live elsewhere.

The Tarnished Golden State

California Net Migration   (The difference, in thousands, between the number of people moving into the state and those moving out.)

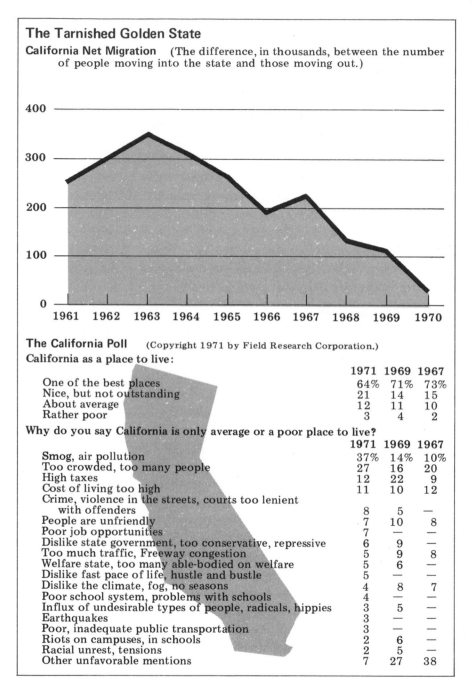

The California Poll   (Copyright 1971 by Field Research Corporation.)

California as a place to live:

	1971	1969	1967
One of the best places	64%	71%	73%
Nice, but not outstanding	21	14	15
About average	12	11	10
Rather poor	3	4	2

Why do you say California is only average or a poor place to live?

	1971	1969	1967
Smog, air pollution	37%	14%	10%
Too crowded, too many people	27	16	20
High taxes	12	22	9
Cost of living too high	11	10	12
Crime, violence in the streets, courts too lenient with offenders	8	5	—
People are unfriendly	7	10	8
Poor job opportunities	7	—	—
Dislike state government, too conservative, repressive	6	9	—
Too much traffic, Freeway congestion	5	9	8
Welfare state, too many able-bodied on welfare	5	6	—
Dislike fast pace of life, hustle and bustle	5	—	—
Dislike the climate, fog, no seasons	4	8	7
Poor school system, problems with schools	4	—	—
Influx of undesirable types of people, radicals, hippies	3	5	—
Earthquakes	3	—	—
Poor, inadequate public transportation	3	—	—
Riots on campuses, in schools	2	6	—
Racial unrest, tensions	2	5	—
Other unfavorable mentions	7	27	38

The "net migration" statistic is a combination of two things, the movement in and the movement out, and each factor responds to rather different forces. But demographers generally agree that people move to California mainly for economic reasons.

"They say that as long as it snows in Chicago, people will move to California," said Arch Hardyment, an economist for the Security Pacific National Bank. "But the great bulk of people who move have to know there is a job here for them."

Historically, California has had a succession of economic booms to provide those jobs: gold, motion pictures, oil, home building, aerospace. But in the last year employment in the state has dropped. The jobless rate, now 7 percent, reached a peak of 7.4 percent in April. With the national rate at 6.1 percent, most people have a better chance to find a job at home.

The immediate cause of this economic slump is the drastic decline of the aerospace industry. In June, 434,400 workers were employed in aerospace here, a drop of 181,800 since the end of 1967. And every hard industrial job supports two related service jobs.

Other industries have also suffered. Rising costs have driven most movie making out of Hollywood. Until recently, the construction market was squeezed by high interest rates. Foreign imports, particularly from Japan, have captured large chunks of the electrical equipment and automobile markets.

In addition, say the economists, the California economy has reached "maturity," making a certain slowdown inevitable. Professor Werner Z. Hirsch of the University of California campus here put it this way: "Until the end of World War II, the predominant portion of goods used in California and the West were imported. After the war, the area reached a critical mass, a threshold, and it became profitable to produce out here for the home market. A large number of industries grew up to supply California and the West.

"These industries built up tremendous capacities and capital investments. But at some point in time you have built up that capacity, and once you've done that, all you have to do is produce at that level, or slightly higher, to accommodate the natural growth rate. California has caught up: It's come of age."

The same economic ills that crippled California's drawing power infected people already here. Some who lost their jobs pulled up stakes and went elsewhere. Moreover, the twenty-year boom of the postwar era has left a terrible fallout: smog, traffic, and over-crowding, oil on the beaches, gashes in the hillsides, and crime in the streets. To people like the Evanses, even a good job is no longer worth the trouble.

"We're taking a 50 percent cut in income, but money isn't that important to us," said Mrs. Evans, who is 34. "Like my husband says, he's out of the house at 6:30 and doesn't get home until 6. At night he watches TV and on the weekends there is always yard work to do. We're not the kind of people who go bar-hopping or to the Music Center or to fancy restaurants, so this area is just not for us."

"Yakima has 48,000 people, and that's quite a bit different from Los Angeles," Mrs. Evans added. "L.A. is not the best environment to raise a family. I'm worried about the drug traffic and the high rate of crime. I realize we'll run into some of that when we move, but it won't be as prevalent. While we were up there looking around, I saw maybe two boys with long hair who badly needed a bath, but the majority of the kids looked clean-cut, what I was used to when I was growing up."

Mrs. Evans touched on another powerful motivation: the desire for a simpler, more personal style of life. If California is a harbinger of the future, many people would just as soon stick with the past. Kent Greenwald is a native Californian, but in twenty-five years he has seen the state grow up around him, and now he is moving to Phoenix.

"We felt that California was becoming too crowded, the air was becoming too bad, and there was too much anonymity," said Mr. Greenwald, a financial analyst for the American Cement Corporation. "If you transact business here you most likely never see the people again. In Arizona you get to know people by name, there's more of a friendly, small-town atmosphere."

For some, this search for a sense of community means going back home, or to a town where relatives already live. Economics is often a contributing factor. California is a high-wage area, but prices are also high, and people who could afford a house in their home towns are squeezing into apartments here.

Judith Gorham and her family are moving to Hartford, Connecticut. Her husband's sister lives in Westport, and their families are all in the East. "We got very discouraged about home prices out here," said Mrs. Gorham, whose husband is a sales representative for Xerox. "And we're starting to realize that as the kids get older, they're becoming more aware of grandparents. We just thought it would be better for all of us to be within driving distance, instead of flying distance."

The political climate here is also a factor. A. W. Skidmore took a 15 percent pay cut to move from Susanville, California to Ely, Nevada, where he works for the state parole and probation department. "Taxes were the main thing," said Mr. Skidmore, who has four children. "Just before we left, our property was reassessed for the third time in nine years, and our taxes would have doubled from $360 a year to $600 a year. All the tax money was going for welfare. It got to be old stuff."

Mrs. Ann Esler, an instructor in dental hygiene at the University of Oregon Medical School, had a different view: "We weren't very pleased with the politics. Reagan isn't interested in health or education, and what he did at Berkeley, where he made a lot of hay, really irks me."

"The greatest migration in human history," as the westward movement to California has been called, is now over, at least for the present. To many analysts, the slowdown is a great blessing. California, they feel, has grown too fast. It needs a "breathing space," an opportunity to evaluate the past, and plan for the future.

"This gives us a chance to do things we haven't done before," said George E. Marr, director of research for the Los Angeles County Regional Planning Commission. "Maybe we can build some necessary facilities, rehabilitate the older areas, and buy up some open space."

Maybe, but even as the net migration levels off, the per capita consumption of resources continues to soar. People are using more electricty and driving more cars than ever. The bulldozer, not the golden bear, is still the most appropriate symbol of California. If "planning" is still the vogue word right now, "profit" has never lost its appeal.

And as Alfred Belser, former planning director for Santa Clara County, put it recently, "Good planning and the current popular value system are completely irreconcilable."

1971

The Death of the Desert

Barstow

All that glitters here in the California desert is not gold. Usually it's broken glass, or a discarded beer can, or a motorcycle leaping over a sand dune. Strange as it sounds, some experts fear the desert is dying.

The California desert covers more than 16 million acres of jagged mountains and sweeping plains, small rodents that never drink water and drab cacti that burst forth with sudden stabs of color. This arid wilderness is really two deserts, the Mojave and the Colorado, stretching from the Sierra Nevada and Death Valley on the north to Mexico on the south, from the Colorado River on the east to the mountains surrounding Los Angeles on the west. The total area is as big as West Virginia.

Once the desert was considered a barren, hostile place, the last barrier before reaching the Promised Land of Southern California. But today it is the great sandy backyard for 11 million people, a weekend refuge from Paradise-on-the-Pacific.

The Federal Bureau of Land Management, a part of the Department of the Interior which supervises about three-quarters of the desert, put it this way: "Try to picture the California desert, not as a vast expanse of open space, but as a constantly shrinking landscape, surrounded by sprawling cities."

In 1970, according to the bureau, the desert absorbed 8 million visitor days—one person spending one day. Only two years before the estimate was 5 million. This weekend alone, as on most holidays, more than 100,000 are expected. And these visitors, as they have so often done elsewhere, are threatening to ruin what they came to enjoy. "Unless we act soon," the bureau said in a report last year, "the desert faces damage and destruction because of people pressure."

Few believe that the desert should be roped off, that people in the crowded coastal cities should not have an escape. But planning, officials feel, is essential; anarchy can only end in destruction. "We have to let people enjoy the public lands," said one. "And yet keep the natural environment intact. That is always the rub."

The damage takes many forms: erosion of the land, destruction of vegetation and wildlife, the defacement of ancient Indian petroglyphs, the plunder of ghost towns, the loss of historic relics, and everywhere the mark of modern man—trash.

"Everybody thinks of the desert as indestructible," said J. R. Penny, state director of the land management bureau, "but it's just the opposite. The desert is one of the most fragile environments we have."

It has been more than a year since the bureau warned of the imminent "destruction" of the desert. In that time, the spokesman conceded, it has "been able to do darn little" to stop the process. A ranger at the Joshua Tree National Monument south of Barstow said efforts to protect the desert "have been like throwing water up Niagara Falls." The Bureau of Land Management has roughly one man in the field for every one million acres, not nearly enough to patrol its vast domain. Moreover, the bureau has always been geared to supervise land, not people, and its agents have no training or authority to enforce the law. As a result, most use of the desert is completely unregulated.

The desert is hardly virgin territory. It has been violated for years by miners, squatters, ranchers, and people who just wanted a convenient dumping ground for an old automobile. But recently, a much more serious threat has developed, the off-road vehicle. A novelty only five years ago, there are now 800,000 in the state—motorcycles, mini-bikes, jeeps, dune buggies, gyroplanes—most of them within striking distance of the desert.

What is happening to the land can be seen a few miles east of Barstow. Out here, ruts and gashes criss-cross the land like a child's aimless scribbles. Every arroyo has become a freeway, and on weekends the more popular paths remind one of the beach roads on a summer Sunday. Scattered everywhere are the corpses of desert plants, like casualties on a battlefield, white and stick-like, deprived of life-giving moisture. Some of the remaining bushes are festooned with unnatural colors: orange ribbons marking racing trails, bright blue paper blown away from some abandoned campsite. In the dry desert climate, even paper lasts for years.

People often camp in large groups here, as if they were afraid of the desert or too used to cramped quarters to break the habit. And they leave their mark: an egg crate, a child's sneaker, the rusting hulk of an automobile, so many bottle caps and cans they almost look native to the region. The refuse serves one purpose—as targets for amateur riflemen. When they run out of cans and cars they shoot at signs and rest stations and rodents; nothing escapes their tell-tale pock marks.

"You get to the top of some hill and you think no one has been there in 200 years," said Bill Halligan, a young cyclist out for a weekday spin. "Then you see a beer can."

The most drastic impact of the vehicles is on vegetation. "Desert plants are not rugged, they're very delicate," said Ranger Donald M. Black of Joshua Tree, who is a naturalist. "They develop very shallow root systems and wax and cork coatings to retain moisture, and once they're broken, they don't usually heal before they dehydrate and die. The right conditions for growth might not come again for 10 or 20 years." Moreover, the vehicles compact the soil, causing the rare desert rainfall to run off quickly, rather than percolate into the soil. And their tracks are practically indelible. Scars left by General Patton when he trained his African armored unit here during World War II are still visible.

As people have invaded new areas of the desert, the wildlife has retreated. The big horn sheep, which are very sensitive to man, "are like an encircled band, restricted and confined more and more," according to Ranger A. B. Sansum of Joshua Tree. As he talked, Ranger Sansum got a call from a colleague. A young coyote was dying near a campground, apparently from eating human garbage and waste.

Another threat to wildlife are clubs of "varmint hunters" who track down coyotes, foxes, and similar species. "There is a very delicate balance of nature between the varmints and other types—the varmints weed out the weaker animals," said Ranger Black. "But for some reason these people feel they have a religious duty to kill varmints. I just don't understand them."

One of the major results of the off-road vehicle is noise. As Ranger Sansum put it: "People pay $2 a night to camp where it's peaceful and quiet. And then some dingaling comes in with his motorcycle and does nothing but drive around and around and around, often with the silencer off his muffler. He has no thought that people might be tired of all that noise they get all the time. On a heavy weekend, this place sounds like the Culver City speedway."

Off-road vehicle enthusiasts talk about the "freedom" they have and the chance to reach once inaccessible areas. But those areas often contain Indian petroglyphs—pictures scratched in the soft rock—valuable archaeological sites, and remnants of the white man's early days here. Many of these have been picked clean by rock hounds, bottle hunters, and plain vandals. One example is a wooden plank road built across the desert by early pioneers. Most of it has now been burned for firewood.

What lies behind this destruction, and what can be done about it? Part of the problem is sheer numbers, and many officials feel that developing more facilities might make things worse, since they would only attract more people. Recently the Bureau of Land Management returned to the Federal Treasury $250,000 earmarked for a campground near Trona, because it felt the ensuing visitors would destroy the area.

Another part of the problem is just ignorance, and the bureau hopes to get money for an educational program that would make people more aware of the limits of the desert. But the issues go deeper. Many people who come here are not concerned with the esthetic value of the area but its recreational potential according to Ranger Sansum. "They want to know how they can use it—collect rocks, or take plants, or drive over it," he said. "And this is where we bang heads with them."

There is also a small group of openly destructive vandals, the type who burn privys and shoot up signs. "I don't think they have a grudge against us," said Ranger Black, "I think they're striking out at their situation in life. They can't get back at their boss, or a cop, so when they come out here, with no restraints, they strike out at anything."

Last Labor Day weekend, thousands of people camping out in the Imperial County sand dunes stopped a train and broke its windows. When a county sheriff went out to investigate they chased him away.

Officials agree that off-road vehicles must have some place to go; so do rock hounds and bottle hunters. The problem, as always, is balance and planning, reconciling conflicting demands, establishing some order, preserving the land even while it is being used.

A few things are being done. A Boy Scout troop is fencing off a particularly valuable Indian rock painting. Several large areas near here have been reserved for off-road vehicle use. But as Gordon W. Flint of the land management bureau office in Riverside said, "We haven't begun to scratch the surface of what's needed."

What is needed, according to conservationists, is a thorough survey of the desert, a plan to allocate different areas for different uses, and enough manpower and authority to enforce the regulations. The bureau asked Washington several months ago for $28 million to pay for drafting a master plan and setting up an "interim management" program.

But others add something else to the list of needs—a new attitude on the part of the public. As one writer put it, "Up to now men have treated the deserts as if they made no difference. One of these days, when survival can no longer be taken for granted on a crowded, used-up earth, they may make all the difference."

Time is probably the rarest commodity in this ageless place. With 11 million people "poised like some gigantic tidal wave," as the bureau put it, eager to escape the smog and stress of daily life, crisis is a mild word. "We can't afford to wait five years," said Mr. Flint. "Things like the petroglyphs will be totally destroyed, rare animal species will possibly become extinct, the danger to desert visitors who lack protection will increase. The beauty the California desert now holds will be diminished to the point where people won't want to use it. Would you want to stand up to your neck in beer cans?"

1971

Smog: A Curse on the Spirit

Riverside

Smog almost accomplished here recently what snow, rain, heat, and gloom of night have never done—stopped the mailmen from the swift completion of their appointed rounds. Several weeks ago, the director of the Postal Service's local district declared that all mail deliveries and pickups would be halted during a "smog alert," an announcement that the choking, smarting, grayish brown haze had exceeded the safety level.

The service's western regional director was horrified and rescinded the order the following day, but the point had been made. Man is giving Mother Nature a run for her money when it comes to messing things up.

Nowhere is this more obvious than in Riverside, a town of 145,000 about 50 miles east of Los Angeles. This is a lovely, sunlit place with the charm of old Spanish architecture, the convenience of modern shopping malls, and the bucolic touch of citrus orchards and grape vineyards.

Unfortunately, Riverside sits squarely at the intersection of two "atmospheric sewers." Prevailing westerly winds blow the smog from Los Angeles and Orange Counties through two funnels formed by a series of hills and mountains, and it all ends up here.

For seventeen straight days last month, the city suffered through alerts. In 1971, the smog exceeded the minimum danger levels on 241 days, up from 192 in 1970. As one resident put it, "We don't breathe the smog here, we chew it."

Most mailmen were disappointed when the order was retracted. "We're not getting any help from the big people, so the individual has got to do something," said Gene Gilmore, as he backed his truck up to the post office. "All we've been hearing for years and years is talk, talk, talk."

"The little man has got to take over," Mr. Gilmore continued. "It's gotten to the point where maybe a vigilante committee should take over and get something started. We pay taxes on top of taxes for smog prevention, but nothing ever happens. It's just as bad as ever, maybe worse."

Smog blights everything in Riverside—work, recreation, plants, mental and physical health. Above all, says James N. Pitts, director of the Statewide Air Pollution Research Center here, it is a "curse on the spirit." "It's depressing as hell," said the chemist, who bounces around his office like a rubber ball. "You get up in the morning and you think, 'How can I face another day of that yuck.' "

At Dave McNair's auto repair shop, output drops about 25 percent on bad days. Dan Alfaro, a house painter, adds, "You feel like you've just finished an eight-hour day when you're just starting."

Pine trees in a nearby national forest, a recreational resource for 11 million people, are dying from the smog. A bad attack can kill an entire crop of lettuce or spinach. A nurseryman finds he can no longer raise petunias in the area. Citrus crops exposed to pollution fall 40 percent below normal.

Doctors say their patient load doubles during a severe siege, and people with respiratory problems are regularly advised to leave town. When an alert is called, school children must stop all physical activity.

Debbie McCormick is 19 years old, a new bride who works as a bank teller. "I'm not going to have children in the smog," she said during her lunch hour recently. "I'd like them to grow up in a better environment. We're thinking of moving up north, past San Francisco," she explained. "So many people want to get away, but can't because they're too rooted in. We'd like to move away while we're still young, before we get stuck."

Real estate sales have been down for the last four months. Businesses find that even in the tight market, they cannot get employees to move here. Enrollment at the University of California campus has also dropped, and as one faculty member put it, "A kid would be a damn fool to come here if he could get in somewhere else."

Just what can be done, nobody really knows. Governor Ronald Reagan keeps saying that the problem is getting better, but to most people here, he sounds like an American general in 1965 predicting a quick end to the Vietnam war.

"Tornadoes or floods are one thing," fumes Mayor Ben Lewis, "but we're doing this to ourselves!"

One severe frustration is that most of the smog is imported. Mayor Lewis recently suggested that Governor Reagan declare a state of emergency and order all cars in Southern California to convert to natural gas, since the automobile accounts for 90 percent of the pollution. But the Governor replied that he did not have such powers.

That might sound like an extreme measure, but most people here believe only drastic action will have any effect. Bob Craven, a local newspaperman who writes frequently about smog, noted that if he wanted to, he could convert his own car to natural gas at a cost of about $400. "But I haven't done it; I will have to be forced to by legislation," he said. "People won't do anything voluntarily. They won't give up their own car to join a car pool, and if you had mass transit, they wouldn't take advantage of it."

Dr. Pitts insists that even if the auto companies make technological improvements, and even if motorists were willing to spend money on them, problems would remain. What is needed, he said, are "societal changes," such as limits on population, on the use of cars, and on the consumption of energy. And he knows, by looking into himself, that such changes will be grievously difficult. "I'm very discouraged," he conceded. "I'm a polluter. I'm not necessarily willing to give up my car. I'm a sinner, and I recognize human frailties."

The only hope, Dr. Pitts says, is for people to change their values. But he is not placing any bets. As he put it, "What worries me is that people are becoming used to it. They're becoming used to not seeing the mountain, to calling their kids into the house, to watching the citrus drop off the trees. What's really terrifying, damn it, is what we're giving up.

"The most important message coming out of the students the last ten years is to look at things that are really important. You can't put a value on it, but my God, it's important to see that mountain."

Then he left, in his car.

1972

EPILOGUE:
SUMMING UP AND LOOKING BACK

"Around the West by Camper" has not been published
previously and I include it here with a special
satisfaction. Spiro Agnew attacked the press for the
wrong reasons, but there was some truth in his claim that
we were "elitists" who did not pay enough attention to
common people and their problems. I got dozens of
requests to write about Cesar Chavez and Ronald
Reagan, but I could seldom interest a magazine editor in
the ordinary folks I write about here.

"Old-Fashioned at 27" is also about average, rather
than exotic people, and while it might seem a bit odd to
include it here, Bayonne tells you a lot about California.
I grew up in a house my grandfather built with his
own hands. I had a sense of place, of community. My
children, raised in a rented house on a Malibu hillside my
grandfather never saw, cannot say that. But Bayonne
also exemplifies the other side of community—the
entangling relationships, the suffocating pressures to
conform—that have always sent young people fleeing
from small-town life. One day after High Holy Day
Services in Los Angeles my wife and I were standing
outside the temple, musing about how nice it would be to
belong somewhere, to have ties to something. A friend
came up and moaned, "I just saw half my class from
U.C.L.A., and they kept asking me when we could get
together." She showed us a handful of small pieces of

paper and explained, "They all gave me their phone numbers. But the reason I haven't called them is that I can't stand them!" And she threw the papers on the ground.

Since "Old-Fashioned at 27" first appeared, I have gotten more letters and comments about it than about all the other articles in this book put together. Most people in Bayonne hated it; what I meant as affectionate ribbing they took as snide put-downs. The local newspaper, where I had my first job in journalism, wrote an editorial attacking me, and even my grandfather, who was still in business at the time, wrote a letter to *The New York Times* disassociating himself from his wayward relative.

Readers outside Bayonne generally liked the piece. It seemed to strike a chord somewhere. So many people my age felt the same way—uncomfortable in the present, unsure of the future, caught in a cultural crunch of shifting values, a sense nourished, I'm sure, by my years in California. I still feel old-fashioned, but four years later, it does not bother me so much. Growing older has its advantages. You see things change. You know that today's fad might be tomorrow's foolishness. You see more of the forest and less of the trees. You relax a bit. If I were to write about my tenth reunion from college this year I might call it "Almost Content at 31."

Around the West by Camper

Los Angeles

One day I looked at my file drawer. It was liberally sprinkled with such topics as communes and countercultures, Indians and Chicanos, Angela Davis and Daniel Ellsberg. There was one slim folder labeled, for lack of a better term, "Middle Americans." This is an endemic problem all journalists face. We tend to write about the fringes rather than the mass, the exotic rather than the average. Reams have been published about the girls who ran away with Charlie Manson, virtually nothing about the ones who stayed behind and became vice-presidents of the PTA.

Obviously there is a reason for this. Unusual people and events stimulate more public interest. They also indicate where the leading edge of society is going. But I decided that what millions of Americans did every summer should also be news, and my editors agreed. So in early July I rented a camper and packed up the whole family—wife Cokie, son Lee, 2¾, and daughter Rebecca, 10 months—for a three week trip through the West.

What follows is something like a journal of that trip. Looking back I have two major impressions. One is of the extraordinary decency of my fellow Americans; wherever we went, people were friendly and helpful. Stereotypes just don't fit very well. A man might rant about "lynching" criminals, as one did, and then spend an hour helping you fix your camper. The second impression is that many people are quite unhappy. They seem bored with their jobs, worried about their families, uncertain of their worth and direction. Our industrial society has given them the time and money to take a vacation, to buy a boat or a camper or both, to grill steaks instead of hot dogs. But the cost has been high. There is a void in their lives, and they do not know what to fill it with.

J U L Y 6. We went to a dinner party the night before we left, and the other guests unanimously agreed that we were insane. They seemed sure that we could not survive three weeks on the road together, and as we prepared to go, I began to think they were right. The refrigerator was barely cool, and I hastily packed an ice chest; Lee kept running the water, and every time I stopped him, he cried. Cokie announced the camper made her seasick, and we hadn't left the driveway. At the crack of noon we pulled out and made it to Santa Barbara, where we had a nice picnic near the beach. But we forgot the pin which holds the refrigerator closed, and as we drove away the door opened, allowing the food to crash to the floor. A few miles later acrid gray smoke started billowing from the front end, and the wheel screeched when I turned. Lee offered his advice, "Let's take this camper back to the camper store." Thanks, kid.

Finally we limped into a campground at Cachuma Lake, a beautiful reservoir in Los Padres National Forest. The place holds more than 400 campers, and we had no trouble finding a spot on a finger of land, surrounded on three sides by water. During the Fourth of July some people waited up to six hours for a site and never got one. Across the road a ball game was in progress. A little girl named Shelley was at bat, and with the help of her mother, she managed to hit the ball. Great excitement. Everybody yelled at her to run. So she did—straight for the pitcher's mound. Her older brother grabbed her roughly and pushed her toward first base, where she was tagged out. Tears flowed. Mother explained, "Shelley doesn't know where first base is yet." Ah, Innocence.

Cokie said the water was backed up in the shower. (We had a huge camper, 24 feet long and 10 feet high, with a refrigerator, four-burner stove, hot water heater, toilet, and shower. The only thing rough about the trip was the cost—$175 a week plus 5 cents a mile.) I went to investigate the outflow pipe. Within seconds a man sauntered over from the next campsite and said something very knowledgeable about a "gasket." Then he showed me how to empty the pipe and the shower problem was solved. The man was six feet tall and well-built, with a long, narrow face and hair cut so close his tanned scalp shone through. His name was Fred, and he was a deputy in the Los Angeles County Sheriff's Department. "I don't like it much," he said quickly, "but a man's got to stick it out where he can make a living and provide for his family."

We stood around talking, feet scuffing idly at the dust. Fred had tried to get away once. He went to Alaska and joined the state police, but he was back within seven months. The money wasn't very good, and he did not like the job. "The force wasn't professional enough," he said. "Like the kids coming out of college—you couldn't tell them there was a better way to do things." The county sheriff's department was professional, but it had other drawbacks. "I'll give you some idea the way things have changed," he went on. "The first 11 years on the force I had one murder, in the last two years I've had three."

There were other things eating Fred. Like many people we met, he seemed frustrated by forces larger than himself. He had moved his family out to Lancaster, a desert community on the fringes of Los Angeles County, but now there was a proposal to build a huge jetport nearby. "I moved out there so I could get out of the city, out of the rat race," he explained. "My daughter is in 4-H, she raises animals, we live like people used to live. Nine out of 10 people moved out there for that reason, and now they want to put in an airport. We don't have any place else to go."

After dinner Fred wandered over again, obviously troubled. His daughters had been talking to a "hippie" couple camped across the road. "I like to be liberal, you understand," he said, "but that girl started telling my daughters about the trips she'd been on and free love and how when they were in Texas the cops used Gestapo tactics on their friends and searched their house without a warrant and broke one of the guy's fingers. The more my daughter told me the madder I got. It would be one thing if they were 15 or 16, but they're only 9 and 11. I just went over there and told them they'd better not talk to my daughters again or they'd wish they were back in Texas with the Gestapo." Fred sipped some coffee and went on: "I'm not sure I did the right thing. Now my daughters are embarrassed, and maybe the next time they won't tell me where they're going." The incident really bothered the man, and later he brought it up again. "I took a shower this morning and saw the hippie guy in there," he admitted "I figure anyone who keeps clean can't be all bad." Then he invited me to go fishing in his boat, a little three-seater he had bought at Sears. But getting up at 5:30 didn't thrill me, so I declined.

J U L Y 7. The next morning Fred called me over for coffee he hadn't gone fishing either—and showed me his campsite. The family slept in sleeping bags in a roomy tent. Fred proudly displayed his gadgets: a lantern, a gas-powered stove, a space-heater. Two plastic chaise lounges sat under a tree. "I like it up here, nobody knows me," he said. "When you're a cop it's hard to take your wife to a bar or something. The guy sitting next to you could be someone you once threw in jail. We like to go up to Bakersfield every once in a while. We get someone to stay with the kids for a few days and go up there and drink and dance, that sort of thing. If I have a few too many nobody cares."

Fred showed me where to fill up the water tank and we were off. Soon the steering wheel balked again; the hose containing the power-steering fluid was broken, and it took two hours to get it fixed. Back on the road, the engine started roaring. A gas station attendant in Pismo Beach said the muffler had become disconnected. I simmered as he banged it back together. The machines are rebelling! They're holding us prisoner! But the attendant was able to fix the troublesome part, and away we went. By nightfall we made Big Sur.

J U L Y 8. Our campsite was on the bank of a sparkling little river; more important, two little girls quickly adopted Lee and swept him off to the playground. After breakfast I wandered up to the village of Big Sur—a post office, a store, and a restaurant—to talk to some of the youthful hitchhikers who were passing through. They were very different people, but most of them shared at least one thing: they were on the road because they did not like where they came from. For some, it was a testing time, a chance to escape the padded environment back home and prove themselves. A red-haired youth from a wealthy suburb of Chicago said, "I want to learn how to function without my parents. Our parents are 2000 miles away now and anything we do is on us. When I get home I'll feel better, I think I'll learn a lot of stuff." For girls, especially, hitchhiking also meant freedom from deceit. "I live with my mother," said a 20-year-old from Toronto, "and I have to hide a lot of things from her so she won't be hurt. If I stay out all night with a boy I tell her I was at a party."

Yet there is an almost frightening aimlessness to these kids, with their guitars and organic apple juice and orange nylon backpacks. I sat down next to a guy named Terry Delugo. He had a dollar in the pocket of his tattered coveralls and was holding up a sign that read "Vancouver." Why Vancouver? "I don't know. I haven't figured that out yet," he replied. "I'd like to go to Alaska or Canada or back East, wherever the Lord tells me to go." A bit of a put on, but typical. The sign seemed to give Terry some sense of purpose, but it was completely arbitrary. Mark Heazle, 19, and Glenn Holdren, 18, were heading north, too. Why? "I just got tired of sitting around Denver," said Mark. "Besides, they cut out all the rock concerts after Red Rock, that was a big concert with Jethro Tull. I was sticking around to see Poco but they canceled them, and Denver was really dead."

The long hair might frighten the tourists, but most of the hitchhikers I met were card-carrying passivists. If a ride did not stop, the road was afflicted with "bad karma." If someone said, "Let's go to Seattle," they went. If they met a Jesus freak, he was "cool"; if they met a yogi, he was "cool," too. Tina Scholnick, 18, was hitching with a girlfriend from Long Beach. "I've been working off and on, but I'm going to school in the fall," she said. Where? "I don't know where." Why are you going? "My parents really wanted me to go."

A few youths, very few it seems, finally reach some place and stop traveling. Russ Harrop was on his way back to Los Angeles to save enough money to move to Ananda, a meditation retreat in the foothills of the Sierras. Marcia Hendrick, the girl with him, was already living at Ananda. She had flowers in her hair and a deep smile on her face as she related how she had moved there. "Back in April I went to a spiritual festival at Davis, and some people from Ananda were there. I was working in Los Angeles at the time, cleaning houses, and I was miserable. I was supposed to be back at work on Monday and I never went back. I left everything, all my possessions and all that junk. I just had my sleeping bag." Her parents, Marcia admitted, were "shocked" but not unhappy. "They're kind of glad I've settled down, I've been there three months," she said. "I tell them everything and they've been through everything with me—drugs, and all that. They don't really understand, but they think it's O.K."

J U L Y 10. We spent several days at the River Bend Trailer Park near Guerneville, California, a typical result of the tremendous boom in recreational vehicles. The place had good facilities—electricity, showers, washing machines—and almost no room. It looked more like a parking lot than a campground. Cokie worried that our children would disturb the neighbors, a problem that never crossed our minds at home. I could not understand at first why people would come to a place like this. Why not just stay home?

The answers all touched on one idea: like the hitchhikers, people were not going somewhere, they were getting away. It did not matter much where they wound up. Richard Phillips, a young lawyer who was sitting under the awning of his small trailer, explained it this way, "It breaks the monotony of the job. You come home from work and you go into your house, and the job and home are all tied up in your routine. This is a way of saying I'm leaving it all behind . . . you break the chain. You leave the telephone, which is always holding you to anything that's happening. One thing I enjoy more than anything is getting away from the TV, I feel so stupid when I sit and watch it." I asked John Rickard, a forklift driver, what he did. He smiled wryly and said, "I get through five days and come up here." Carol Phillips, Richard's wife, put it another way, "Sometimes it's more of a hassle to get ready than to stay home, but if you stay home, you don't do anything different." Richard added, "I enjoy waking up here. I'm not in the same old grind."

The words sound trite: routine, grind, rat race. But they describe a pervasive fact of life. Many people do not enjoy waking up in the morning. At least there are no schedules, no bosses, no telephones. A drowning man is very grateful for a few gulps of air.

The other thing that struck me is that the trailers and campers become an end in themselves; people derive enormous satisfaction from tinkering with their rigs. Phillips was rather embarrassed to admit his delight when he found a piece of carpeting to fit the entrance of his trailer, or when his wife spent days making a cover for their propane gas tanks. He introduced me to a furniture mover who ticked off the gear he had assembled in his trailer: a stereo, a tape deck, a citizen band radio, a color TV. It is not unusual to see a camper pulling a boat, with several motorcycles strapped to the side. One gets the feeling there is a big hole somewhere that people are trying to stuff with anything they can grab. Bored? Buy a tape deck. On the other hand, many people really want conveniences and companionship; they do not want to traipse off into the woods and sleep on the ground, and that's fair enough. I also wonder whether the traditional definition of "creative" is too narrow. Isn't wiring a complex electrical system creative? What about sewing a dress or banging a fender back into shape? Work is becoming shorter and more stultifying. The question hovers over River Bend like charcoal smoke: What do we do now?

J U L Y 11. You can drive most places in America and never leave home. The Holiday Inns and Texaco stations and McDonald's hamburger stands are there at every turn, grasping the traveler in their comforting vinyl embrace, eliminating any possibility of culture shock. The country has become Sanderized ("look for the big bucket goin' round and round in the sky, with the Colonel's face a-shinin' down on ya"). Highway 1 north of San Francisco is wonderfully different. A winding, twisting road, overlooking surging scenes of water and rock, it is made for enjoying, not driving. The little lumber towns on the coast still have a distinct character and a visible history; they don't look like they were bolted together last week on an assembly line.

We reached Van Damme State Park near Mendocino feeling refreshed. In the next campsite a group of aging beatniks were earnestly debating some unknown topic and drinking from large jugs of wine. I guessed that they taught English somewhere, and I was close; they taught at an art school in Mendocino. Lee, as usual, drove his toy motorcycle over to investigate the new neighbors. They promptly chased him away with a "scram, kid" attitude. That had never happened at Cachuma or River Bend, and I began to feel uneasy for the first time on the trip. "When it comes to kids," said Cokie, "I think I prefer Middle Americans."

J U L Y   13. At about 3 o'clock a palpable tension begins to crackle across the highway. Should we stop now? What if the campground is full? We pulled confidantly into Prairie Creek Redwoods State Park at about 5. "Have any campsites?" I asked, with the same false jauntiness one uses for such questions as, "Are you going to buy the article?" or "Do you like my new outfit?" I got back the Bad News Look. "You can try," said the ranger, "there might be a few left." We rushed toward the campground. There's one! Nope, reserved. Another! Also reserved. I began to curse those well-ordered souls who Planned Ahead. Two circuits, no campsites. Then Cokie remembered—the map showed a smaller campground nearby. One site left! Cokie perched on the picnic table to stake our claim. Soon the "overflow area"—that limbo reserved for those who dawdle too long on the road—began to fill up. Fathers, their faces twisted with failure, could not face their glum families. Another night in Overflow! I felt like I had just found a gold nugget in Prairie Creek.

J U L Y   14. Wandering around the park I ran into a delightful elderly couple named Gilbert and Ivy Schryver from Sebastopol, California. They had a small trailer behind their car and a poodle named Sandy, their "juvenile delinquent." Mr. Schryver, a retired warehouseman, said they were going home. "Being retired we don't have to buck the crowds," he said. "After Labor Day we hope to go out again, if we have the money." What did they like about traveling? "I haven't seen a news report and I haven't seen TV," he replied. "You get a mental rest. One more month of this and I'll say, 'Nixon, who's he?'" Ivy chimed in, "I love the outdoors, I love the trees, I don't like being cramped up." Her husband smiled affectionately, "She'd make a good pioneer."

The Schryvers said they had sold their house and moved into a mobile home, but they were dissatisfied. "They told us there would be no maintenance, no worries, no trouble," said Mr. Schryver. "But that's just it. You need some trouble, it's the dullest place imaginable. You have the feeling that if you disappeared, no one would miss you. That's what happens when you retire, you find out the world gets along fine without you, and that's a heck of a comedown." Ivy added, "So you join the trailer owners association, and you become the secretary, and you do a little work, but that's nothing."

A few campsites away I heard the babble of children and walked over. Two families were camped together, the Hallbergs of La Crescenta, a Los Angeles suburb, and the Boehners of Santa Cruz. The two men, both high school teachers, are old college buddies and the families try to get together every year. With their husbands away for a few hours on a fishing trip, the women were primping, even out in the woods. Rita Boehner's long, dark hair was wound around pink plastic curlers; Velores Hallberg, a slim blonde, looked fresh and pretty from a shower. For the Hallbergs especially, the trip to the redwoods was an escape from urban life. "If you live in L.A. it's impossible to live alone," said Mrs. Hallberg, who teaches English at a junior college. "There's no place you can go without seeing other people. The kids can't even ride their bikes where we live because it's too busy." More than that, it is a chance to strengthen and rejuvenate the family unit. The nuclear family might be passé to some, but to Rita Boehner, "everything is based on family happiness."

We talked some more about families, as half a dozen kids provided a steady flow of background noise. A fire licked at the blackened bottom of a coffee pot. "We only have girls," said Mrs. Hallberg, "and I used to think it was only important for boys to have a male model, but now I know it's important for girls to have Dad around, too." She was clearly thinking about something, and after a few moments went on, "Out of 13 kids in my girl's Brownie troop, three had parents getting divorced this year. Out of my seven closest friends in high school I'm the only one still married to my first husband. But the critical time is coming up—my husband is turning 40 this year. I realize it could happen to me."

Velores Hallberg is a bright, attractive, independent woman, but divorce frightened her. Her family gave her life meaning. "It's very hard to identify with the world or humankind," she said, "and we have to get away from nationalism, it's been very destructive. Most jobs don't provide any identity, and religions sort of blend together. How will people find an identity? Going back to the old family unit is the way people will find it. What makes you, you? What makes you different? I think it's your family, the people you're with."

J U L Y 15. I was up and out of the camper around 8:30, and when I looked around, I was stunned. The campground, full the night before, was almost deserted. "Getting an early start" is the unquestioned credo of the American road. So what if you're camped in the middle of the redwoods. No time to look. You have to be somewhere else by nightfall. The ranger told me that 50 percent of the visitors who camp here stay only one night. For them, the park is a convenient motel which happens to have, as Lee put it, a few "tall, tall trees." People seem truly grateful to flee their jobs and home, to escape the tyranny of time and regimentation they face every day. But many of them recreate a whole new schedule, just as rigid and domineering. Part of it is the "machismo" thing of "making miles." Less than 300 a day and your virility could be questioned. Part of it is the sheer drive to compete. "It's the American idea of bigger and better," said Herb Schneider, a rather mordant physical therapist who was camped across the road. "Every holiday we try to kill more people." And part of it is that many people seem afraid of spontaneity. If the hitchhikers carry freedom to the point of aimlessness, at least they can say, "I dig this place, I'll stay awhile." The average traveler could say that about as easily as he could burn an American flag.

The rangers at Prairie Creek have trouble getting people to look up from their charcoal grills long enough to see the trees. But a few miles up the road, they were packing them in at something called the Trees of Mystery. The attraction was not redwoods in their natural setting, but oddities: strangely shaped branches, trunks you could walk through, etc. Dozens of tourists clustered around the "cathedral trees," a lovely group of redwoods that had been outfitted with an altar, canned music, and a sign. On the sign was a prayer, which read in part, "Sink down, O Traveler, on your knees/God stands before you in these trees." He might have been there once, I thought, but He must have left right after the Muzak was installed.

The Trees of Mystery tour is so arranged that you have to leave through a gift shop, and I noticed the changing styles in souvenirs. The traditional gewgaws run to leatherette coin purses, carved coconuts, and wooden plaques with such messages as, "Good bread, good meat, good gosh, let's eat." At least the wallets and T-shirts say where you've been; they are slightly different from the treasures sold at the Grand Canyon. The new style souvenir is totally unidentifiable: scented candles, colored soap, paper flowers, all in bright oranges and purples. Instead of the plaques there are posters, misty, windswept scenes with captions like, "Blessed Are Those Who Are Close to Nature," and "Love." We bought Rebecca a bib which said, "Trees of Mystery," and Lee two books, about Smokey the Bear and Paul Bunyan ("Paul Onion" to Lee).

Across the highway we had lunch at a coffee shop, our first restaurant meal of the trip. I had forgotten the stomach-gnawing anxiety of waiting for the food, hoping vainly that your child would not empty the sugar on the floor or hurtle into the next booth. I had also forgotten the cost: $8.50 with tip. We had been spending about $7 a day for food. The economies of camping, both financial and psychological, seemed evident. As we left, Cokie said, "Was that restaurant on a tilt, or am I just used to a tilt?" I didn't know.

We stopped that night near Cave Junction, Oregon. All along the heavily traveled tourist roads, farmers have turned fallow fields into makeshift campgrounds, and we stayed in a delightful spot, with a pear tree drooping over the table and a creek rushing past a few feet away. Lee headed for the water. There is something about a stone and a stream that makes a little boy want to throw one into the other. We strolled slowly along the bank, tossing twigs into the swift current, drinking in the dying summer light. Lee, of course, soaked his shoes, but it didn't matter. The world was far away.

J U L Y 17. After a few days I had realized that our original plans were far too ambitious; instead of heading for Yellowstone we turned around at Cottage Grove, Oregon, a lumber town that was holding an annual festival called Bohemia Mining Days. All of us trooped over the railroad yards for a "buckaroo breakfast," and sat down at a long table next to a retired grocer named Mel Gans. The breakfast, he told us, was sponsored by the Shriners, of which he was a member. An unlikely crew—an electrician, a plumber, a sand and gravel man—were deftly turning out platters of pancakes, ham and eggs. I asked how they did it. "These guys have been doing this for years," laughed Gans, "each one knows exactly what to do and what his job is." They were among the rare people we had met who could say that.

I left my family at a swimming pool and headed for the gravel pits outside of town, the site of the annual hound dog water race and treeing contest. Hound-doggers are a small and tightly-knit group, with real manure on their jeans, real calluses on their hands, and real affection for their animals. They stood in small groups, shuffling and talking, the masculine ballet of camaraderie and competition. Six dogs at a time are placed in a cage at one side of the pond. Then they are given the scent of a raccoon, who is placed in a cage on a small float. As the dogs are released the coon is pulled across the pond. First dog across wins the heat; a process of elimination produces the grand champion. As we waited, the banter was light and easy. "I've got the only water dog with aquaphobia. . . . That coon is so damn spoiled he won't work without a can of pop. . . . I came to give you guys some competition . . . you've got it!"

The president of the local hound dog association was Kenner Peterson, a younger man with a small beard. Why was he a hound-dogger? "Have you ever been out with a pack of hounds at night?" he asked. "The music is beautiful, it sends the hair up the back of your neck. Also it's the competition, to know you've got a good dog." Another man chimed in, "It's a great feeling when you're out hunting with your dogs. No one is bothering you, and you're not bothering anybody." Carl Bergman, one of the veterans in these parts, had another view, "It's just a sport. It makes as much sense as chasing a little ball all over a green field."

That night I went to Bohemia City, the little fairgrounds set up for the festival. Every hour or so, a group of young men in Western garb would stage a shoot out, complete with blank but very loud pistol shots, to entertain the crowd. The group called itself the Lemati gang—that's what the Indians called this area—and they were clearly the local heroes. Little kids crowded around them between acts, asking questions and touching their guns and their glory. It was play-acting, but the men took it very seriously. "I lived about a hundred years too late," said Jack Cook, who was dressed like a frontier judge. "I think most of us feel that way. You take us out of these clothes and put us back on the street and we're different people." Don Farris, who works in a lumber mill, broke in: "It's a way of life we ought to go back to, the way things are starting to look these days. I believe people were happier then. You could walk up to anyone and in general he'd treat you right. Now they're too busy for you. It was rougher in some ways, but better in others. If women had the chores they used to have in the old days less of them would be getting divorces and getting into trouble."

Farris and Cook were seeking one escape from Cottage Grove; the teen-agers were taking another route. Across the fairgrounds was a booth run by The People Center, a new organization in town which is trying to deal with a growing drug problem. Jay Critchley, a VISTA volunteer, helped organize the center; he was dressed like a gypsy, playing the barker for a fortune-telling booth, but he took a few minutes to talk. "There is just nothing in this town," he said. "Everyone is freaked out on drugs. There's a lot of speed in town and everything else." Why? "There's a lot of peer group pressure, but the main thing is the myth about what it means to be cool. The people who had the original hippie ideals are gone, but the myth has been built up, and a lot of young people are coming up who are growing long hair and taking drugs. It's the same trip as the fifties, when everyone was into drinking beer and driving motorcycles."

It was getting late, and Cokie was staying with the kids. I stopped at a pie stand run by the women of the Trinity Lutheran Church. I heard one lady talking about a trip to Hawaii. "It's the 30th anniversary of Pearl Harbor coming up," she said, "and my husband was there when it was attacked." Pearl Harbor was closer to 130 years ago, I thought, eating my pie. It was great. I had another piece, bought one for Cokie, and went home.

J U L Y 22. Red Bluff, California, was settled during the Gold Rush era, and the roots of its people lie deep in the land. I visited the Tehama County Fair one day, and talked to the 4-H kids who were standing around a barn, waiting for the chance to show off their pigs, sheep, and cows. Many had parents hovering around, helping to comb a steer or shove a reluctant lamb into the arena. Here fathers still had something to teach their children; they did not have to go camping to spend time together.

David Stroing, 17, was a freckle-faced lad sucking the remains of a coke through a reluctant straw. His pig—"my brother gave it to me"—had won reserve grand champion, or second prize, and his steer was also in the finals. What were his plans? "I'll probably end up back here," he said cordially. "I know I'll be in the country somewhere. I was born and raised right here in Red Bluff and I don't think I could live in a city. We live up in the mountains—our closest neighbor is 7 miles away—and we can do anything we want to. Me and my brother do all kinds of stuff. We go fishing every day and chop down a bunch of alders just for the hell of it."

"My grandfather came here in 1877 and we've lived here ever since," he went on. "He was from Germany and couldn't speak any English, and he had a tag on him that said, 'Red Bluff, California,' so they just sent him here. He worked in town for a while and then homesteaded out in the sticks. We live right next to his old land. Most of my uncles and aunts live around here too, most of them on the same road. There were 12 kids in my grandfather's family, and most of them are still here. About half of Tehama County is related to us."

Nearby, Rodney Little was holding the halter of a large black angus bull, a registered bull, he quickly informed me. He told me there had been some fights in his high school between "cowboys" and "hippies." "They don't dig long hair around here," he said, eying the locks which curled over my ears. "I went to a fair last year where the cowboys got some longhairs behind a barn and gave them a sheering. Long hair was made for women, not men."

Rodney considered himself a "cowboy," a word he pronounced with great reverence. What was a cowboy? "To me," he replied, "a cowboy knows cattle, he really gets into it. It's someone who looks decent and doesn't lay around and take drugs. It's someone willing to get out and work." Didn't people have the right to wear their hair any way they wanted? "No, I really don't think so," he shot back. "They say they did it in the olden days, well big deal. Short hair has been the going thing for a long time, and if you have a lot of guys with long hair it don't look good for the school. And if you get all doped up and drive a car you can kill someone." A girl sitting on the fence rail next to Rodney smiled sweetly and said, "You can do the same thing if you're drunk."

Over in the exhibit hall, one booth was run by the National Association to Keep and Bear Arms. The group sold bumper stickers saying, "Register Communists. Not Firearms," as well as the Dan Smoot Report and other right-wing literature. A hard-eyed woman came over, and I asked her the purpose of the group. "Adam and Eve were put in the Garden of Eden and they were immediately tempted," she replied. "We always have to be on guard against evil." Here was a woman who knew her purpose; like Rodney Little, maybe she knew it a little too well. But fighting sin and corruption requires clear and present demons, and they are in short supply these days. Here she had all this literature denouncing trade with Russia, and President Nixon was winging off to Red China. It all sounded like a 15-year-old newsreel. "I think we have a lot of basics to return to in this country," she said sternly.

Rebecca, who was riding in a backpack, had happily torn up the silver foil that was decorating the booth. I hurried away, and found myself in front of a display for a line of biodegradable cleaning products. "When man thinks he's smarter than God it won't work out so good," said the plump woman behind the counter. "He didn't put those synthetic chemicals here for us to eat. I think we need to get back to original things."

I thought of introducing the two women, but decided to go to the carnival instead. On my first try I knocked down three grinning dolls with a softball and won Lee a stuffed blue bear. Now, said my wife, heady with success, win something for Rebecca. Soon I knew how Vida Blue felt trying to win his twentieth game. Quarter after quarter disappeared, and I didn't come close again. Rebecca solved the problem by swiping the blue bear. Lee, who had gone on about 300 merry-go-round rides, was too tired to complain. He settled for a coke.

JULY 26. As we were about to leave Sequoia National Park the muffler broke again, lending a nice symmetry to the trip. Actually, except for a hole Cokie had poked in the side of the camper, the whole trip had worked out quite well. Our friends had been wrong. With the muffler patched up we wound down out of the mountains and into the steaming San Joaquin Valley. In order to ease our re-entry—and because we couldn't face another picnic lunch—we ate at a Plastic Restaurant in Porterville. A few hours later we were crossing the Tehachapis, the last barrier between the valley and Los Angeles. Suddenly we topped a ridge, and a brownish-yellow haze smudged the sky. It was smog. We were home.

1971

Old-Fashioned at 27

When I decided at the last minute to go to my tenth high school reunion, I tried to find the girl whose name was on the invitation. She wasn't listed in the phone book, so I called somebody with the same last name and asked for help. "I don't know a Marie Sestito," said the girl who answered, "but I'll ask my mother-in-law; she knows her." I told the girl not to go to so much trouble. "That's all right," she said. "My mother-in-law lives upstairs."

That tells you something about my hometown, Bayonne, New Jersey. Wooden two-family houses fill narrow lots separated by tiny alleys. In front and back, each house has its little square of hard, barren dirt. About 75,000 people squeeze into Bayonne's 5 square miles, and land is so scarce that they are building houses in swamps and next to sewage plants. But even the new brick boxes somehow look weathered.

It is a close-knit town, rather isolated and parochial, Eastern, ethnic and industrial, the kind of town where one's in-laws are likely to live upstairs. I would be surprised if there are a dozen couples in all of Southern California, where I now live, who share a two-family house with one partner's parents. The old folks are back in Queens or Cleveland or maybe Sun City, and besides, a two-family house in California is practically a historic landmark.

A week after the phone call, I was landing at Newark Airport on one of those deceptively sunny fall days that leave a chilly aftertaste. I saw Bayonne clearly, a key-shaped peninsula on the west side of New York Harbor. It is so close to the city that my twin brother and I could see the Statue of Liberty from the window of the bedroom we once shared. As the plane made its approach, consumptive smokestacks coughed noxious chemicals into the bleary sky. Grime caked bridges, factories, and homes. The tanks from the oil refineries, long the town's major industry, looked like giant, rusty checkers. Newark Bay itself seemed corroded. To call it a body of water would be to stretch the definition of water considerably. When some people think of home they remember tree-shaded streets or a particular park or maybe a river. I think of the soot of Bayonne and its smell, an aromatic combination of barbequed garbage and smoldering inner tubes, with a dash of sulfur for tanginess.

One of my fellow passengers was a middle-aged woman with carefully set black hair and multicolored sparkles on her eyeglass frames. As she deplaned she was met by two teen-age girls. One wore curlers in her hair and a purple jacket with a legend on the back announcing that she was a high school cheerleader. The other was a nun, in full habit. (No new-style nuns here. In this part of New Jersey, ecumenism means that the Irish now speak to the Italians.)

The girls symbolized two of the area's principal cultures. Sports is practically the highest calling a youth can have—not sissy games like tennis or chic ones like pro football, but such sweaty, traditional sports as baseball, bowling, and, above all, basketball. If Bayonne has a heartbeat, it is the thump of a basketball being dribbled on concrete by a 12-year-old boy. Making the high school varsity is like being admitted to a pantheon of ineffable greatness. Your picture was enshrined on the dusty wall of a school corridor, your name chiseled into the base of a brass-plated trophy. You had torn a tiny shred of immortality from the sweatshirt of history.

And Bayonne is about 80 percent Roman Catholic—mainly Irish, Italians, Poles and other Slavic groups. Many families settled there soon after arriving from the old country. They kept to their own enclaves, their own churches, and modernity made surprisingly few inroads, at least until recently. One of the great tests for a young newspaperman there was to write a Polish obituary and spell all the names right. The priests were extremely powerful, if for no other reason than that they had an education. When I was a teen-ager the city still had a commissioner, Stanley Fryczynski, who could barely speak English. But as an undertaker he probably knew more families in town than anybody except "the good fathers." Jews accounted for most of the rest of the population, and I grew up thinking that Protestants were a tiny minority group. In the fifth grade a boy named Johnny Powers joined our class, which was replete with DeMartinos and Wyroskas and Turtletaubs, and I remember thinking that he had a queer last name. I was completely unaware of the Anglo-Saxon sound of my own name, which had been changed from the Russian, Rogowsky.

For some reason, Bayonne seems particularly prone to scandal and disaster. While I was in high school, we made front pages across the country when a train fell off a drawbridge someone had casually neglected to close, killing several dozen passengers. A few years later, an imaginative entrepreneur helped bankrupt a Wall Street investment house by swinging a big deal in which a huge supply of salad oil was to serve as collateral. The tanks which supposedly contained the stuff were in Bayonne. They were empty.

Next to oil refining, Bayonne's biggest industry is probably crime. It took me years to realize that those men talking furtively into telephones in the backs of candy stores were taking bets. Some investigators have linked Bayonne's congressman, Representative Cornelius Gallagher, to the Mafia, in particular to a gentleman known as "Joe Bayonne" Zicarelli, which could give "Joe Bayonne" an uncommon advantage in his line of work.

For years our most famous natives were Sandra Dee, the actress known for her deathless portrayal of the title role in *Gidget Grows Up*, and Dick Brodowski, who once pitched for the Boston Red Sox against the New York Yankees—and lost. Now the town claims Arthur Burns, the head of the Federal Reserve Board, and Frank Langella, the young actor who plays a callous stud in *Diary of a Mad Housewife*. "Bayonne people," a friend once said, "always tell you where they're from because they're so proud of having risen above such humble beginnings."

When I came back for the reunion, I had not been to Bayonne for several years. My parents moved to Lakewood, in central New Jersey, after I graduated from college, and only my grandfather still lives there. As I walked through Newark Airport the passing faces kept looking familiar. Several times I had to stifle a greeting when the face turned out to be that of a stranger. After renting a car and checking into a motel near the airport, I tried unsuccessfully to take a nap. Feeling a little like a varsity member about to play a big basketball game, I changed my shirt and drove the few miles to Bayonne.

The party was being held in the Hi-Hat Club, a "hall for hire" with a doorway edged in orange neon. It was not a Jewish place, so I doubt if I had ever been there before (in Bayonne, such ethnic distinctions are not taken lightly). I was greeted by Marie Sestito, a jolly girl draped in floor-length pastel, who professed to remember me. On a side table were name tags and favors—small glass bowls with six gold plastic toothpicks. "They're nice for olives," said one girl. Slowly the crowd gathered.

Ten years ago last June we graduated from Bayonne High School, old B.H.S., with the school song ringing in our well-scrubbed and clearly visible ears. ("Oh, Bayonne, we'll strive for thy glory/ To our alma mater we'll be true.") High school had been a torturous time in many ways. With acne on my face, braces on my teeth, and a skinny body one local sports writer insisted on calling "elongated," I had an inferiority complex that was probably justified. I was the sort of social incompetent who learned every new dance after the cool kids had moved on to something else. Yet it was also a marvelously uncomplicated four years. Grass was what the sign said not to walk on in the county park. Sex was something that happened to somebody else. Some of the bolder guys carried condoms around "just in case," but they usually crumbled from age and disuse.

Most of us were blissfully ignorant of politics, at least until the spring of our senior year. Then we rooted for Hubert Humphrey, the great liberal hero, against John F. Kennedy, the political wheeler-dealer, in the West Virginia primary. Blacks—still called "colored" in Bayonne—were virtually invisible except for an occasional athlete or class clown. The heaviest reading undertaken by many of my friends was the gossip column in *Bayonne Facts*. The apex of culture was a Frankie Avalon concert in the school gym followed by pizza at Dido's, a dimly lit joint where they served the watered Cokes so fast you finished one before the pizza came and had to order another. Pizza was a staple in our diet, despite its pimple-producing properties, and I spent my youth with a mouth perpetually seared by bubbling tomato sauce and mozzarella cheese. We heard vaguely of "beatniks" and "foreign movies," and maybe we braved Greenwich Village once or twice for a cup of *cappuccino*, but for all we knew Jack Kerouac could have been a third baseman for the Dodgers. I once went to a Shakespeare play at the old Phoenix Theater in New York and fell asleep.

Bayonne was a working-class town. Only about a quarter of the kids went to college, and most of those attended state or trade schools. Many who went right to work either could not afford college or got no encouragement from home to further their education. The school was seldom more helpful. To this day, they shuttle some of the brightest girls into commercial programs, which often condemn them to a life sentence in front of a typewriter. I learned later that a number of these kids had eventually gone to college, sometimes at night, often at considerable sacrifice. A few are still going.

There are, of course, some people in Bayonne who care deeply about culture and education. I was fortunate enough to have two of them for parents. Both my mother and father had gone to college—although a combination of inertia and family ties kept them in Bayonne—and nothing was quite so important to them as their children's education. I also had one or two teachers who viewed the learning process as something more than the regurgitation of freeze-dried facts. But neither my brother nor I would have applied to Harvard if the older brother of a girl I once dated had not urged us to make the stab. His name was Barney Frank, and he was a senior at Harvard at the time. When we went to Cambridge for our interviews we stayed with him, and I was deeply disappointed that the chatter centered more on female pulchritude than politics. When I inquired about the absence of a genuine intellectual collegiate bull session—or what I thought of as a bull session—Barney pointed to his two roommates. "We've been roommates for three years," he laughed, "and whatever there is to be said about politics has been said." We were interviewed the next day by an admissions officer who had spent the war at the Bayonne Naval Supply Depot, and—maybe out of sympathy—he let both of us in.

According to questionnaires they filled out for the reunion, many of my classmates have been married six or eight years, a few as long as ten. Yet only a few have more than two children, an indication that many Catholics are not listening to the Pope on birth control. Most of them have decent, average jobs: salesman, dentist, insurance agent, accountant, hair dresser, office clerk, mortician, computer programmer, airplane pilot, fireman, toll collector on the New Jersey Turnpike. The strangest job was running ten-day sailing cruises in the West Indies. The most successful and the least successful apparently did not come back; my brother, a professor of economics at Harvard, was absent, and so were the guys who pump gas. Many of the reunioners had moved to the suburbs, quenching the land hunger inherited from their immigrant forebears. Under "places traveled" in the questionnaire, a few listed Europe, and a sizable number mentioned Florida and the Caribbean. Many had gone no further than Washington, D.C., or the Jersey Shore. Only two said they had been in Vietnam. Many of my classmates who joined the Army young missed the war, and most of us who had college deferments managed to escape altogether. One mother of three answered the question about travel with, "Are you kidding?"

As we downed our first drinks, I looked around. A few had lost some hair, others (including me) had gained weight. The Lord giveth, I suppose, and the Lord taketh away. Most of my old basketball-playing buddies reported that various physical calamities had relegated them to golf or motorcycling. It struck me that if my wife had been there—our month-old daughter kept her home—she would have been one of the few girls with long, straight hair, a style which is practically universal in California. Most of the girls wore it short or piled high on their heads in stiff, elaborate twists that looked a bit like Italian pastries. Later, dancing close to one of those lacquered confections, I felt a rush of memory; one whiff of hair spray and I wanted to go neck in the front parlor. The female fashion show included a few pants suits or hostess pajamas or openwork knit dresses, but the favorite was the traditional spangled sheath in pastel silk. Some of the guys were sporting modest moustaches or sideburns or collar-length hair, but there was only one true freak, the husband of a class scatterbrain, who turned out to be, of all things, a newspaperman. In general, the gathering could have passed for the annual banquet of the Junior Chamber of Commerce.

The background sounds ranged from casual chatter ("I don't know what it's like not to be pregnant. . . . We saw them last week in church") to shrieks of recognition ("I don't believe it. I don't believe it!"). I started talking with Walter Gonsiewski, one of those amiable jokesters everyone always liked, whose neck was gleaming from a fresh haircut. What was he doing? "Working, right? What else?" he laughed. "I'm a mechanic at Humble Oil; I fix the trucks." Did he like it? "I care for it, it's for me, that's my kind of work. I never was much of a book man. I like tinkering with things—I'm a wrench pusher."

We traded notes. Each of us had been married four years, each had a boy and a girl. "They're hot stuff, aren't they?" Walter asked enthusiastically. "It's the best time of a man's life, when his kids are this age. He can really enjoy them. I wouldn't trade it for the world. Thank God everything is as good as it is." When Walter thanked God, I felt he meant it. At that moment his wife, the former Marion Sudamack, came up. Ethnic ties are strong and open in Bayonne, and with a look of affection she said, "I married this Polack here." Was she still a nurse? "I wouldn't let her go back to work," said Walter. "You won't get me to baby-sit, not this guy." What did he do in his spare time? "Work around the house, like everybody else."

The conversation with Walter set the tone for the evening. What really concerned my classmates were private things—family, job, home. I had to shift gears a bit. As a reporter I spend most of my time talking to the exotic or the active. I sometimes get the feeling that most of the world is either grooving on brown rice or working for peace candidates. Yet some things don't change; in the middle of writing this I had to replace my son's diapers and read him a bedtime story.

Because I went away to Harvard and have the kind of job I do, many of my friends are strivers, achievers. They want to have an influence, preferably on a national scale. What's more, they feel they deserve regular doses of passion, of intense experience, whether through drugs or art, sex or skiing. They want—or at least talk about—life with a capital L. Not my high school classmates. They are neither ecstatic nor depressed, and they do not expect to be. They are neither movers nor shakers, and that is all right. They are content. They get along.

Take Jay Slomovitz, Dr. Jay Slomovitz. Always pudgy, he is now a hefty young dentist practicing in Staten Island. "This guy needed someone in his practice when I was looking," explained Jay, whose pretty wife was pregnant with their second child. "I'm more or less my own boss. I have a lot of freedom. I don't mind going there; it beats punching a time clock." Politics? "I go along my own way. I feel I'm a good listener. I'm not against the war and I'm not for it. I spent two years in the service, and I found out a lot that other people don't know." How did he feel? "Things could be better, they could be worse. I never think about it. I work hard and I come home and unwind. I don't do much of anything. My day is over at 6 o'clock, and I come home and relax."

But beneath the contentment, other currents are running. Mike Lipman was one of the social leaders of our crowd, the epitome of coolness. Now he is married to a classmate, Brenda Appelbaum, and teaches physics at Bayonne High. He finds it difficult. "The kids are changing and the schools aren't," he said. "We have the same administrators, but the kids know more; they're better informed. They're not satisfied with commands, they want reasons, but too many teachers say, 'Do it my way.' The administrators just can't administer. Their solution to a problem is to turn around and hide from it and hope it will disappear." Was he happy? "Sometimes I am, but sometimes I wonder if I'm doing any good to anybody, including myself." We talked some more and Mike mused, "I think we just missed out. The last five years have really been the turning point."

I heard that comment several times during the evening. We had "just missed out" on most of the great changes of the sixties: We were out of college by the time the Vietnam war escalated, the civil-rights movement turned bitter, dorms went coed, pot became more popular than beer, college health services gave out birth control pills, and assassination and confrontation became a regular part of our political life. By and large, we did what was expected of us. "Do your own thing" was still an unborn cliché.

Mike's frustrations were shared even more intensely by the girls. I joined a conversation between two fellow members of Home Room 322, Joyce Frank Fishberg and Judy Kiesnowski Czarneski. (If these two are classic examples of ethnic solidarity, many others are not. Arlyne Greenhill was married to Frank Fricchione, Jean Reilly to John Semanchick and Mary "Gigi" Barresi to Peter Jaroszewski.) Joyce now lives in the suburbs with her husband, who works for a chemical company. "I felt like a duck out of water when I moved to the sticks," she said. "There's a rooster down the street, for God's sake."

After several years as a secretary in New York, she is now the full-time mother of a little girl, and she is not overjoyed. "I have to get back to work," said Joyce, who always had a sharp-edged prettiness and fit well into a tight black dress. "But I'd really feel guilty if I left my daughter at this age. She needs me. I like Women's Lib, but I've been brainwashed by the old school—I'd still feel guilty if I left my child. Work is much more rewarding than cooking or changing diapers or hearing 'Mommy, Mommy, Mommy' every minute of the day. I can't take it. There's got to be more to life than this. I wasn't meant to be a servant, I don't think." Judy taught high school for a while, but quit when the first of her three kids was born. What makes her happy? "When my kids are quiet, that's when I'm happy."

Pat Blihar also belongs to the old school. She met her husband—Sergeant Brian Connors of the Bayonne Police Department—in a candy store his sister owned on Pat's corner. Her mother lives across the street and is an "excellent babysitter" for the three little Connorses, aged $4\frac{1}{2}$, $2\frac{1}{2}$, and 15 months. She worries about Brian. "I don't like my husband being called a pig," said Pat, who wore a lime-colored silk suit. "I think he's a fair cop because I know he's a fair person. It's the overall disrespect for authority that bothers me. I don't want some nut taking a potshot at my husband because he hates cops. My husband is there to do a job, and he does it."

But Pat worries even more about her children, two girls and a boy: "I hope I'll be able to meet their needs as they get older. Each day is another problem, and I only hope I can handle it in the right way, especially with values changing so rapidly. I'm kind of old-fashioned—not puritanical but old-fashioned—even compared to a 21-year-old. Sometimes being a mother is a very awesome thing." How was she old-fashioned? "I still think the father should be head of the family and the mother should be home caring for the kids. Not that she shouldn't go out and have a part-time job, but it shouldn't interfere with her home life. I also think religion should be instilled in children. People place less and less importance on this, but kids need something to be guided by; they need to know there's a higher being. Fewer and fewer families attend mass; it seems like it's breaking down."

As we sat down to dinner, it was obvious that the cliques of ten years before had been well preserved. The wealthier Jews, those who had lived in the same neighborhood and had gone to the same totally white elementary school, mostly sat together. So did a group of bright, non-Jewish girls, many of whom had gone to local colleges. Some of the cheerleaders, the "personality kids," were together. So were some of the athletes. I was asked to sit at the Jewish table (I had gone to that elementary school) by several girls who, in high school, would not have asked me for the time. On my left was Arlyne Greenhill Fricchione, and I was stunned to realize that I had met her in kindergarten, twenty-three years ago. The talk was of old friends. ("I used to talk to Marley, but she cut it off. So she's not married. You'd think she had the bubonic plague.") Of old times. ("Remember the party we had in your basement and Phyllis came running in and said she was pregnant, but it was really her mother?") And of the years apart. ("I was teaching in Elizabeth and I taught a boy they called the Hatchet Murderer. They said he killed some people, but he's all right in my book.")

Arlyne is a sensitive girl, now the wife of a musician after an unhappy first marriage. Looking smashing in an aqua pants suit, she talked about teaching biology in a suburban high school: "The kids are so lost, the world is so ugly to them. When I was in high school I had nothing on my mind except whether I was going to the [Jewish Community] Center tonight and what I would wear. These kids are so involved in life, they're so much more

serious. I feel sorry for them. They're not kids anymore, they're adults."
Vicki Shandler Bernfeld, the wife of a New York lawyer now living on Long
Island, overheard. "I keep getting so frightened," she said. "What am I
going to tell my son?"

Vicki, like so many wives, faces the classic dilemma. She wants to
work—she once taught art—but she also wants to raise her children. This
year she decided to take art lessons, and one night a week her husband
comes home early to take care of the two kids. It is an imperfect solution,
but working is no panacea, either. David Bernfeld is as unsettled as his wife.
"I react to day-to-day things," he said. "Nixon and Agnew got me bugged,
but not enough for me to get actively involved. I do some volunteer legal
work, but like all of us, I'm still finding myself." The problem, of course, is
where to look.

Gigi and Peter Jaroszewski came over. Peter and I had played softball
together in the fourth grade. In high school I had admired Gigi from afar,
but I had been too afraid of the religious problem to ask her out. (Like many
things, religious differences seemed so big then, so small now. Six years after
graduation I married a Catholic.) With Gigi's support, Peter earned a degree
in civil engineering, and now he works for a company trying to abate water
pollution. "We try to treat this stuff and those big companies just keep
dropping it in," he said. "I think they'd rather spend the money on fines
than on stopping pollution." The Jaroszewskis have no children, but they're
still concerned about young people. "Kids today are stupid," said Peter;
"they don't enjoy high school the way we did. All they want to do is cause
trouble. But maybe we just don't understand them." Gigi made a face.
"How can they neck with someone who has long greasy hair?" she asked.

Public issues intruded into only a few conversations. When they did, it
was usually because of personal experience. Living in northern New Jersey,
for instance, makes one keenly aware of the pollution problem. Several
people talked wearily about ending the war, but at least one fellow said, "If
we don't fight them there, we'll fight them here."

The smoldering resentment against longhairs flared up when one girl
started attacking the freaky newspaperman and his wife, who was wearing a
gypsy-style gown. "She was mad at me because I didn't have children," the
newspaperman's wife explained the next night. "She assumed I was selfish
and didn't want them, just because of the way I looked." She said she had
had several miscarriages.

The reunion conversation also included a tirade against welfare. "It was like a Grade B flick," said my friend Helene Holder at the postmortem. "They were still using the old stereotyped arguments, and I found myself giving stereotyped replies."

One guy with a beef was Ray Poplaski, known as "Moose" when we played in the Biddy Basketball League because of his slight build. Ray works for an investment house on Wall Street, and takes a few courses at night. "I'm not complaining," he said. "I didn't go to college and I can't expect the breaks but I'm not afraid to go out and hustle." Recently his wife was attacked on the subway. "I think the coloreds are getting too much handed to them," he said. "They don't want to work. Fifteen- or 16-year-old kids roughed up my wife and ripped her dress. It really shakes the hell out of you. There were four white guys standing there, and not one of them told the kids to knock it off. This is it. No one wants to do anything about it. Give, give, give. If me or you roughed somebody up, we'd sure as hell get arrested."

The band for the evening, the Blue Chips, wore pink shirts and clip-on bow ties and featured a lot of accordion music. When they played a lively polka, dozens of couples jammed the floor. The Bunny Hop was a big hit, as was the Charleston. Occasionally they dredged up a song from our youth—"Blue Suede Shoes," for example—and a few couples with good memories went out and jitterbugged. As I watched the jitterbuggers I realized how unsexy the dance was. It had been a big thrill for us to do a "slow" dance and feel the jab of two small, pointed breasts as we maneuvered closer, palms sweating. For years now, of course, the more expressive high school dancers have been in danger of arrest for simulating sexual intercourse in a public place. Yet they dance alone now, without touching. We always touched hands, we were always together. (What did Arlyne call her students? Lost?) The band played the Bayonne High School fight song ("Bayonne goes marching down the line/ Everyone is feeling mighty fine") and closed. Most of the people were already gone, and the evening ended on a sort of down note. "I feel like it's a dream," Arlyne had said earlier, and Vicki had replied, "Everybody has their own life; that's what it is."

The next day I drove around Bayonne. Everywhere were the signs of family things, private things: a man painting his porch railing; a young couple polishing their car; a grandfather walking his tiny charge; a group in hats and white shirts off to visit relatives, cake box clutched in hand; a boy nuzzling a girl in the doorway of a shuttered store; a parade of cars parked in front of a church, decorated with pink streamers, waiting for the wedding party. The churches are the grandest buildings in town, great stone structures now as grimy as the factories where so many of their parishioners work. They serve not only as places of worship but as community centers. At Assumption, the main Italian church, a giant bowling pin affixed to the school dwarfs all else. At St. Henry's, the Irish citadel, a sign advertises "Bingo Every Saturday Night."

Bayonne is that rarest of entities, a genuine community. My grand-fathers, both refugees from Russia, came to the town about fifty years ago, when it was still mainly dairy farms. My mother was born there. She lived in a house her father had built with his own hands—a house I lived in, too, until I was 13. I drove by. It is still there, very much the same except for a coat of bright green paint and the latest local rage, an address written out in script. I thought of some longhairs I met recently in Taos, New Mexico. The thing they wanted to do most in the world was live in a house they had built themselves.

A remarkable web of relationships enmeshes you in a town like Bayonne. Just driving around I saw Iorio's Shoe Repair (I went to elementary school with Janice Iorio), Hourihan's Liquor Store (Mary Hourihan was my freshman algebra teacher), Cherow's Housewares (I took Renee Cherow to the junior prom), Kavula's Bar and Grill (Tommy and Johnny Kavula were on my Little League team). A real estate firm whose signs sprinkled the city is run by the husband of my mother's girlhood chum. Around the corner from my old house, Mr. Levine, now well into his 70s, still tended his tiny fish and vegetable store, wearing—I swear—the same gray sweater he did twenty years ago. A few blocks away I went to see my grandfather, my father's father, who still owns a business in Bayonne. His long, varied, and largely unsuccessful career included running an amuse-ment park, promoting boxing matches, building houses, and selling lumber. "Most of the chicken coops in Toms River are built with my plywood," he remembered. On the mantel was a framed photograph of his family, including a dark-eyed sister named Rebecca, my daughter's name. He was the only one who ever left Russia. One sister is still alive in Moscow, but he talked about going back to what he considered his true home, Israel. He had lived there for several years as a youth, and worked on some of the first roads built in Tel Aviv. "All I want," he said, "is plenty of fish, plenty of fruit, peace of mind, and *The New York Times*."

I stayed in town an extra day so I could visit the high school, and I looked up some of my old teachers to ask what had changed. For one thing, there was a new dress code; girls could now wear slacks, and when the classes changed it was obvious that most of them took advantage of the new rule. It was also obvious that their straight, flowing hair had seldom been tortured like their older sisters'. The blacks now had an Ebony Culture Club, the rate of illegitimate babies was up, teachers were required to take a course in drug prevention. The few really good teachers complained that there still weren't enough kids willing to think for themselves, but one of the others was distressed. "The place is falling apart," she told me. "I never ran up against this before. I tell them what I want and they resent it and talk back."

Later I went to see the principal, Alexander X. O'Connor, known with something less than affection as "The Ax." He kept using words like "dialogue" and "communication," but what he really wanted to communicate about was sports. "Our participation in sports is excellent," he said, his face lighting up. "We've won a couple of county championships recently, and that really helps." What about drugs? "For a while there was some glue-sniffing and marijuana smoking," he said. "We've found some empty glue bottles, but I think it's fairly well controlled." When I kept turning the conversation away from football, Mr. O'Connor got a bit uneasy. "These kids go to the theater and see these movies and hear all those four-letter words," he said. "I may be old-fashioned, but I still like to say 'yes, sir' and 'no, sir'. There are certain niceties you shouldn't throw out the window." What about student complaints that they did not have a large enough role in the school? "The day of exercising dictatorial power is over," he conceded, "but they have to realize that I also get directives I don't like. I have a superior, too." I had the feeling that old B.H.S. was as it always had been; my sharpest memory was of the agony of waiting for the bell to ring.

One of my old teachers had given me a copy of *The Bayonne Free Press*, the high school's first underground paper. It was an amateurish, barely legible job, but it demonstrated clearly that a lot more had changed in ten years than the dress code. One article told how to get an abortion in New York; another attacked the use of a park to build a new City Hall (the city has also sold several parks for housing developments, a novel way to balance the budget). An editorial entitled "Get Out!" declared, "We must continue to oppose this immoral war in every possible way." One could almost hear the beer glasses being slammed in anger on the bar at the American Legion post. On the culture page, one critic wrote about hearing a rock concert while stoned. Another called *Getting Straight* a "fantastic film" and with great relish quoted a line of Elliott Gould's: "Last week all that kid wanted was to get laid. Now he wants to kill somebody." When I was editor of *The Bayonne High Beacon*—now temporarily suspended because of a bureaucratic foul-up—I thought I was being really radical when I wrote editorials deploring the lack of school spirit or the rising number of traffic accidents.

I looked up the editors of *The Free Press*, Richard Dulee and Debbie Warnock. We talked in Debbie's living room under the watchful eye of her weary mother, who made it clear that she did not approve of the abortion article. Why an underground paper? "We felt there was too much censorship by the advisers to *The Beacon*. We want to control what we put in our own paper," said Richard, a sincere, thoughtful youth. For instance, the advisers had slashed an article telling kids where to get draft counseling and had decreed that all articles must apply to students. "There's no world outside, right?" Richard said wryly. Were drugs "fairly well controlled," as the principal had said? "They're available all over the place," answered Debbie, who will have to work next year to afford college. "Each year they're more and more in the open. Now you can hear kids yelling in the halls, 'I've got to cop some stuff tonight.' " The pressures, added Richard, were enormous. "If you don't do drugs, you're not a chicken—you're just not hip, which is worse." Did he do drugs? "I'm more of an individual than most kids; I can say no and still feel good about it."

Feeling good. It so often comes down to that. Wandering through the high school I ran into Joyce Lauton Nestle, literally the girl next door, now an English teacher. She was a year older, but we had played together as children, and I asked her about her friends. "You know, when we were in high school, we used to do skits about how horrible suburbia was and sit around and laugh. Now we're all living that way." She thought a bit and added, "We're scared whether we're going to make it. We believe in the new ideas, but we don't know whether we can live with them. Like the idea of property. I like the idea of a commune, but I'm used to the old way. I don't think we're flexible enough for the changes that are coming, and it hurts so much to be insecure."

Joyce touched on something I had seen reflected in many of my classmates. We had "just missed out" on many things—Vietnam, drugs, even the Beatles. More deeply, we had missed out on the changes in so many basic assumptions. We had been shaped in the dying years of a world that no longer exists. We had been taught that you play by the rules, that you respect authority, that reason is the source of all wisdom, that caution is a virtue, that sex is dirty, and that a woman's place is in the home. We could just as easily "let it all hang out" as fly to the moon. At 27, we are old-fashioned. And that is not a very comfortable thing to be these days.

1970

About the Author

Steven V. Roberts, 31, sold his first newspaper story when he was 15, graduated from Harvard University magna cum laude, and has been with *The New York Times* since 1964. The following year he became a reporter on the metropolitan staff and in 1969 was named Los Angeles bureau chief, a post he held until early 1974, when he assumed his present duties as head of the Athens bureau. Mr. Roberts has written more than fifty magazine articles for publications such as *Playboy, Esquire, Atlantic, Commonweal,* and *Redbook.* Other credits include a Pulitzer Prize nomination for his *Times* reporting on a California earthquake and appearances as a commentator on TV shows in New York and California. Mr. Roberts, a native of Bayonne, New Jersey, now lives in Athens with his wife Cokie, a TV producer and journalist, and their two children, Lee, 5, and Rebecca, 3.